"This is a long overdue book for Chris _____
be widely read, studied, and preached i _____
trated that the media has largely made _____ ...rmation worse. We
need more clear-headed scholars to be heard. Faith and not coercion is
a believer's walk. Humility and integrity are vital. Love and Truth are the
paths forward."

—**Steve Hassan**
author of *The Cult of Trump* and *Combatting Cult Mind Control*

"Christians believe in the literal embodiment of truth, Jesus Christ. We also
confess the One who is Truth to be the creator and sustainer of all things,
including the human faculty of reason. Editors Michael Austin and Gregory
Bock have assembled an outstanding collection of essayists who help us
use these epistemological anchors and others to recenter our faith, worldview, and interpretation of reality. During a time of competing fantasies
and deceptive and destructive conspiracy theories that play on our hearts
and minds, this book is a gift to the people of God. Individuals, churches,
schools, and denominational bodies will find *QAnon, Chaos, and the Cross*
an effective tool to protect themselves and their communities from falling
prey to a real and present danger while deepening their relationship to what
is ultimately and consummately true and good."

—**Rob Schenck**
president of the Dietrich Bonhoeffer Institute

"This collection of essays, largely from evangelical Christian scholars, offers a generous and substantive engagement with the problem of conservative Christian susceptibility to conspiracy theories. Most essays appear to
be written by authors who live within contexts in which conspiracy theories
such as QAnon have been fairly widely embraced. Thus, the book is interesting both for the virulent conspiracy thinking that it addresses and for
the rhetorical and reasoning strategies now being attempted by scholars
within such contexts."

—**David Gushee**
Distinguished University Professor of Christian Ethics
at Mercer University

QANON, CHAOS, and the CROSS

Christianity and Conspiracy Theories

EDITED BY

Michael W. Austin and Gregory L. Bock

WILLIAM B. EERDMANS PUBLISHING COMPANY
GRAND RAPIDS, MICHIGAN

Wm. B. Eerdmans Publishing Co.
4035 Park East Court SE, Grand Rapids, Michigan 49546
www.eerdmans.com

Published 2023
Printed in the United States of America

29 28 27 26 25 24 23   1 2 3 4 5 6 7

ISBN 978-0-8028-8265-3

Library of Congress Cataloging-in-Publication Data

A catalog record for this book is available from the Library of Congress.

CONTENTS

Contents

Contents

CONCERNS ABOUT
CONSPIRACY THEORIES FOR CHRISTIANS

Michael W. Austin and Gregory L. Bock

Yesterday, as I (Mike) walked back to my office from class, I noticed that a middle-aged man had set up some posterboard near the main campus dining hall, on which was written the question, "Was the moon landing faked?"[1] As I passed by, he was talking with a student and pointing toward the sun, apparently as part of his argument that the earth is flat. Perhaps he could see the skepticism on my face as he asked me if I knew of the evidence for the claim that the landings were faked. I said I'd read the counterarguments to his view and found them convincing. In reply, he informed me that "NASA are liars." I kept going. But my heart broke when I learned that he's also a professing Christian.

Throughout the history of the church, Christians have been susceptible to belief in conspiracy theories. Christians scapegoated Jewish people during the Black Plague. In the 1980s, many believed the false claim that the president of Procter & Gamble admitted to worshiping Satan, and that satanic symbols were on their products. The number of conspiracy theories related to end-times prophecies and predictions is legion. And at least one

---

1. As an exercise in understanding both the initial plausibility of a conspiracy theory and how a closer look at the evidence undermines that plausibility, check out the debunking of the claim that the moon landings were faked at the History Channel website; Becky Little, "The Wildest Moon Landing Conspiracy Theories, Debunked," The History Channel, updated July 18, 2019, https://www.history.com /news/moon-landing-fake-conspiracy-theories.

conspiracist comes to university campuses in Kentucky, seeking to persuade people that the moon landings were faked and the earth is flat.

Belief in conspiracy theories is not just a historical problem; it is a pressing contemporary one, too. A recent survey by Lifeway found that 49 percent of Protestant pastors agreed with the statement "I frequently hear members of my congregation repeating conspiracy theories they have heard about why something is happening in our country."[2] Significant numbers of Christians in America believe at least some of the claims of QAnon.[3] Many believe conspiracy theories related to the 2020 presidential election, the coronavirus pandemic, mask wearing, and vaccines, and that there is a deep state at work in our country.[4]

We are deeply concerned about this recent trend toward belief in conspiracy theories for many reasons. First, the theories are often demonstrably false. As Christians, we are to love the truth and pursue wisdom. Belief in false conspiracy theories hinders this. Second, belief in these theories fosters tribalism in society and the church, while undermining civil discourse and Christian unity. Third, this trend damages our credibility as we seek to share the gospel of the kingdom of God and work on its behalf in our world. Lastly, many aspects of belief in conspiracy theories hinder us in our quest to love God with all our heart, soul, mind, and strength, and our neighbor as ourselves. Let's briefly consider each of these causes for concern.

The first reason is that such theories are often demonstrably false. The wording here is crucial. Such theories are *often*, rather than *always*, false. Some conspiracy theories are in fact true. But many, even most, are simply false, and often demonstrably so. This is a particular problem for Christians who believe or propagate such theories, for many reasons. We are to be lovers of truth and pursuers of wisdom, as followers of Jesus, "in whom are hidden all the treasures of wisdom and knowledge" (Col. 2:3 NRSV).

---

2. Aaron Earls, "Half of U.S. Protestant Pastors Hear Conspiracy Theories in Their Churches," Lifeway Research, January 26, 2021, https://lifewayresearch .com/2021/01/26/half-of-u-s-protestant-pastors-hear-conspiracy-theories-in-their -churches/.

3. Jack Jenkins, "QAnon Conspiracies Sway Faith Groups, Including 1 in 4 White Evangelicals," *Christianity Today*, February 11, 2021, https://www.christianitytoday .com/news/2021/february/white-evangelicals-qanon-election-conspiracy-trump -aei.html.

4. Daniel Burke, "How QAnon Uses Religion to Lure Unsuspecting Christians," CNN, October 15, 2020, https://www.cnn.com/2020/10/15/us/qanon-religion -churches/index.html.

Truth is central to Christianity. Our faith is grounded in many truth claims, including most centrally claims about the life, death, and resurrection of Jesus of Nazareth. Truth is serious business for followers of Jesus. We must carry that conviction into our assessment of conspiracy theories.

Second, as recent years have made all too plain, belief in conspiracy theories undermines unity in the church and in society. It hinders civil discourse. Civil discourse and unity are under threat for several reasons. Many people equate their religious beliefs with their political beliefs and create strange combinations of the two. Often, political belief determines religious belief, on the right and on the left. For example, consider the following from DeAnna Lorraine, whose 2020 run for Congress in California's Twelfth District failed:

> [God] also sees us as being good, and anyone who is doing good deeds should not be living and hiding in the shadows behind a mask. A mask is a symbol of fear. You're living in fear. If you have a mask on, it means you actually don't trust God. You don't have faith . . . the Marxist globalist Satanists that are pushing all this, they are trying to invert reality and pervert God and Christians, and they want to isolate us from God, isolate us from other humans, and deprive us of that faith so that we rely on the government, the media, telling us what to do and telling us whether to be fearful or not instead of God. I prefer to have faith. I will live by faith instead of by fear.[5]

It is difficult to have a rational discussion with someone who claims that wearing a mask during a global pandemic means you don't have faith in God. It is also difficult to see how unity could be experienced with such a person. It's one thing to disagree about mask mandates. It's quite another to claim wearing a mask is antithetical to faith in God and that it's all being forced on us by "the Marxist globalist Satanists."

It is difficult to have a rational discussion with someone who believes she has been magnetized by the COVID vaccine, who doubles down on the claim even after her attempted demonstration with a key and a bobby pin fails, as occurred during an Ohio statehouse hearing in 2021.[6] But civil

5. Kyle Mantyla, "DeAnna Lorraine Claims That 'God Does Not Want Us Wearing Masks,'" *Right Wing Watch*, July 17, 2020, https://www.rightwingwatch.org/post/deanna-lorraine-claims-that-god-does-not-want-us-wearing-masks/.

6. Mia Jankowicz, "An Anti-Vax Nurse Tried, and Failed, to Make a Key Stick to Her

discourse seems to be threatened as well, as parents attack school board members, public health officials are threatened, and, to be frank, so many exemplify an arrogant overconfidence in their abilities to "do their own research" that conflicts with the consensus of experts over and over again. An important question to ask here is whether the conspiracy theories we believe, or are drawn to, tend to reinforce and reflect our preexisting political beliefs. If so, that's a serious warning sign that we aren't being drawn to them by evidence, but rather by something else. The cliché used to be about a church splitting because of the color of the new sanctuary carpet. Now, churches are divided over vaccines, masks, and mask mandates. Misappropriations of 2 Timothy 1:7 and many other passages from the Bible abound. We would prefer a good debate about carpet colors.

Third, when Christians advocate conspiracy theories that are likely to be or even are demonstrably false, we undermine our own credibility as ambassadors for Christ and his kingdom. While God is bigger than our credibility, and there is power in the message of the gospel, those who want to be faithful ambassadors for Christ must be credible and trustworthy. If your neighbor, coworker, or friend doesn't think you are a credible witness to truth because of your belief in one or more conspiracy theories, why would that person take your claims about Christ, the resurrection, God's grace, or God's heart for the poor seriously? We fear that too many fail to consider this question very much, if at all.

Finally, many aspects of belief in conspiracy theories hinder us in our quest to love God with all our heart, soul, mind, and strength, and our neighbor as ourselves. While many are suspicious of masks and vaccines, many others argue that wearing a mask during the pandemic, or getting one of the vaccines, is a way to love our neighbor as ourselves, especially our neighbors who have underlying conditions that make them more vulnerable to serious illness or death if they get COVID. Belief in conspiracy theories also has a tendency to propagate an *us versus them* mentality, which hinders us from loving our neighbor as ourselves. We may see those who fall prey to a conspiracy as sheep, brainwashed individuals, or fools. Or, like DeAnna Lorraine, we may question the very faith of those who deny the truth of the conspiracy. This goes both ways, sadly. For some it is easy to dismiss those who believe in conspiracy theories, too. The answer, or at least part of the answer, is to focus on the arguments and the evidence, es-

---

Neck as Proof That COVID-19 Vaccines Make You Magnetic," *Yahoo! News*, June 10, 2021, https://news.yahoo.com/anti-vaxx-nurse-tried-failed-092354565.html.

chewing personal attacks. The overarching lesson here is that all we think, do, say, and are should be brought under the Great Commandment to love God and our neighbor as ourselves (Mark 12:28-34).

The contributors to this book bring a wide variety of expertise to bear on Christianity and conspiracy theories, from the fields of theology, biblical studies, philosophy, communications, history, political science, education, and information science. For this and other reasons, there are a variety of definitions of "conspiracy theory" in this book. We think this is good, as it enables a variety of unique perspectives and doesn't lock authors into a particular view of such theories. Each chapter stands on its own, so the chapters can be read in any order, though it will be helpful to start with the first chapter as a way of understanding a Christian framework for thinking about these issues. The contributors have written their chapters not for other scholars but for thoughtful followers of Christ, and really anyone else, who want to think hard and well about these issues. Some chapters require a bit more of the reader than others. A few chapters may require you to look up a word or two. But it is worth a little extra effort, given what is at stake. We are confident that each chapter will be useful to you as you seek to understand the various connections between Christianity and conspiracy theories. And we trust that it will not only help you work through the concerns we have discussed here, but will also help you navigate these issues in a way that is honoring to Christ and loving to your neighbors, wherever you and they stand on these issues.

JESUS AS THE TRUTH

Stephen T. Davis and Eric T. Yang

"The Democratic party is run by a secret cabal of pedophiles!" So says a conspiracy theory that appears to be held by not a small number of people. Despite the lack of evidence for such a belief, this claim appears to be popular. Conspiracy theories like this are not uncommon, and many are even held by Christians. But how should Christians approach conversations with people who accept these claims? Is there a Christian framework for thinking about conspiracy theories?

Christians have always been deeply interested in truth. After all, Jesus said, "I am the way, and the truth, and the life" (John 14:6).[1] And Paul tells us to "fasten the belt of truth around your waist" (Eph. 6:14). As Christians, then, the foundation of our framework is this starting point: Jesus is the truth. There is no doubt much that can be said about that claim, both theologically and philosophically. But for our purposes, we want to focus on one crucial implication of it, which is that Christians must be committed to what is true. Truth is not a matter of opinion. We are not relativists.[2] Someone may sincerely believe something, and yet it may turn out to be false. Being passionately committed to a belief doesn't make it true. We believe that the framework that begins with Jesus as the truth can help Christians

---

1. All Scripture quotations in this chapter come from the New Revised Standard Version.

2. Relativism is the view that what is true is relative to who is speaking; that is, what is true for one person or community may not be true for another.

think more carefully and critically about conspiracy theories and engage more effectively with those who accept and propagate them.

In this chapter, we begin with a brief definition and characterization of conspiracy theories. Then we unpack what we mean by a Christian orientation toward truth, discussing two important biblical themes that we believe are relevant to thinking about conspiracy theories. We then offer some lessons that the phenomenon of conspiracy theories, in our view, ought to teach Christians. Finally, we provide some practical suggestions for Christians who want to respond to this cultural phenomenon.

What Is a Conspiracy Theory?

What exactly is a conspiracy theory? We accept a definition given by Jared Millson: "A conspiracy theory is an explanation of some alleged fact or event in terms of the actions undertaken by a small group of individuals working in secret."[3] As Millson points out, conspiracies are common in human experience, and some conspiracy theories are harmless and some are even true. The conspiracy theory that the 1972 Watergate break-in was sponsored by the Republican National Committee was at first widely disputed, but it turned out to be true. However, we are interested in those conspiracy theories that the vast majority of sensible people consider false or even obviously false, for example, that Dwight Eisenhower was a secret Communist, that NASA faked the moon landings, that the 9/11 attacks were brought about by the CIA or other American groups, or (more controversially) that Biden's election in 2020 was stolen away from Trump.

Why do conspiracy theories occur, and what characterizes them? There seem to be typically five steps in the evolution of a conspiracy theory. (1) Some event occurs, often a bad or catastrophic one, and people are fearful, in part because they feel that they have no control over or influence on it. (2) The question naturally emerges: Why did this happen? Who is responsible for this event? Here is the heart of a conspiracy theory: a group of conspirators are then accused; they are to blame. (3) A conspiracy theory is then propounded and publicized, and so-called research (which may often be no more than scouring one's favorite websites or social media pages) is done to support its claims. (4) More people are brought onboard to accept the conspiracy theory; in our Internet age, this can readily be ac-

3. Jared Millson, "Conspiracy Theories," 1000-Word Philosophy, December 17, 2020, https://1000wordphilosophy.com/2020/12/17/conspiracy-theories/.

complished. (5) Objections to the conspiracy theory are answered, usually by offering *ad hoc* additions to it. These additional explanations are *ad hoc* because they lack independent support for accepting them other than the fact that they save the theory from the objections. Thus, the conspiracy theory becomes immunized from virtually any critique.

Conspiracy theorists are often highly suspicious of government officials and reports, as well as the opinions of scientists or experts. The accusation is that such people are withholding or distorting the truth, either because they are biased or because they are intentionally aiming to manipulate others to achieve malicious ends (for example, to undermine certain political or religious groups). Conspiracy theories tend to give their advocates a false sense of security or confidence, as in, "I know the truth and you don't." Conspiracy theorists are typically not relativists on truth ("You have your truth and I have mine"); they are fully convinced that their theory is true.

Discernment and False Prophets

We believe two important biblical themes are relevant for Christians responding to conspiracy theories: discernment and false prophets. Discernment is the ability to distinguish between truth and falsity. First Thessalonians 5:21 enjoins us to "test everything," including the words of prophets. Hebrews 5:14 speaks approvingly of "those whose faculties have been trained by practice to distinguish good from evil" (see also Phil. 1:9–10). Unfortunately, we are living in a time of increasing biblical and theological ignorance, even among churchgoers. Discernment seems to be a rare thing; it is easy for people to be "blown about by every wind of doctrine" (Eph. 4:14). We believe that studying Scripture, theology, and even philosophy and logic is of great practical importance in developing our facility for discernment.

While we believe the Holy Spirit primarily assists Christians in becoming discerning, we also believe that discernment takes some effort. It's much easier to belong to or follow a particular individual (such as a pastor or media personality) or particular group (such as a Christian organization or news source) and decide to believe whatever is presented. But this exhibits intellectual laziness and a lack of intellectual humility. Our favorite speakers or media personalities can be mistaken, and Christians should be willing to test everything they read or hear, first on whether it is compatible with the teachings of Scripture, but also on whether it is reasonable or supported by the available evidence. If we are truly humble, as we are commanded to be, then we should recognize that we might be mistaken. The people or organizations we rely on might also be mistaken. Accordingly, we need to engage in the labor of trying to figure out the truth.

Additionally, both the Old Testament and the New Testament severely criticize false prophets, that is, those who speak falsehoods purportedly on behalf of God (see Jer. 14:14; 23:1, 21; Zech. 10:2; 1 John 4:1). Now conspiracy theorists do not usually claim to be speaking for God. But there are important similarities between them and false prophets: both try to deceive people on important (not trivial) points and often succeed in misleading many people. Jesus points toward an important criterion in deciding which of the people who claim to speak for God are false: "You will know them by their fruits" (Matt. 7:16). Accordingly, we must ask: Are the consequences of their teachings good or bad? We can ask the same question about the teachings of those who promulgate conspiracy theories.

What Can We Learn from Conspiracy Theories?

What can or should Christians learn from the phenomenon of conspiracy theories? We suggest three things.

The first lesson is this: trust in God. It is said that the most frequent command in Scripture is "Do not be afraid" (see, for example, Isa. 8:12–13). Conspiracy theories often arise out of fear.[4] We certainly do live in a world in which terrible things happen that we are powerless to prevent or even shape. Yet, in the face of such events, God wants us to trust our lives and the lives of our loved ones to him. It is true that we are powerless to stop many of the events that we worry about, but God is in control. In this sense, a conspiracy theory can constitute a spiritual problem for Christians who are committed to it: they focus on it rather than trusting in God.

If this happens, we think Christians should go back to the fundamental claim—that Jesus is the truth. Along with the myriad of things this claim implies, it tells us that Jesus is fully in charge and has not lost control. In the Upper Room Discourse (captured in John 13–17), the disciples are troubled by what they are hearing from Jesus. His response is for them to have full confidence in him, trusting him even when things seem shaky and uncertain. If all authority has been given to Jesus (Matt. 28:18), then our anxiety does not have to lead us to embrace an answer that blames the problems

---

4. For more on this tendency, see Karen M. Douglas et al., "Understanding Conspiracy Theories," *Advances in Political Psychology* 40 (2019): 3–35.

on some secret organization or group of conspirators. Maybe there is one, maybe there isn't. But we won't feel the compulsion to jump to the conclusion that there is a conspiracy afoot. Once we have total trust in Jesus, we can work toward discerning whether what we are hearing or reading is true or false, and we can examine the fruits of those ideas as well as the fruits of those who write or speak (and you should be doing that to us, the authors writing this very chapter!).

Once our sense of security is placed in the fact that Jesus is in control, we can see that it is often reasonable to trust proper authorities in their specific areas of expertise. We accept that there are authorities in different domains: religious authorities, moral authorities, scientific authorities, political authorities, and so on. In order to function as a community, we need trust—trust in others but also trust in authorities.[5] This does not imply that we shouldn't question what we hear from those authorities. Still, our attitude to those who have spent years training and studying should be one of trust and not one of suspicion (unless, of course, there is good reason to be suspicious). Scientific investigation is not easy, as it often involves higher mathematics and probabilistic reasoning, and many people have not been adequately trained to understand the calculations that support scientific hypotheses. It is reasonable, then, for us to trust those who are experts in these areas. One caveat: it is easy for experts in one field to slip into talking about some other area where they are not experts, and their authority does not carry over. So, discerning Christians must try to figure out if and when this sort of thing is happening.

Not only should we investigate the claims of media sources and alleged experts, but we should also be willing to scrutinize the claims coming from our own group. There may be a tendency to give those from one's own religious, political, or ideological brand a pass—as long as they are on the "right side." However, we should care about truth. Perhaps someone's own side is giving a bad argument or spreading falsehoods. Followers of Jesus who love the truth should be willing to speak up against these things; not harshly, but honestly—and always "speaking the truth in love" (Eph. 4:15). Even Paul was willing to rebuke Peter when he saw Peter acting in a way that was not in step "with the truth of the gospel" (Gal. 2:14). Rather than criticizing opposing religious or political parties or agendas, we should first look at ourselves and at our own affiliations—after all, there's a good

---

5. For more on this, see Linda Zagzebski, *Epistemic Authority* (Oxford: Oxford University Press, 2012).

chance there is a beam in our own eyes while we are obsessing over the speck in another's (Matt. 7:5).

The second lesson is to be reminded that gossip is a sin. As Paul says, we must not be slanderers or "inventors of evil" (see Rom. 1:28-30). First Peter 2:1 reads, "Rid yourselves . . . of . . . all slander." And 2 Timothy 2:23 says: "Have nothing to do with stupid and senseless controversies; you know that they breed quarrels." Like conspiracy theorists, those who engage in gossip often see themselves as exerting power, as in "I know an important secret that others do not know until I tell them." One motive, then, for entertaining conspiracy theories may be a sinful desire to be part of what C. S. Lewis calls an "Inner Ring." Lewis worried that such a desire would "be one of the chief motives" in a person's life unless one "takes measures to prevent it."[6] This is the desire to be "in the know," or to have membership in an exclusive group that somehow has not been duped like the rest of society. Now, sometimes people find themselves in situations where they are privy to insider knowledge, and that is not necessarily bad. What does seem problematic is the inordinate desire to be on the inside, and that can be sinful.[7]

The third lesson is to be careful not to become obsessed with conspiracy theories. We believe that Christians should be spending their time not on propounding conspiracy theories but in thinking about positive things. As Paul says, "Finally, beloved, whatever is true, whatever is honorable, whatever is just, whatever is pure, whatever is pleasing, whatever is commendable, if there is any excellence and if there is anything worthy of praise, think about these things" (Phil. 4:8). In other words, we need to look at the world, and at our own lives, from God's perspective—not from the perspective of the secular world.

The draw of conspiracies is, in part, that they are fascinating. Conspiracy theories, like gossip, are often alluring—they shock and surprise. Sadly, the discrediting or demise of another person can become entertainment

6. C. S. Lewis, "Inner Ring," in *The Weight of Glory and Other Addresses* (New York: HarperCollins, 2001).

7. Furthermore, as sin often yields negative consequences, the pushing of false or unsubstantiated reports can yield disastrous results, such as death threats received by restaurant owners on account of the conspiracy theory stated in the first sentence of this chapter (which led to "Pizzagate"). Many thanks to Susan Peppers-Bates for this point.

for us. And it is easy to get sucked in, going deeper and deeper into the labyrinth, into websites that offer click-bait to draw people in to the "real truth" of the matter. Not only is there usually no evidence or support for the conspiratorial claims, but the stories are often not edifying to the reader or listener. And the claims spread when people start sharing this alleged information, when they try to exhibit that they are "in the know." But as Christians, we should ensure that "no evil talk come[s] out of [our] mouths, but only what is useful for building up" (Eph. 4:29). Jesus even warns that on the day of judgment, people will have to give an account "for every careless word" they speak (Matt. 12:36). Even if there is a political, religious, or secular group that we strongly disagree with, speaking falsely or uncharitably should not be the disposition of a truth-loving follower of Jesus. If someone is in sin, we are not to gossip, slander, or bask in entertaining stories but are to find ways to help that person overcome the sin by the Spirit's help. And if it seems that we are unable to do anything, because it has to do with powerful people or with the government, Christians can always pray.

Encountering Conspiracy Theories

We now offer practical suggestions we have gleaned from observing the cultural phenomenon of conspiracy theories. The first suggestion focuses on direct interaction with those who embrace conspiracy theories, and the second offers a long-term strategy for Christians.

Christians encounter conspiracy theorists frequently, even among friends and loved ones. Indeed, some Christians are committed to certain unreasonable conspiracy theories. We believe this can do great harm to the cause of Christ (for some of the reasons stated in the previous section). But what should we do when we encounter such folk? First, avoid the temptation to argue; at least, don't argue right away. They often have replies to objections already worked out; arguing with them or claiming that their responses are *ad hoc* will usually only deepen their commitment to their favored conspiracy theory.

A prudent approach is to follow a three-step procedure developed by Seth Freeman, a professor at Columbia University's School of International and Public Affairs and NYU's Stern School of Business and an eminent expert on conflict resolution and negotiation strategies. Seth is also a Christian. His strategy is primarily designed for conversations between people who disagree strongly about politics and public policy, but we believe it can be fruitful in conversations about conspiracy theories as well. His procedure involves *paraphrase*, *praise*, and *probe*.[8]

Suppose you are talking to friends or loved ones who strongly accept a conspiracy theory. What should you do? First, politely ask them to explain their point of view. Listen carefully to what they say without interruption. Then attempt to paraphrase their viewpoint as fairly as you can. That is, mirror back to them their own views, stressing important thoughts and feelings.

Second, praise them for something—anything—that you approve of. Say something like, "I can tell that you've studied the problem a lot," "I can see that you've thought about this issue a great deal," or "I appreciate your passion and concern for this question."

Third, gently and respectfully probe, that is, dig deeper and offer alternative views. You can say things like, "Here is where I am confused," "Let me get your take on this particular problem," "Here is where I am seeing problems in your view," or "I'm going to push back now."

We think this will produce a better result than arguing at the drop of a hat or simply clamming up. You may not convert friends or loved ones away from the conspiracy theory, but you might help them to become a little more open-minded, or plant a doubt or two that lead to such a conversion. At the very least, you haven't shut the door on conversation, and you've opened yourself to being a caring dialogue partner who wants to know what is true. In discussions, we're not trying to show that we are right; rather, we are trying to find out what is true, because Christians are committed to the truth. Accordingly, we need to model our own openness to revising our own beliefs. But on the assumption that the person you are talking to is holding to an unreasonable conspiracy theory with almost no evidence and is offering *ad hoc* explanations for every criticism, keeping that door open is important, as the hope is to help fellow Christians become equal partners in our mutual pursuit of truth. This may take time and may require plenty of patience, but we must remember that Jesus was extremely patient with his disciples (and is always extremely patient with us!), and so we should likewise exercise the same kind of patience with others.

8. This was taken from an online presentation to the Claremont Colleges Christian Scholars Group on February 16, 2021. This idea was drawn from Rapoport's Rules, which was developed by game theorist and conflict management expert Anatol Rapoport.

Engaging Conspiracy Theories

Our second suggestion is this: while some Christians are called to withdraw from society, we believe that more Christians should actively enter into those institutions that appear to be undermining truth. For example, in the early to mid-twentieth century, it seemed that the university, and especially philosophy departments, was a hostile place for Christians. Around that time, a few Christian philosophy professors began to do good scholarly work, calling Christians neither to be afraid of the profession nor to hide their Christian commitments.[9] Since then, a large number of Christians have entered into the discipline of academic philosophy, and it is difficult to find a philosophy department in a well-respected college or university that does not have at least one Christian in it. From almost no Christians to the plethora of Christians and Christian scholarship that we see now, we've witnessed formerly hostile environments become places where Christians can thrive and carry out their vocation in pursuing truth as they follow Christ.

Similarly, one area today that receives much criticism, especially by some Christians, is the news media, particularly what is labeled the "mainstream media." Now there are Christian journalists, but there seem to be too few of them. And news sources do seem to exhibit bias or perpetuate political agendas to boost ratings, whether of a conservative or a progressive bent. What is needed are Christians in journalism who are willing to speak the truth and not merely what is popular or what will satisfy or flatter their fan base. Sometimes it is hard to take a stand and call out something as wrong or evil when the rest of your group or party disagrees. However, Christians who are committed to the truth should be courageous and willing to do so. Moreover, the media is often criticized for being unreliable, given its biases and hidden (or not-so-hidden) political agendas. But organizations can regain trust by becoming places that are trustworthy and by filling them with trustworthy people.

Now, we understand the source of frustration for many Christians. We have read or seen many news reports that paint Christians or Christianity in inaccurate or unflattering ways. Often, the problem seems to be ignorance of what Christianity even is.[10] And we are not called to take an eye

---

9. For one notable example, see Alvin Plantinga, "Advice to Christian Philosophers," *Faith and Philosophy* 1 (1984): 253-71.

10. While there are many differences among Christian branches and among

for an eye (Matt. 5:38). Just as there has been a rise of Christians in philosophy and academia, we hope for a rise of Christians in the media, especially those willing to speak the truth at the cost of unpopularity. We would expect such individuals to be willing even to admit mistakes and rectify them, being okay with such admissions, since all sources of information apart from Scripture are fallible. However, we hope that all Christians who are committed to the truth would not consume only media that reinforces their current allegiance but would exercise discernment and avoid sources that include slander or denigration of people who are experts in their fields. Perhaps this may seem idealistic to some. But to us, this looks like Christianity at work in the media.

Conclusion

Our starting point in thinking about conspiracy theories is to claim that Christians should value truth because Jesus Christ is the truth. Pursuing truth involves reading widely, assessing evidence carefully, and valuing the opinions of those who are in a position to know. We must also practice discernment and reject those who speak in flattering ways but do not bear fruit. The lessons we have learned are to deepen our trust in God, to avoid gossip and slander, and to unglue ourselves from unedifying obsessions—and this may help us steer clear of problematic conspiracy theories. Our hope is that Christians will engage in more productive conversations with each other—paraphrasing, praising, and probing each other's views. Finally, we long to see more Christian journalists who are willing to stand up for the truth. These may be lofty hopes, but we also believe in the power and presence of the Holy Spirit, and so we maintain that our hope is rational. We are striving to live our lives seeking truth, and we hope to be joined by all who are following in the way of Jesus, who is the truth.[11]

Christians, there is much overlap as well, and much of what is depicted seems at best to be a caricature of any real Christian or Christian commitment.

11. Thanks to Charles Barker, Gaston Espinosa, David Frederick, Seth Freeman, Craig Friske, Alan Padgett, Susan Peppers-Bates, John Baptist Santa Ana, and James Smith for helpful comments on earlier drafts.

References

Douglas, Karen M., Joseph E. Uscinski, Robbie M. Sutton, Aleksandra Cichocka, Turkay Nefes, Chee Siang Ang, and Farzin Deravi. "Understanding Conspiracy Theories." *Advances in Political Psychology* 40 (2019): 3-35.

Lewis, C. S. "Inner Ring." In *The Weight of Glory and Other Addresses*. New York: HarperCollins, 2001.

Millson, Jared. "Conspiracy Theories." 1000-Word Philosophy, December 17, 2020. https://1000wordphilosophy.com/2020/12/17/conspiracy-theories/.

Plantinga, Alvin. "Advice to Christian Philosophers." *Faith and Philosophy* 1 (1984): 253-71.

Zagzebski, Linda. *Epistemic Authority*. Oxford: Oxford University Press, 2012.

2

IS IT ALWAYS WRONG TO BELIEVE A CONSPIRACY THEORY?

Chad Bogosian

Throughout the 2016 and 2020 US elections, there appeared to be a boom in conspiracy theories to help *explain* what was going on in our national circus called "politics." For example, we heard reports of Russian election interference, Ukrainian meddling, Pizzagate, and Q'Anon.[1] Conspiracy theories[2] are nothing new, yet they seem attractive to either those who

---

1. Nina Jankowicz, "How an Anti-Trump Flash Mob Found Itself in the Middle of Russian Meddling," *Politico*, July 5, 2020, https://www.politico.com/news/mag azine/2020/07/05/how-an-anti-trump-flash-mob-found-itself-in-the-middle-of -russian-meddling-348729; Julian E. Barnes and Matthew Rosenberg, "Charges of Ukrainian Meddling? A Russian Operation, U.S. Intelligence Says," *New York Times*, updated May 27, 2021, https://www.nytimes.com/2019/11/22/us/politics/ukraine -russia-interference.html; Alex Nelson, "What Is Pizzagate? The Fake News Scan- dal Involving Hilary Clinton and Wikileaks Explained—and Why It's Trending amid Epstein Inquiry," *Scotsman*, July 22, 2020, https://www.scotsman.com/news/politics /what-pizzagate-fake-news-scandal-involving-hilary-clinton-and-wikileaks -explained-and-why-its-trending-amid-epstein-inquiry-2879166; Adrienne La- France, "The Prophecies of Q," *Atlantic*, June 2020, https://www.theatlantic.com /magazine/archive/2020/06/qanon-nothing-can-stop-what-is-coming/610567/.

2. It's important to acknowledge that there's a difference between "conspira- cies" and "conspiracy theories." Below I define each, and I believe there is not a big difference between them, which is why I treat them together in this chapter. In everyday popular dialogue, however, some speak as if "conspiracies" are more likely candidates for rational beliefs, because we know that people conspire all the time to do A or B. However, "conspiracy theories" are irrational because these are

don't like what's going on in the political arena such as losing an election, or those who wish to dismiss as irrational a potentially damning claim such as one's husband being guilty of sexual relations with a subordinate political aid.[3] Like many, I have been deeply concerned and embarrassed about the readiness of many—especially Christians—to espouse conspiracy theories in these election cycles. While I was initially of the persuasion that conspiracy theories are irrational by definition, I have changed my mind, though I will not argue for the veracity of any particular one below. Rather, I will argue that it is sometimes reasonable to believe a conspiracy (theory), though there are multiple ways most are undermined.

What Is a Conspiracy (Theory)? Satan, Sex, and God

Whether it is rational or irrational to believe a conspiracy depends in part on what qualifies a claim or theory under this label. Let us begin by stating some well-known conspiracies/conspiracy theories in order to help define the term:

1. The United States government orchestrated the attacks on 9/11.
2. The Russian government interfered with the 2016 US election.
3. A cabal of Satan-worshiping pedophiles running a global child sex-trafficking ring is plotting against Donald Trump, who is battling them.
4. Accusations that President Clinton had sexual relations with a subordinate is the result of a "vast right-wing conspiracy."
5. There exists a benevolent tripersonal God who is advancing his good and beautiful kingdom through his son Jesus of Nazareth. Jesus invites all wayward humans to follow him and become coconspirators with him to overcome evil with good.[4]

---

just false beliefs or explanations people hold for a range of bad reasons. My definitions below should partially expose this way of differentiating them as incorrect. In addition, all claims or theories must be candidates for being true or false, so it won't do to define either concept in such a way as to make them false by definition. This too should become clear below, and I hope our way of talking about these concepts will improve in light of my arguments.

3. David Maraniss, "First Lady Launches Counterattack," *Washington Post*, January 28, 1998, https://www.washingtonpost.com/wp-srv/politics/special/clinton/stories/hillary012898.htm.

4. Dallas Willard, *The Divine Conspiracy: Rediscovering Our Hidden Life in God* (San Francisco: HarperSanFrancisco, 1998).

What makes each of these claims a *conspiracy*? Philosopher Jared Millson offers a helpful definition: "Conspiracies are actions or plans undertaken by a small group of individuals working in secret to achieve shared goals. These goals need not be sinister: the African National Congress conspired for decades to bring down the apartheid regime in South Africa—a noble aspiration."[5] Notice here that two key aspects of this definition are *a small group* and *secrecy or hidden actions unknown to everyone*. These help us see why number 4 in our list *may* not be considered a conspiracy, because "the right wing" is a group too large to work together in secret to take down the president of the United States. Of course, a small group of right-wingers could conspire against the president, in which case it would pass our definition. Assuming so, then, numbers 1-5 are conspiracies due to the secrecy and size of the groups.

A *conspiracy theory* is usually a set of claims that offers an *explanation* of alleged facts or events by pointing to its underlying (hidden) causes.[6] Claims 1-3 above attempt to explain why a particular candidate won or lost a presidential election, or why hundreds of lives were tragically lost when planes flew into buildings on 9/11/2001. Interestingly, in number 5 above, Christianity teaches that a triune God who is spirit is working behind the scenes to guide human history toward good ends. As part of his plan, he has "shown up" through prophets, his followers, and Jesus of Nazareth, making himself and his ways known to morally wayward human persons who are ready and willing to hear, receive, and follow him and his ways. They become coconspirators to advance God's good will for other humans and the cosmos. Of course, this explanation of good and evil in the world can be ignored, suppressed, or rejected, but it is taken by Christians to be the best explanation of what's going on in the world around us as well as the hopeful end toward which the world is headed.

Why Do Some Dismiss Conspiracies as Irrational?

There are at least three reasons why people dismiss conspiracies or conspiracy theories as irrational. First, we might think them irrational by definition, because their claims sound strange, far-fetched, or wildly implausible.

---

5. Jared Millson, "Conspiracy Theories," 1000-Word Philosophy, December 17, 2020, https://1000wordphilosophy.com/2020/12/17/conspiracy-theories/.
6. Millson, "Conspiracy Theories," para. 2. See also M. R. X. Dentith, *The Philosophy of Conspiracy Theories* (New York: Palgrave Macmillan, 2014); M. R. X. Dentith, "The Problem of Conspiracism," *Argumenta* 3, no. 2 (2018): 327-43.

The problem with this approach is twofold. On the one hand, we all believe some conspiracies are *true*. For example, most believe in Watergate or that the 9/11 attacks on the Twin Towers were orchestrated by al Qaeda, or that Dietrich Bonhoeffer conspired to take down Hitler. Each of these satisfies our definition of "conspiracy," since a relatively small group worked in secret to bring about the events in question; and each of these beliefs is rational because it is directly supported by a body of available evidence.

On the other hand, people hold many other kinds of beliefs that might strike us as strange or implausible, but this wouldn't be enough to dub those beliefs irrational for them to hold. For example, religious or irreligious beliefs often strike the other side as being either strange or implausible, yet they are not irrational. Atheist philosopher William Rowe has argued for a view he calls "friendly atheism"[7] where atheists should view theists as *rational but wrong* about their theistic beliefs. After he considers all the relevant evidence, he sees how theists arrive at belief in God. However, he has good counters to that evidence as well as good reasons to believe God does not exist. In light of the available evidence, he views his opponents as having false but rational beliefs. Might we view those who believe (some) conspiracies the same way?

Second, one might be inclined to dismiss conspiracies because some who hold them act out violently as a result of their belief(s). We can and should condemn violence enacted by those who believe conspiracies, while at the same time highlighting that violence is *not* an *inherent feature* of these beliefs. Nonconspiracy ideological beliefs have also led to mass violence and human rights violations (e.g., communism, religious extremism, etc.). What's common across these belief types are *additional* moral beliefs about how to treat those who believe differently than we do.

Finally, one might find conspiracy beliefs irrational because they are not verified repeatedly by the sciences through scientific method. It is tempting in our proscience age to find this approach attractive, but it runs afoul in two ways. On the one hand, it makes many beliefs conspiracies that are in fact not conspiracies. Consider your beliefs about where you were born, your legal parents, and where you went to high school. You probably have some good evidence from testimony, memory, and written records (such as a birth certificate, yearbook, and diploma) that these beliefs are true. But you lack repeated scientific verification of the relevant sort. Thankfully,

---

7. William Rowe, "The Problem of Evil and Some Varieties of Atheism," *American Philosophical Quarterly* 16, no. 4 (October 1979): 335–41.

most would think your evidence for these claims is sufficient for these beliefs to be rational even while you lack scientific verification.

On the other hand, this definition implies that we can't trust or believe claims in history, literature, math, philosophy, or religion, because they too fail to meet this narrow criterion for rational belief—that is, repeated scientific verification. While scientific evidence and the scientific method are important, science isn't the only way to support beliefs or gain knowledge of ourselves and the world. What this means is that conspiracies or conspiracy theories can be rational to believe, but if they are, it's because they have good evidence to indicate their truth. This naturally leads us to inquire about how and why we should support our beliefs, as well as what counts as good evidence.

How Should We Form Beliefs Generally: What Counts as Good Evidence?

Many years ago, philosopher William K. Clifford wrote a thought-provoking paper about how we should form our beliefs and why it matters. He asks us to consider a shipowner whose ship has been on many voyages and is now resting in port. Upon inspection, the shipowner discovers it is severely worn from its time at sea and requires many repairs to travel safely again. But the owner is concerned about time and money, and keeping it in port for repairs would be too costly. So, the owner reasons that it is a good and trustworthy ship that has been on many successful voyages and has returned to port safely each time. The ship is likely to make a safe voyage one more time. Unfortunately, however, he sends out the battered ship full of people, and a bad storm sinks it, killing everyone on board. The moral of the story is, we should be the kinds of people who form beliefs responsibly on the basis of good evidence, rather than whimsical people who ignore and suppress evidence relevant to our beliefs. Additionally, being people committed to valuing truth and evidence is essential to building a good, just, and safe society. Our beliefs are like rails that our lives run on.[8] Since belief formation is a high-stakes game, "It is wrong always, everywhere, and for anyone, to believe anything upon insufficient evidence."[9]

8. Dallas Willard, *Knowing Christ Today: Why We Can Trust Spiritual Knowledge* (New York: Harper One, 2014), esp. 13–50, where he discusses the nature of belief, knowledge, faith, and assent.

9. William K. Clifford, "The Ethics of Belief," in *Lectures and Essays* (London: Macmillan, 1879).

But what counts as "good evidence" in support of one's beliefs? Evidence to support our beliefs might come from a handful of sources, such as perception, experience, testimony, memory, conceptual insight (e.g., "all bachelors are unmarried"), and cognitive intuition. Worth noting is that a single belief need not have support from all these sources. Rather, it needs *direct evidence* from one or more of these sources, depending on the belief in question. For example, the belief that I should pull my car over to the side of the road when I hear sirens is *directly* supported by my perceptual inputs as well as my memory about related driving laws. Or believing that a person on trial is guilty beyond a reasonable doubt is *directly* supported by multiple testimonies to the person's guilt in the courtroom. Or a Christian-theist might have a body of evidence from reason, history, and experience to *directly* support one's religious beliefs.

What counts as good evidence is sometimes debated case by case, but generally, we should seek out the best quality of evidence from each source relevant to the subject matter. On the topics of science, religion, morality, and politics, reliable and trustworthy sources might include *direct evidence* from original or other quality documents, knowledgeable persons who seek the truth, as well as expert testimony. Additionally, good evidence might include *indirect evidence* about the topic at hand: what experts have to say about the direct evidence, that politicians are often deceptive and conniving, and the fact that both experts and your intellectual peers disagree about the topic. Wishful thinking, conjecture, blind leaps, gut feelings or hunches, opinionated friends on social media, etc., are generally considered *poor quality evidence*. While you might turn out to have a true belief about something you wish for, this is likely a matter of cognitive luck, since wishful thinking doesn't typically generate true beliefs.

How Should We Critically Evaluate Our Beliefs or Conspiracy Theories?

More could be said about the nature of evidence and how it may support one's beliefs, but it is time to consider how this applies to critically evaluating conspiracy theories. Generally, if a person lacks good evidence from any of the sources mentioned above, or if the person believes a conspiracy (theory) on a whim or on the basis of some other sketchy source, then the belief would be irrational. However, it is *possible* for a conspiracy theory to be supported by evidence from one or more of the good sources named above. For example, one's perceptual and testimonial evidence might be strong that there was Russian interference in the 2016 election. Or a Christian may have undergone a transformative spiritual experience that led to knowledge of Christ and subsequent conversion to the divine conspiracy. In either case, these conspiracy theory beliefs would have supporting evidence (that could be overturned), so the person believing the theory could be seen as rational. There's an important distinction between supporting and persuasive evidence. One might have good supporting evidence for the conspiracy theory that fails to persuade one's friends. Not being able to persuade one's friends wouldn't count against a particular conspiracy theory (or any other) belief. What matters most is that one has good evidence which supports one's beliefs. That's what counts toward the rationality of the conspiracy theory belief (or any belief) in question.

While it may *sometimes* be rational to believe a conspiracy theory, there are at least three ways one's conspiracy theory belief might be *undermined* or *defeated*. Remember, an irrational belief is one we should abandon or at least suspend judgment on if the evidence is inconclusive, weak, or undermined. First, conspiracy theories are often undermined, because they lack *publicly available support* for their truth. While it might *seem* to one that the conspiracy best explains the event or issue in question, this seeming is not strong enough to counter the publicly available evidence that the conspiracy is false. What would better support a conspiracy theory is leaked evidence revealing what's going on. An insider or whistle-blower could reveal documents, recordings, or firsthand testimony attesting to the details of the conspiracy.[10] But leaked evidence is usually lacking, perhaps out of fear that the leaker would be punished. Nevertheless, this lack of supporting evidence is a strong reason to discount and not believe a conspiracy theory.

Second, a conspiracy theory is undermined when parts of its explanation include additional *erroneous* claims that are either in conflict with the official story or that cannot be explained by the official story. Granted, the official story *could* be incomplete or misleading, but that is beside the point. Without salient direct evidence, the official story *is* incomplete or misleading, and it would be unreasonable to maintain this. To do so allows entry into one's body of evidence speculation or wishful thinking that degrades the quality of one's total evidence. Since wishful thinking has a relatively negative track record in reliably supporting beliefs or theories, we should

10. S. Clarke, "Conspiracy Theories and Conspiracy Theorizing," *Philosophy of the Social Sciences* 32, no. 2 (2002): 131–50; P. Mandik, "Shit Happens," *Episteme* 4, no. 2 (2007): 205–18.

not adopt a theory to explain events or other data simply because we wish, hope, or want it to be true. If we do, we allow errant beliefs or other cognitive states to enter the picture, reducing our level of rational responsiveness to the world around us.

Additionally, if the conspiracy theory is only a partial (rather than a full) explanation of the events or data in question, this counts against the truth of the conspiracy theory. A helpful example here is that some 9/11 conspiracy theories are unable to explain why there is a video of Osama bin Laden claiming responsibility for the attacks.[11] Conspiracy theorists might reply that their explanation, while partial rather than full, is simpler than the official story. Simple explanations are to be preferred over complex ones, so the conspiracy theory is a better explanation.[12] While I agree that preferring simpler explanations over complex ones is a good approach generally,[13] simplicity by itself is not sufficient to render one explanation the best among its competitors. Another mark of a "best explanation" is that it plausibly and thoroughly explains all the data. If explanation A (the official story) does this while explanation B (the conspiracy theory) does not, then explanation B's being simpler fails to render it the overall best explanation (at least for now).

Third, a conspiracy theory might be undermined because it fails to include the testimony of experts in its explanation of the data in question, and these experts often provide counterevidence to the conspiracy theory. Experts possess knowledge that many of us lack, so we trust their testimonies on many issues. Disregarding expert testimonial evidence requires a good reason. One reason conspiracy theorists might offer is that the experts themselves are coconspirators, so they can't be trusted with the "official story." Granted, expert coconspiring is possible, but we need direct evidence that this is going on, something more than a hunch, whim, or wish.

Another, and I think stronger, reason one might disregard expert testimony is due to *disagreement among experts* about the topic or purported conspiracy at hand. Expert disagreement provides one with evidence that may cancel out the weight of expert testimony regarding the official story,

11. Clarke, "Conspiracy Theories and Conspiracy Theorizing," 131–50; M. R. X. Dentith, "Conspiracy Theories on the Basis of the Evidence," *Synthese* 196, no. 6 (2019): 2243–61.
12. Millson, "Conspiracy Theories."
13. This expresses a common explanatory principle called Occam's razor.

thereby leaving one with the remaining evidence to weigh for or against the conspiracy theory. This doesn't mean one is automatically rational to believe a conspiracy theory any time experts disagree; rather, it indicates that expert testimony can be neutralized or defeated. That said, it's possible that dissenting experts may be debunked for various reasons, and this must also be considered carefully before dismissing expert testimony and believing a conspiracy theory.

In the end, it is sometimes reasonable to believe a conspiracy or conspiracy theory, but only when it is supported by good evidence and all objections to that evidence have been carefully addressed. Many conspiracy theories will be unreasonable to believe, because they either insufficiently explain the data, lack publicly available evidence, or fail to take expert testimony into account. And some purported conspiracies, like claim 4 in our list above, will turn out to be so in light of good evidential analysis. As Christians, an *agapē*-centered intellectual life and ethic require that we love God with our minds, and this includes loving the truth, being careful to acquire good evidence, seek understanding, and willingly suspend judgment when our beliefs about the world are on shaky ground. Being these kinds of persons help us thrive intellectually, relationally, and socially.[14]

References

Barnes, Julian E., and Matthew Rosenberg. "Charges of Ukrainian Meddling? A Russian Operation, U.S. Intelligence Says." *New York Times*, updated May 27, 2021. https://www.nytimes.com/2019/11/22/us/politics/ukraine -russia-interference.html.

Clarke, S. "Conspiracy Theories and Conspiracy Theorizing." *Philosophy of the Social Sciences* 32, no. 2 (2002): 131–50.

Clifford, William K. "The Ethics of Belief." In *Lectures and Essays*. London: Macmillan, 1879.

Dentith, M. X. R. "Conspiracy Theories on the Basis of the Evidence." *Synthese* 196, no. 6 (2019): 2243–61.

———. *The Philosophy of Conspiracy Theories*. New York: Palgrave Macmillan, 2014.

———. "The Problem of Conspiracism." *Argumenta* 3, no. 2 (2018): 327–43.

Jankowicz, Nina. "How an Anti-Trump Flash Mob Found Itself in the Mid-

---

14. I want to thank Dan Churchwell for comments that helped me clarify and tighten my chapter.

dle of Russian Meddling." *Politico*, July 5, 2020. https://www.politico.com/news/magazine/2020/07/05/how-an-anti-trump-flash-mob-found-itself-in-the-middle-of-russian-meddling-348729.

LaFrance, Adrienne. "The Prophecies of Q." *Atlantic*, June 2020. https://www.theatlantic.com/magazine/archive/2020/06/qanon-nothing-can-stop-what-is-coming/610567/.

Mandik, P. "Shit Happens." *Episteme* 4, no. 2 (2007): 205–18.

Maraniss, David. "First Lady Launches Counterattack." *Washington Post*, January 28, 1998. https://www.washingtonpost.com/wp-srv/politics/special/clinton/stories/hillary012898.htm.

Millson, Jared. "Conspiracy Theories." 1000-Word Philosophy, December 17, 2020. https://1000wordphilosophy.com/2020/12/17/conspiracy-theories/.

Nelson, Alex. "What Is Pizzagate? The Fake News Scandal Involving Hilary Clinton and Wikileaks Explained—and Why It's Trending amid Epstein Inquiry." *Scotsman*, July 22, 2020. https://www.scotsman.com/news/politics/what-pizzagate-fake-news-scandal-involving-hilary-clinton-and-wikileaks-explained-and-why-its-trending-amid-epstein-inquiry-2879166.

Rowe, William. "The Problem of Evil and Some Varieties of Atheism." *American Philosophical Quarterly* 16, no. 4 (October 1979): 335–41.

Willard, Dallas. *The Divine Conspiracy: Rediscovering Our Hidden Life in God*. San Francisco: HarperSanFrancisco, 1998.

——. *Knowing Christ Today: Why We Can Trust Spiritual Knowledge*. New York: Harper One, 2014.

3

THE COST OF DEBUNKING CONSPIRACY THEORIES

Scott Culpepper

Christian comedian Mike Warnke paced the stage of an independent interdenominational church near Chicago in the fall of 1991. He stood at the height of his influence without realizing it. Warnke was worth millions of dollars and jetted from one performance to the next aboard a private plane. His label, Word Records, proclaimed him the number one Christian comedian, and the title was legitimate.

The Satan Seller

It turned out that his title was the only legitimate thing about Mike Warnke. The nets were closing in on the self-proclaimed former satanic high priest. Warnke had spent two decades spreading the tale of his immersion in the occult and escape through conversion to Christianity. He popularized that story in *The Satan Seller* (1972), using the book as a means to build his platform as a Christian comedian and supposed expert on satanic ritual abuse. His "expertise" connected with the emerging "Satanic Panic" in the 1980s, giving him opportunities to consult with law enforcement and appear on mainstream television shows such as *20/20* in 1985 and Geraldo Rivera's now infamous "Devil Worship: Exposing Satan's Underground" in 1988.

Warnke knew the jig was up. He spotted two journalists in the crowd that night, Mike Hertenstein and Jon Trott. Trott and Hertenstein worked for *Cornerstone*, the flagship publication of a Chicago-based Christian communal group, Jesus People USA. Warnke's associates at his ministry headquarters in Lexington, Kentucky, had told him Hertenstein and Trott were seen investigating Warnke Ministries' financial records at a local courthouse. That night, Warnke announced to his stunned audience, "There's a bunch of people right now launching a campaign to drive me out of the ministry. And, you know what? There's only one way I'm leaving this ministry. Jesus will tell me that he's finished with me and then I will sit down. Or, you will have to pry my Bible out of my cold, dead hand. And that is the only way."

The anticipated storm broke in the summer of 1992 when Trott and Hertenstein's article "Selling Satan" appeared in the June/July issue of *Cornerstone*. Their exposé told the story of a pathological liar, serial adulterer, and extortionist who had built a reputation as "America's Number One Christian Comedian" on a foundation of fraud. Extensive interviews with Warnke's college classmates at San Bernardino Valley College revealed that it was not possible for Warnke to have been involved in the occult during his one-year stint at the college. Pictures of Warnke at the time he claimed to be a drug-addicted long-haired satanic high priest showed him as a somewhat "square" college student with short hair and understated dress. Warnke inserted his first wife, Sue, into the narrative of *The Satan Seller* in place of his actual fiancée at the time, Lois. Maybe Warnke wanted to eliminate her from the narrative because Lois was prone to say things like, "If he says he was a Satanist between September of 1965 to June of 1966, he's lying. How could I not know my boyfriend was into satanism? I don't remember there ever being a time when we didn't see or talk to each other every day." *Cornerstone* shredded Warnke's testimony with detailed accounts contradicting Warnke's assertions at every turn.

Equally shocking revelations about Warnke's conduct after his ministry began filled the latter half of the article. Warnke was married four times and accused of cheating on some of those wives with other women. He cheated on his first wife with a classmate, Carolyn Alberty, while he was attending Bible college in Colorado. Alberty married Warnke, but they divorced in 1979 amid allegations of physical abuse and death threats. His third wife, Rose Hall, married Warnke in 1979 and became a critical component of his ministries' administration. Rose was taking in almost as much salary as Warnke in the mid-1980s. She released *The Great Pretender* in 1985, in which she wrote, "Satan provided a woman to fill the gap in Michael's life." He eventually left Rose in 1991 for Susan Patton, wife number four and fellow alumnus of Rim of the World High School.

Warnke admitted to financial abuses and placed himself under the accountability of an elders group following the release of the article.

Subsequent investigations by both Christian and mainstream reporters supported and extended the original findings of Trott and Hertenstein. Although he admitted to the financial improprieties and apologized for his marital transgressions, Warnke insisted that his involvement with satanism was true. Even after ten years had elapsed, Warnke repeated his claims in *Friendly Fire: A Recovery Guide for Believers Battered by Religion*, published in 2002. In a pattern now sadly familiar to students of contemporary American evangelicalism, Warnke cast himself as the victim and his detractors as pharisaical busybodies who cared more about exposing sin than proclaiming the gospel of grace. His defiant tone permeates the book and equates his years of public deception to someone suffering from local church gossip. He sidestepped accusations of fabricating his satanic past by insisting that he had only exaggerated certain aspects of his tale. For instance, rather than leading a satanic cult of 1,500, he had actually led a cult of 15 or so. Warnke wrote in *Friendly Fire*, "On January 25, 1993, I issued a public written statement in which I stood by my original testimony as to former satanic involvement. At the same time, I clarified and acknowledged some exaggerations and embellishments in the story that were due to old and perhaps faulty memories as well as deliberate attempts to 'protect the innocent.' Exaggeration is also an integral part of comedy, but in some cases in my concerts I had stepped over the line, forgetting my responsibilities as a minister of the gospel for the sake of being good at my 'job.'" Warnke, now an ordained "independent bishop," continues to minister on a smaller scale and sticks to his claims about satanism.

Unmasking the Satanic Panic Underground

Why does this matter? After all, didn't Warnke lead all kinds of people to Christ during the years he was lying about his past and raking in millions? Surely the myths that inspire us are more important than the disappointing realities that may lie behind them. Who was he really hurting? Do conspiracy theories really need to be debunked if they do some good in the midst of the harm?

There are a number of good responses to those questions. It's important to understand that Mike Warnke was far from alone in his deceptions. A number of Christian leaders created a whole culture of belief about satanic practices in America that equals the work of J. R. R. Tolkien and George R. R. Martin in their creation of fantasy worlds. What looks at first glance like a spontaneous eruption of unconnected observations about satanic ritual abuse is revealed to be an interconnected web of popular speakers and writers feeding off each other's mythologies and adding their own embellishments to the mix. *Cornerstone* started down the path to their exposé of Mike Warnke due to several exposés on alleged satanic cult survivors and the pushback their investigations provoked from fellow Christians.

Laurel Rose Wilson adopted the name Laura Stratford and published *Satan's Underground* in 1988. It's no coincidence that Geraldo Rivera's special, released later that year, carried the subtitle "Exposing Satan's Underground." Stratford was promoted by Johanna Michaelsen, a staunch Warnke ally, and by Warnke himself. Michaelsen published her own tale of escape from the occult in 1982, titled *The Beautiful Side of Evil*. She claimed psychic power inherited from her grandmother and told stories of her flirtation with occult phenomena before converting to Christianity. Stratford gained the endorsement of popular prophecy writer Hal Lindsey through Michaelsen, his sister-in-law at the time. Lindsey himself published *Satan Is Alive and Well on Planet Earth* in 1972, the same year Warnke published *The Satan Seller*. One of the great ironies about the Satanic Panic is that those who imagined conspiracies everywhere were themselves linked in collaborations that mimicked their wildest fantasies. Stratford claimed to have been a baby breeder for a satanist group and participated in the sacrifice of her own child as part of a satanic ritual. She said she also gave birth to two other children who were killed in snuff films produced by the satanists. A *Cornerstone* investigation gathered testimony from friends and family, including her parents, sister, and ex-husband. They said they had never witnessed any satanic influence in Stratford's life, nor was she ever pregnant. Following the reveal by *Cornerstone* in the early nineties, Stratford disappeared for a while, only to reemerge under the name Laura Grabowski. She claimed in this guise to be a Holocaust survivor. Like Warnke, Stratford influenced the legal system. Stratford inserted herself into the infamous McMartin preschool trial, insisting that she had witnessed satanic ritual abuse at the preschool and that she had a lesbian relationship with preschool owner Virginia McMartin. The allegations collapsed in the early nineties, as no evidence of satanic ritual abuse was found.

Furious attacks waged against the *Cornerstone* journalists by Stratford's defenders furthered the Warnke story. The magazine published its story about Stratford on December 8, 1989. Lindsey used radio appearances and his show on the Trinity Broadcasting Network to raise doubts about the integrity and motives of the *Cornerstone* journalists. Words like "muckrakers," "pharisees," and "legalists" were tossed at the reporters by Lindsey, Michaelsen, and many lesser-known advocates of satanic ritual abuse myths. More dangerous were the accusations that *Cornerstone* and Jesus People USA were acting as a front for the satanic conspiracy in the guise of an anticult ministry. Bob and Gretchen Passantino, a husband-and-wife team who ran a ministry called Answers in Action in California, assisted Trott in the research and writing of the article about Stratford. They received some of the most vigorous attacks from fellow Christians, because of heavy support for Stratford among some evangelicals in Southern California.

Trott and Hertenstein described conversations with ABC producer Ken Wooden, who had produced a 20/20 program on Stratford. Wooden advised all parties to hold their questions about Stratford's veracity because investigators were on the trail of the cult she exposed in her book, and further attention now would wreck the investigation. The individuals in Stratford's account were never identified, and Wooden refused to join Stratford's media defense once it became clear that her story was false. Stratford's publisher, Harvest House, attempted to defend her at first, but then they withdrew the book and a planned sequel from publication in January 1990, offering no explanation for the cancellations. Harvest House released the rights to a small Louisiana publisher called Pelican Books. Hertenstein and Trott wrote in *Selling Satan*, "The pragmatic outlook of the Christian public surprised the journalists. The many defenders of Stratford put false sincerity and therapeutic authority over substantiated fact. Again and again, in the face of the mass of evidence compiled, callers asked Trott how he could question someone professing Christ."

Similar fallout ensued as Warnke ministries imploded in 1991 and 1992. *Cornerstone* investigated Warnke because all the satanic ritual abuse testimonies they had previously exposed pointed back to Warnke's for validation, even though the sensational details now common to the new breed of satanic abuse survivors were not a part of his story. Also, Jesus People USA had enjoyed a close working relationship with Warnke in the seventies and promoted some of his events. Even then some leaders in the group knew that Warnke had problematic tendencies. Some *Cornerstone* journalists saw tackling the Warnke tale as an act of justice too long delayed.

The hostility stemming from their previous articles offered a small preview of the exponentially larger roasting *Cornerstone* and its allies received from Warnke's defenders. In an infamous November 1992 *Christianity Today* article, Rose Hall Warnke said that *Cornerstone*, the Christian Research Institute, and the Passantinos were part of a satanic cult and that *Cornerstone* would kill *Christianity Today* reporter Perucci Ferraiuolo if he published their side of the story. When Ferraiuolo did just that, Mike and Rose denied what they said. Ferraiuolo played the audio of their interview to several media outlets to prove that his quotes were genuine.

Kingdoms of Lies and Legacies of Misinformation

Mike Warnke, Laura Stratford, and hosts of other Christian advocates of satanic ritual abuse myths could not maintain their fiction alone for as long as they did. So many people had to look the other way. Publishers, record companies, churches, pastors, and many other people within the evangelical subcultures of the seventies and eighties ignored suspicious activity before *Cornerstone* gathered the evidence that had been sitting in plain sight for years. *Cornerstone* enjoyed an advantage in the sense that Jesus People USA already stood apart from the mainstream of popular Christian publishing and media. However, the evangelical cultural gatekeepers supported and promoted too many Christian celebrities with dubious backgrounds for far too long, until it became absolutely impossible for them to do so any longer. Even as I write this in 2021, a podcast series produced by *Christianity Today* is wrestling with the destructive influence of Mark Driscoll. Kristin Kobes Du Mez's book *Jesus and John Wayne* has laid bare the destructive influence of masochistic cultures supported and defended by popular evangelical gatekeepers. David Barton, Eric Metaxas, and a host of lesser-known imitators peddle fantasized versions of American history to eager popular Christian audiences. QAnon conspiracy theorists circulate stories about satanic pedophile rings plotting the downfall of America while they ravage the young. It seems that we have learned little since the days of Mike Warnke and Laura Stratford. That makes revisiting their stories of paramount importance.

There is also the religious liberty issue. And I don't mean the fantasies of radical "New Agers" seeking to control the levers of education and government in the name of Satan promoted by the likes of Frank Peretti. The Christian Satanic Panic mythologies cast people practicing alternative religions in the worst light possible. If anyone was battered by religion, it was not Mike Warnke, but the hosts of people he slandered and libeled through his fantasy world. One feels little sympathy for Anton LaVey and his Church of Satan, in part because LaVey was being intentionally provocative when he created the satirical church. Little did LaVey know that the Manson murders in 1969 and the cultural shifts of the early seventies would convince people that the atheistic group really was worshiping Satan and sacrificing children. The sympathy here goes to practitioners of Wicca, Druidry, and a host of other neopagan religions that had nothing to do with satanism, real or imagined. These people suffered the stigma of association with child abuse and blood sacrifice until pop culture came to their rescue in the late nineties with shows like *Buffy the Vampire Slayer* and *Charmed* that began to cultivate a friendlier image of paganism. Far too many Christian apologists attacked cruel straw-man depictions of these religious groups rather than engage with the real differences between Christianity and these religious movements.

A host of Generation Xers like myself grew up hearing diatribes against Dungeons & Dragons, the Smurfs, He-Man, and many other pop culture icons. Heavy metal music would melt the brain and drive one to suicide. The net result was a generation raised to believe the world was scary and binary, poised between absolute good and evil with no room for gray. The notion that good and evil run through the soul of every human, that we all can be both sinners and saints, gets lost in that constant warfare perspective. Horrifying consequences flowed from these kingdoms of lies. Imagine the defendants whose fate rested in occult "expert" Mike Warnke's hands as he fed information to the police on satanic ritual practices that was sheer fabrication culled from a variety of equally untrustworthy sources.

Costly and Consequential Christian Debunking

Conspiracy theories need to be debunked for the good of Christian communities. Unfortunately, Christian communities make that harder when they attack the messengers rather than weigh the validity of evidence being presented. Logic would argue that communities more readily accept criticism from their own rather than from outsiders, that Christians would naturally resist exposure of their own by "secular" media outlets thought hostile to the faith while being more open to friendly correction from inside. However, the examples cited throughout this chapter indicate that Christians can be just as hard, if not harder, on insiders who dare to question cherished myths. The cost rises immeasurably higher for insiders. Outsiders are spurned by a community already predisposed to reject them. Insiders stand to lose their faith community, family connections, and possibly even their livelihood. None of these things will be easy to recover for insiders, because they have made commitments as part of the community that prevent them from easily turning to the outside for all those things. Christian insiders who dare to tell the truth, following the very principles of the faith they were taught by their faith communities, face exile by those same faith communities for living out the very calling they were taught to observe. Christian debunkers know the proverbial rock and hard place well.

Sadly, willingness to resist conspiracy theories in one area does not ensure that Christians, their communities, and their subcultures will apply critical thinking consistently. *Cornerstone* deserves a fair share of the credit for discrediting satanic ritual abuse myths in mainstream cultures. Journalists from the magazine, most of them also committed members of the Jesus People USA communal experiment, applied rigorous investigative standards and a high commitment to truth to that end, from the seventies to the early nineties. In 1993, Jesus People USA faced criticism from sociologist Ronald Enroth over allegations of abuse within the community, including emotional and sexual abuse. Many of the same individuals who pursued cases of satanic panic mythologies with such determined zest for transparency circled the wagons and defended their community in ways reminiscent of evangelical gatekeepers defending their favorite stars. *Cornerstone* itself went the way of so many other periodicals in the age of social media, publishing their final issue in 2003. Controversy has continued to haunt the community in the first two decades of the new century, with investigative reporting by various media outlets, accusations of an authoritarian abusive atmosphere, and a lawsuit filed in 2014 and dismissed in 2015.

Human nature clamors for certainty to ease our fears and vindicate our hopes. Charismatic individuals, some well intentioned and others unscrupulous, will always appear to tell us what we want to hear. Sometimes even the horror stories they tell are preferable to the hard work of facing the world as it actually is. If Christians are truly a people of truth, Christian communities should welcome discerning voices with the courage to set the story straight and help us view reality in all its amazing complexity.

References

Ferraiuolo, Perucci. "Warnke Calls Critics Satanists." *Christianity Today*, November 9, 1992.

Hertenstein, Mike, and John Trott. *Selling Satan: The Evangelical Media and the Mike Warnke Scandal*. Chicago: Cornerstone, 1993.

Lindsey, Hal, and C. C. Carlson. *Satan Is Alive and Well on Planet Earth*. Grand
    Rapids: Zondervan, 1972.

Stratford, Laura. *Satan's Underground*. Eugene, OR: Harvest House, 1988.

Warnke, Mike. *Friendly Fire: A Recovery Guide for Believers Battered by Religion*.
    Shippensburg, PA: Destiny Image Publishers, 2002.

——. *The Satan Seller*. Plainfield, NJ: Logos Associates, 1972.

4

CAN WE TRUST SCIENCE?

Garrett J. DeWeese

The headlines blare (and scare): "Nasa Faked Moon Landings, Filmed on a Hollywood Sound Stage!" "New Evidence Proves Earth Is Flat!" "Vaccine Contains Microchips! The Government Can Track You!"

Are there conspiracy theories in science? Surprisingly, yes. Discussions of these three, and many more besides, can be found across the Internet, with many slick productions on YouTube.

However, this chapter will not directly address conspiracy theories in science. We will instead consider a broader—and more important—question: Can we trust science?

Is This Really a Problem?

We live in a truly amazing age of scientific discoveries and their fruit in technological innovations. Science and technology have, in the main, made our lives immeasurably easier than the lives of our grandparents, and have raised billions of people out of abject poverty and disease. And yet, public trust in science is surprisingly low. A 2019 Pew Research Center survey showed that only 35 percent of Americans trust science "a lot."[1]

Trust between individuals, and within and between communities, is

---

1. "How to Build Community, Connection, and Trust in Science," Pew Research Center, October 2, 2020, https://www.pewtrusts.org/en/research-and-analysis /articles/2020/10/02/how-to-build-community-connection-and-trust-in-science.

essential for human flourishing, so a lack of trust in a major institution like science is a problem. Science—theoretical or applied—lies behind much in our lives. Building codes are developed so houses don't fall down on families and office buildings can withstand (many) hurricanes. Auto safety standards are similarly based in applied science. Science is employed in designing the electrical grid to get power from the generators to your refrigerator, and again in assessing why the grid failed in particular circumstances. And in the current coronavirus pandemic, science in the form of virology, epidemiology, molecular biology, and so forth has informed public health advice relied on (or not) by politicians making public policy.

This latter example highlights what happens when trust in science to inform wise policy is eroded by dissonant voices. An authoritative "Be quiet and listen to the experts" falls flat in the face of mistrust of the experts.

So, yes, the issue of whether we can trust science, and why, and in what matters, is very important. But to make progress toward an answer, we must begin asking just what we mean by "science."

What Is Science?

It is widely acknowledged that "science" cannot be rigidly defined in a way that includes everything that is legitimate science and excludes everything that is pseudoscience or nonscience. But science can be adequately characterized by pointing to the most salient characteristics of paradigmatic cases of science, both historical and contemporary. The resulting characterization will be sufficient to include most of what we regard as legitimate science and exclude most of what we would not regard as science. While there will likely be a shadowy region where we are unsure about a particular activity, such is the nature of the case. At any given time, some research programs or projects may be "in" that once were "out," and vice versa.[2] And there will probably be several moving through the shadow region, either toward acceptance as science or toward rejection. So I'll characterize science this way:

---

2. Astrology was once accepted as sober truth (even by such giants as Johannes Kepler) but is not regarded as science anymore. Conversely, continental drift was regarded as laughable when Alfred Wegener proposed it in 1912 (although it had been suggested by Ortelius in 1506), but found empirical support and wide acceptance in the mid-1960s, so that plate tectonics is now "axiomatic" in modern geophysics.

Science is a structured, theoretical, cooperative, human enterprise, the goal of which is to offer progressively more accurate explanations of the world, which employs primarily empirical methods, and which delivers publicly accessible and replicable results.

You might wonder why I haven't characterized science in terms of the "scientific method." The reason is simple: there is no such thing. Rather, there is a general method of theoretical work that is common to all theoretical pursuits, with details differing depending on whether the pursuit is history, theology, musicology, or any other theoretical domain.[3] Note also that this characterization is broad enough to cover not only natural science but also what are broadly termed "social sciences."

How Does Science Work?

It's more helpful to think in terms of scientific research programs rather than science broadly conceived. A research program will comprise any number of scientists and research labs, all working in the same area. It will have a history, paradigmatic examples, generally accepted postulates and procedures. Hypotheses are proposed, and empirical tests (experiments) are devised to confirm or disconfirm the hypothesis. Ideally, the confirmed results are explained by an accepted law of nature. Within the research program, some scientists will be working on unanswered questions, others on extending the program to unify different phenomena under a single explanation, and still others on resolving anomalous results that don't fit the general theory. This is the *structured, cooperative, enterprise* part of the characterization.

Further, research programs result in *publicly accessible and replicable results.* These days, scientific results are made available almost immediately as prepublication papers on Internet sites such as arXive.org.[4] The papers then are submitted to a peer-reviewed journal; the reviewers, who are themselves experts in the field, serve a quality-control function, often asking for clarification or questioning explanations, and pointing out any errors they might find. The resulting papers, often in prestigious journals such as *Science, Nature, JAMA,* and so forth, serve as the "state of the art" in

3. I develop this in greater detail in Garrett J. DeWeese, *Doing Philosophy as a Christian* (Downers Grove, IL: IVP Academic, 2011), 271-77.

4. There are more than seventy prepublication repositories for such papers.

a research program and are accessible to the public at large (or at least those who are competent in the technicalities of the field). The published results then will be built upon in further work within the research program. The scientific enterprise has evolved this way of doing business to ensure, as much as possible, that published results are accurate and trustworthy.[5]

So, What Can Go Wrong?

A lot, actually. The scientific enterprise can go wrong in many ways, and reflecting on these matters affects how and when and to what extent we can trust science. Some ways things can go wrong are simply innocent errors. As a *human* enterprise, a research program is susceptible to human error, for example, unexamined but faulty postulates; poorly calibrated equipment; incorrect conclusions drawn from statistical results; or simply lack of awareness of previous results in the field. Generally, these sorts of errors will be "caught" by the peer-review process.

But there are also not-so-innocent issues. The past several decades have seen a number of revelations of scientists falsifying their data, and the deception was not caught in the peer-review process but only later revealed. Why would a scientist risk reputation and position by falsifying data? The usual human vices: pride (academic advancement, fame) and greed (research grants) come to mind.

Apart from falsified results, confirmation bias—finding the results one wants to find (perhaps unintentionally) or disregarding uncomfortable or anomalous data—can affect us all, and scientists are not immune, though most try to recognize and correct for bias.

And then there's the disturbing finding that many scientific studies, it turns out, cannot be replicated, even though replication is one of the hallmarks of scientific methodology. In the early 2010s, in light of a growing number of published results that could not be replicated, the phrase "replication crisis" was coined. It's been estimated that as many as 50 percent of published studies in the "soft sciences" cannot be reproduced by other researchers.[6]

---

5. See Jonathan Rauch, *The Constitution of Knowledge: A Defense of Truth* (Washington, DC: Brookings Institution Press, 2021), especially chaps. 3 and 4, for a more general account of how cooperative enterprises such as science are aimed, quite successfully, at truth.

6. While Wikipedia may not always be the best source, the article "Replication Crisis" is excellent: https://en.wikipedia.org/wiki/Replication_crisis.

Further, statements of laws of nature, or any generalized results of research, will come with a *ceteris paribus* clause—that is, "other things remaining the same." If "other things" is a broad category, there might be many exceptions to the law. Such conditions are almost never stated explicitly in the research publications and are seldom noticed by nonspecialists.[7]

Moreover, science seems always to be changing, as even passing familiarity with the history of science reveals. When the changes appear to be significant, perhaps overturning a previously well-accepted idea, science may come to be regarded as unreliable. Many of us remember press reports in the 1970s citing the danger of global cooling that could result in an era of extensive glaciation. How naïve, we might think today! And in the past coronavirus pandemic year, we have seen respected scientific institutions such as the Centers for Disease Control and Prevention repeatedly change recommendations for dealing with the pandemic. While the changing recommendations are cited by some as evidence that we are being lied to, or that epidemiological science cannot be trusted, a much more charitable interpretation is likely. As more is learned about the novel virus, we should expect changes in recommendations, just as we would expect a weather forecast given a week in advance of a planned picnic to be changed and refined as the date of the picnic approaches. Greater understanding will often lead to revised estimates, forecasts, and recommendations.[8]

Popular media reports of science are also a problem. Science today is so specialized, and results (especially in the physical sciences) are presented in mathematical or statistical language, with a lot of technical vocabulary not easily understood, that it is difficult for journalists to report in an understandable way.[9] Consequently, what often gets reported is an oversimpli-

7. On *ceteris paribus* clauses, especially in the social sciences, see Alex Rosenberg, *Philosophy of Science*, 2nd ed. (New York: Routledge, 2000), 49–52.

8. As I was finalizing this chapter, the *New York Times* had this headline: "Tuberculosis, like Covid, Spreads by Breathing, Scientists Report. The Finding Upends Conventional Wisdom regarding Coughing, Long Thought to Be the Main Route of Transmission." Apoorva Mandavilli, in the October 19, 2021, edition, available at https://www.nytimes.com/2021/10/19/health/tuberculosis-transmission-aerosols.html?searchResultPosition=1.

9. Statistical results in particular provide wide scope for misunderstanding and—unfortunately—outright misinformation. See Jonathan R. Goodman, "How Statistics Are Twisted to Obscure Public Understanding," Social Science Space, September 23, 2016, https://www.socialsciencespace.com/2016/09/statistics-twisted-obscure-public-understanding/.

fied summary of the more sensational, headline-grabbing, clickbait interpretations, thus giving a distorted and sometimes quite erroneous account of the actual science.

To round out the reasons for distrust of science, consider this. Scientists play the role of expert witnesses in society; their specialized training, experience, and accomplishments qualify them to speak authoritatively. This is as it should be. But as trust in all institutions has eroded in recent years, so has trust in experts. Compounding the problem, some scientists have been known freely to offer opinions well outside their area of expertise. A notable astrophysicist or paleontologist, for example, just is not more qualified than the average person to expound on questions in religion or public policy. When we see scientists trading on their authority to hold forth in areas far removed from their expertise, especially in areas where we ourselves have some knowledge (or some "skin in the game"), trust in all such experts is decreased. In my opinion, we see this most egregiously when atheist scientists make claims that God doesn't exist, that the universe had no beginning, or that some scientific discovery clearly disproves some theological claim. The same can be said about celebrities who make claims about technical scientific matters. Or, more controversially, when, say, a chiropractor or radiologist makes claims about virology.

Trust—Broad and Narrow

So it might seem that I've just undercut reasons to trust science, right? I hope not. Instead, I hope I've given reasons not to accept science uncritically as the final word without doing some independent thinking. As a recent *Scientific American* headline put it, "If You Say 'Science Is Right,' You're Wrong: It Can't Supply Absolute Truths about the World, but It Brings Us Steadily Closer."[10] This is the feature of the characterization above that says science offers "progressively more accurate explanations of the world." A poor analogy: for many purposes, we can be content to use 3.14 as the value of pi, while in more critical, demanding contexts (think

---

10. Naomi Oreskes, "If You Say 'Science Is Right,' You're Wrong: It Can't Supply Absolute Truths about the World, but It Brings Us Steadily Closer," *Scientific American*, July 1, 2021, https://www.scientificamerican.com/article/if-you-say-science-is-right-youre-wrong/.

geodetic applications, or precise orbital mechanics), we might have to use at least 3.141592653589—and even that's not exact, of course.

We might say that we trust science in a broad sense to give us those more and more accurate explanations. In general, that is, we can trust what today's science is telling us without placing faith in science to deliver the absolute truth. But in a narrow sense, we might be prepared to be skeptical about a report of the findings of a particular research program, or the claims of an individual scientist.

And indeed, I think that's what we actually do, perhaps intuitively. After all, we use technology grounded in science every day. For example, the accuracy of the GPS in our phones is reliant in part on Einstein's general theory of relativity. But not many of us can understand a simple statement of the theory—what does it mean that four-dimensional space-time is warped by the presence of massive objects?—let alone the mathematical formulation of the theory! That we trust GPS implicitly implies trust in the general theory of relativity (and other things almost as mysterious). Cell phones, LED lights, microwave ovens, and the infrared thermometer your doctor's nurse uses to take your temperature—and much else in modern life—rely on a foundation of scientific theory based in Maxwell's laws of electromagnetism. The most common test for COVID-19 is a PCR (polymerase chain reaction) test, grounded in molecular biology. And examples could be multiplied all day. It seems, then, that we *do* in fact trust science in a broad sense.

I think that trust is warranted. As Christians we should recognize that science as a rational investigation of God's creation is a gift of common grace. God created humanity with the rational powers to search out and understand his creation. We could be grateful for the results of the men and women who employ their intellectual powers to make our lives easier.

So Trust Science, But . . .

My overall claim, then, is this: we can trust science in general, but we must retain a critical (even slightly skeptical) mind-set. What does this mean in practice?

We must be good thinkers in general. We must develop and practice the intellectual virtues in all areas of our life, not just when convenient, or just in certain subjects. A long philosophical tradition has given us a good understanding of intellectual virtues and why they are important. An intellectual virtue is nothing but a disposition of good thinking. What follows is but a brief summary, highlighting some of the virtues I believe are relevant for thinking about and trusting (or distrusting) scientific claims.[11]

1. The first virtue I'll list is *humility*. Let's admit it—we all have sometimes thought we knew it all and acted like know-it-alls. But of course, we don't know it all, or even a tiny fraction of the knowledge available in the world. So a bit of intellectual humility is warranted. We might think of this as a principle of charity: don't be too quick to negatively judge or disregard a claim. I used to tell my students to apply the "smartness of the author" principle (another version of intellectual humility): the author has published on this, and you haven't, so give him or her the benefit of the doubt. Now, that doesn't mean we are naïvely credulous; it just means we are willing to think twice or three times before rejecting a claim or an idea. Humility also means we practice charity to those who disagree with us, resisting name-calling, trolling, or avoiding.

2. *Honesty* means we don't take a claim out of context, making it say something it isn't really saying. We can regularly see such dishonesty in politics and social media. Just because a person advocates for somewhat expanded gun regulations doesn't mean he is trying to take away your Second Amendment rights. And just because a scientist speaks of a scientific consensus supporting climate change doesn't mean she is unaware or is ignoring some contrary evidence or perpetrating a hoax.

3. *Curiosity* may have killed a cat, but it can surely help us think well. I recently read the headline "Vikings Were in the Americas Exactly 1,000 Years Ago." Hmmm. I could have just passed on that, but a bit of curiosity motivated me to read the article, which led to another, and I learned some interesting things along the way. In today's busy world, we don't have time or capacity to follow every interesting-sounding rabbit trail. But curiosity often leads us to greater understanding.

4. A prime virtue is *carefulness*, an antidote to unreasonable beliefs. If you read that the rate of a breakthrough COVID-19 infection in fully vaccinated individuals is 1 in 5,000,[12] you shouldn't immediately conclude that vaccinations are therefore unimportant. A careful reading of the arti-

---

11. An excellent and very readable treatment is Nathan L. King, *The Excellent Mind: Intellectual Virtues for Everyday Life* (New York: Oxford University Press, 2021).

12. According to a Washington State study of some 4 million fully vaccinated people. Lisa Maragakis and Gabor David Kelen, "Breakthrough Infections: Coronavirus after Vaccination," Johns Hopkins Medicine, updated November 23, 2021,

cle would reveal that no vaccine is 100 percent effective, and that break-through cases are quite mild in comparison to the severe cases common among unvaccinated people. This example should also highlight the difficulty of making judgments on the basis of statistics, something I alluded to above. Professors of statistics know well how difficult it is to teach students basic reasoning based on statistical evidence, and how easy it is to deceive using statistics; this is perhaps the reason Mark Twain is reported to have said that there are lies, damned lies, and statistics. Being careful is just another way of saying don't make snap judgments.

5. *Thoroughness* leads us to investigate the source of a claim. Where did you hear or read the claim? I shouldn't need to point out that not all sources are equally reliable. Social media are at the low end of reliability for scientific matters; some websites are better than others. Here the virtue of impartiality plays a role, as we all have sites more in line with our political or religious views. So the *source* guideline asks us to look carefully at the credentials of the source, and whenever possible trace the claim to its origin, even if that means reading some technical material.

6. *Tenacity* implies willingness to study. Not every claim in science is worth our time studying, of course; we must be discerning. But if a claim is made that we want to argue about with friends or on social media, it behooves us to study tenaciously, to do our homework. We all know that claims of global warning are somewhat controversial, and we know that many climatologists and politicians say there should be no controversy at all. Even among Christians the division of opinion is great, as I saw repeatedly whenever I taught environmental ethics. But rather than rejecting the claims of global warming outright, or accepting them uncritically, we need to study the issue. Take the time to read the Sixth Assessment Report from the IPCC (Intergovernmental Panel on Climate Change), or at least the executive summary, which is less technical.[13] Then track down some of the objections. In fact, reading the original source report, as in this case, generally shows that the actual scientific conclusions are much less shocking than the journalism reporting them.

7. While the list could go on, the last virtue I'll mention is *impartiality*. It's difficult, I know, to receive claims or opinions with an open mind.

---

https://www.hopkinsmedicine.org/conditions-and-diseases/coronavirus/break through-infections-coronavirus-after-vaccination.

13. "Climate Change 2021: The Physical Science Basis," The Intergovernmental Panel on Climate Change, accessed June 8, 2022, https://www.ipcc.ch/report/ar6/wg1/.

I mentioned confirmation bias above, the tendency to give greater weight to information that we agree with or that supports our views, or that comes from a person (politician, celebrity, relative, or scientist) we like or respect. The converse, of course, is to discount information that might be contrary to our view. To judge a view as true or false depending on the source is to commit what philosophers call the genetic fallacy. Ultimately truth is conformity to reality, irrespective of the source.

A Final Word

Pontius Pilate, the one who, humanly speaking, held the power of life or death over our Lord Jesus, asked him pointedly, "Are you a king then?" Jesus replied, "You are right in saying that I am a king. In fact, for this reason I was born, and for this I came into the world, to testify to the truth" (John 18:37). As is often said, all truth is God's truth. It is tragic then that the followers of the Lord Jesus too often credulously accept falsehoods, embrace conspiracy theories, or refuse to listen to science. The truth of God is ill-served by such attitudes. May we, followers of Jesus, be known as truth-seekers.

References

"Climate Change 2021: The Physical Science Basis." The Intergovernmental Panel on Climate Change, accessed June 8, 2022. https://www.ipcc.ch /report/ar6/wg1/.

DeWeese, Garrett J. *Doing Philosophy as a Christian*. Downers Grove, IL: IVP Academic, 2011.

Goodman, Jonathan R. "How Statistics Are Twisted to Obscure Public Understanding." Social Science Space, September 23, 2016. https://www .socialsciencespace.com/2016/09/statistics-twisted-obscure-public -understanding/.

"How to Build Community, Connection, and Trust in Science." Pew Research Center, October 2, 2020. https://www.pewtrusts.org/en/research-and -analysis/articles/2020/10/02/how-to-build-community-connection -and-trust-in-science.

King, Nathan L. *The Excellent Mind: Intellectual Virtues for Everyday Life*. New York: Oxford University Press, 2021.

Mandavilli, Apoorva. "Tuberculosis, like Covid, Spreads by Breathing, Scientists Report. The Finding Upends Conventional Wisdom regarding

Coughing, Long Thought to Be the Main Route of Transmission." *New York Times*, October 19, 2021. https://www.nytimes.com/2021/10/19 /health/tuberculosis-transmission-aerosols.html?searchResultPosi tion=1.

Maragakis, Lisa, and Gabor David Kelen. "Breakthrough Infections: Coronavirus after Vaccination." Johns Hopkins Medicine, updated November 23, 2021. https://www.hopkinsmedicine.org/conditions-and-diseases/coro navirus/breakthrough-infections-coronavirus-after-vaccination.

Oreskes, Naomi. "If You Say 'Science Is Right,' You're Wrong: It Can't Supply Absolute Truths about the World, but It Brings Us Steadily Closer." *Scientific American*, July 1, 2021. https://www.scientificamerican.com/arti cle/if-you-say-science-is-right-youre-wrong/.

Rauch, Jonathan. *The Constitution of Knowledge: A Defense of Truth*. Washington, DC: Brookings Institution Press, 2021.

"Replication Crisis." Wikipedia, last edited June 8, 2022. https://en.wikipedia .org/wiki/Replication_crisis.

Rosenberg, Alex. *Philosophy of Science*. 2nd ed. New York: Routledge, 2000.

5

CONSPIRACY THEORIES AND MEANING IN LIFE

Shawn Graves and Marlena Graves

It's reasonable to think that many people want to live meaningful lives or, conversely, to avoid, if at all possible, lives that are rightly regarded as meaningless.[1] Of course, there may be exceptions. Even so, many are still looking for meaning.[2] People want lives that they can make sense of, that are intelligible to them, that in the midst of chaos and disorder seem to have an internal coherence and that fit within their larger sociopolitical and relational contexts. People want lives of purpose, to have something to live for and strive toward, and to be part of something larger than themselves and that goes beyond themselves. People want to belong to some community, to be wanted and cared for, and to have the sense that their lives matter and have significance.

1. According to a September 2020 Lifeway Research survey, "Twenty-one percent of Americans think about the meaning and purpose of life daily. . . . An additional 21 percent ponder the question weekly." In total, the survey "found that 57 percent of U.S. adults during the pandemic say they ponder, at least monthly, the question, 'How can I find more meaning and purpose in my life?'" See Michael Foust, "57 Percent in U.S. Are Searching for More Meaning and Purpose to Life, Poll Shows," Christian Headlines, April 7, 2021, https://www.christianheadlines .com/contributors/michael-foust/57-percent-in-us-are-searching-for-more-mean ing-and-purpose-to-life-poll-shows.html.

2. That same September 2020 Lifeway Research survey found that only "59 percent agree with the statement, 'I have found a higher purpose and meaning for my life.'" See Foust, "57 Percent in U.S."

This natural longing has been exacerbated, working itself into a feverish pitch, due to shifts and changes in Western culture. Since the Industrial Revolution and resultant globalization, American culture has undergone rapid and profound fragmentation. The social fabric is tattered and torn, with many people experiencing loneliness, isolation, anxiety, disintegration, and an unraveling sense of identity and purpose. Given that knowing who one is, to whom one belongs, and the purpose for which one lives is tied to the experience of meaningfulness in one's life, it is no wonder that these changes in Western culture are considered genuine existential threats. As theologian Edward Hahnenberg observes, "We live in a different world today, with a different kind of anxiety confronting us. Our great fear is not the threat of guilt and condemnation but the prospect of meaninglessness. . . . In short, our present problem is not the fear of failure but of never finding our way."[3]

We might assume that this is a relatively recent phenomenon, that this crisis of meaning and belonging began with the advent of the smart phone.[4] No doubt, the smart phone fueled it, along with a mental health crisis, but mention of increasing loneliness and fragmentation can be traced back much earlier.[5] Indeed, at least since the 1830s, American novelists have implicitly and explicitly noted how industrialization and technology have separated us from the land and from each other—the "machine" of progressive technology has entered "the Garden," what some would regard as America's original, and Edenic, natural state.[6] As the Industrial Revolution gained steam, Americans left their agrarian lifestyles, family farms, small towns, churches, and other local networks for the cities to work in factories and other emerging industries. To earn a living, and perhaps to set off on their own in an effort to flee suffocating communal surveillance, people left places, kin, and religious and civic communities, where everyone knew their name, for anonymity. They left a slower lifestyle for a frenetic and

---

3. Edward P. Hahnenberg, *Awakening Vocation: A Theology of Christian Call* (Collegeville, MN: Liturgical Press, 2010), 110.

4. Jean M. Twenge, "Have Smartphones Destroyed a Generation? More Comfortable Online Than Out Partying, Post-Millennials Are Safer, Physically, Than Adolescents Have Ever Been. But They're on the Brink of a Mental-Health Crisis," *Atlantic*, September 2017, http://www.postgrowth.ca/uploads/8/4/9/4/84946882 /have_smartphones_destroyed_a_generation.pdf.

5. Twenge, "Have Smartphones Destroyed a Generation?"

6. Leo Marx, "The Machine in the Garden," *New England Quarterly* 29, no. 1 (1956): 27–42, doi:10.2307/363061.

fast-paced one. Some welcomed the anonymity, isolation, and faster pace. Others did not.

Of course, the idyllic and pastoral American experience epitomized in the public imaginary by writers like Emerson and Thoreau was not the experience of Black slaves, freedmen, the indigenous, and other people of color. They had long known forced separation from family and friends while having to figure out how to forge new relationships and kinship, meaning and belonging, with those in their new location and circumstances. Indeed, the Industrial Revolution and globalization have brought much good, but they have also fractured and fragmented families, churches, communities, and societies all over the world.

Industrialization and globalization have so dislocated people from their places that even if one lives in a neighborhood, one mostly doesn't know one's neighbors, whether next door or those on the other side of the wall in an apartment complex.[7] In churches, people can sit in a row and not even know those next to them while not thinking twice about this being a problem. All this contributes to one's seemingly ubiquitous isolation and alienation, one's experience of meaninglessness, purposelessness, and of being an outsider. It feeds into, as Hahnenberg notes, one's resilient, enduring fear of never finding one's way—that is, one's feeling of being unmoored, disoriented, and hopelessly lost.

Tapping into this fear of social isolation, of never finding one's way, of living a meaningless life, are powerful marketing, retention, and recruiting strategists who work for businesses, organizations, universities, and institutions. For example, one finds the United States Marine Corps explicitly appealing to the search for meaning, the desire to belong and to have a purpose in life, in their recent recruiting efforts.[8] Gangs, extremist organizations, and religious groups do the same thing.

7. See the following: "Survey: 1-in-4 under 40 Don't Know Any Neighbors by Name," Ownerly, accessed June 8, 2022, https://www.ownerly.com/data-analysis /do-you-know-your-neighbors-survey/; Kim Parker et al., "How Urban, Suburban and Rural Residents Interact with Their Neighbors," Pew Research Center, May 22, 2018, https://www.pewresearch.org/social-trends/2018/05/22/how-urban-suburb an-and-rural-residents-interact-with-their-neighbors/; Brian Bethune, "The End of Neighbours: How Our Increasingly Closed-Off Lives Are Poisoning Our Politics and Endangering Our Health," *Maclean's*, August 8, 2014, https://www.macleans .ca/society/the-end-of-neighbours/.

8. See Gina Harkins, "New Recruiting Ad Tells Gen Z to Ditch the Digital World and Join the Marines," Military.com, September 20, 2020, https://www.military

In this chapter, we explore how conspiracies such as QAnon can function in the same way, that is, how they offer a narrative that helps people understand themselves and their world and yields a strong sense of identity, belonging, and purpose and significance to their adherents in a fractured and fragmented world. They provide for people a perceived pathway to meaningfulness, offering rich emotional rewards and satisfying otherwise natural psychological needs. Finally, we will articulate why conspiracies like QAnon ultimately fail to result in a meaningful life and briefly trace what does bring about such a life.

Conspiracy Theories and Counterfeit Meanings

In the immediate context of an industrialized and predatory neoliberal society where communities are fractured and kinship ties are nearly nonexistent, where people feel invisible and unmoored, grand conspiracies can function as the gateway to satisfying the drive to find meaning. Conspiracies promise explanations helping people make sense of their own experiences and surroundings. They can provide individuals with a renewed sense of purpose, a goal to achieve, and a call to action. They may form the foundation for a community of like-minded believers who gladly proselytize and welcome others into their conspiracy-centered community, resulting in a strong sense of belonging and a feeling of being at home in the world. Conspiracies often suggest a much larger sociopolitical project, going well beyond any one individual. Those embracing the conspiracy see themselves as a part of something much larger than themselves, whose significance and value lie outside of themselves. Participating in the community of sleuths trying to figure things out provides camaraderie and a feeling of control in a world that seems to be spinning out of control.[9]

.com/daily-news/2020/09/17/new-call-gen-z-escape-virtual-world-and-join-marines.html.

9. See Zara Abrams, "What Do We Know about Conspiracy Theories?" American Psychological Association, November 18, 2020, https://www.apa.org/news/apa/2020/conspiracy-theories. See also "Speaking of Psychology: Why People Believe in Conspiracy Theories, with Karen Douglas, PhD," American Psychological Association, accessed June 8, 2020, https://www.apa.org/research/action/speaking-of-psychology/conspiracy-theories. Adrienne LaFrance asserts: "Many of the people most prone to believing conspiracy theories see themselves as victim-warriors fighting against corrupt and powerful forces." See Adrienne LaFrance, "The Proph-

Consider QAnon. Here's how Brett Forrest, a reporter for the *Wall Street Journal*, describes them:

> QAnon is a far right-wing, loosely organized network and community of believers who embrace a range of unsubstantiated beliefs. These views center on the idea that a cabal of Satan-worshipping pedophiles—mainly consisting of what they see as elitist Democrats, politicians, journalists, entertainment moguls and other institutional figures—have long controlled much of the so-called deep state government, which they say sought to undermine Mr. Trump, mostly with aid of media and entertainment outlets.

Forrest continues:

> QAnon conspiracy theory alleges that there is a battle between good and evil in which the Republican Mr. Trump is allied with the former. QAnon followers are awaiting two major events: the Storm and the Great Awakening. The Storm is the mass arrest of people in high-power positions who will face a long-awaited reckoning. The Great Awakening involves a single event in which everyone will attain the epiphany that QAnon theory was accurate the whole time. This realization will allow society to enter an age of utopia.

In addition:

> Followers believe that "Q" is a high-ranking government insider, presumably with a military or intelligence background, committed to exposing the hidden truth of what they see as an international bureaucracy scheming against Mr. Trump and his supporters. Some followers believe that "Q" often sends coded signals about his or her existence, using the number 17—the letter Q's placement in the alphabet. Online posts surrounding QAnon conspiracy theories have often described "Q" as a patriot or saint.[10]

---

ecies of Q," *Atlantic*, June 2020, https://www.theatlantic.com/magazine/archive/2020/06/qanon-nothing-can-stop-what-is-coming/610567/.

10. Brett Forrest, "What Is QAnon? What We Know about the Conspiracy-Theory Group," *Wall Street Journal*, February 4, 2021, https://www.wsj.com/articles/what-is-qanon-what-we-know-about-the-conspiracy-theory-11597694801.

QAnon is a recent example of a large movement centered on a grand conspiracy that seems to promise its adherents deep understanding, personal purpose, a committed and expansive community to belong to, a project or agenda much larger than themselves to join, and genuine personal significance. Thus, QAnon is a recent example of a conspiracy-centered movement appearing to offer genuine *meaning in life* proving attractive to people especially hungry and thirsty for meaning. Given that it can foster and fuel the kind of devotion, passion, and sacrifice we find in religious movements, contains multiple biblical allusions, and has a grip on many white evangelicals, some speak about QAnon in quasi-religious terms.[11]

QAnon adherents may experience a kind of joy typically associated with meaningfulness. Importantly, this good feeling is distinct from mere pleasure, fun, or happiness as conventionally understood. Rather, it is best understood as *fulfillment*, as Susan Wolf notes, the sort of feeling one might contrast with existential boredom and alienation.[12] And yet, a fulfilling life can be accompanied by anxiety, disappointment, failure, and frustration.[13] Imagine the life of a medical researcher who strives and strains to find a cure for some terrible disease yet ultimately fails. During the course of her life, she might experience persistent frustration and devastating disappointment. Even so, in her final moments, she may reflect back and declare with sincerity and confidence that it was a fulfilling life, a life she would opt for again if given the chance. She may even describe her life as meaningful, and no doubt many observers would agree.[14]

11. See Mike Allen, "QAnon Infects Churches," *Axios*, May 31, 2021, https://www.axios.com/qanon-churches-popular-religion-conspiracy-theory-c5bcce08-8f6e-4501-8cb2-9e38a2346c2f.html; Katelyn Beaty, "QAnon: The Alternative Religion That's Coming to Your Church," Religion News Service, August 17, 2020, https://religionnews.com/2020/08/17/qanon-the-alternative-religion-thats-coming-to-your-church/; Brody McDonald, "How QAnon Reacts to Failed Predictions," Global Network on Extremism & Technology, March 31, 2020, https://gnet-research.org/2021/03/31/how-qanon-reacts-to-failed-predictions/; and "Religiosity and Conspiratorial Beliefs Linked in Baylor Religious Survey Findings," Baylor University, June 9, 2021, https://www.baylor.edu/mediacommunications/news.php?action=story&story=223733.

12. See Susan Wolf, *Meaning in Life and Why It Matters* (Princeton: Princeton University Press, 2010), 13-14.

13. Wolf, *Meaning in Life*, 13-14.

14. The Pew Research Center seems to tie together meaning and fulfillment in their two surveys on meaning in life conducted in 2017. See "2017 Pew Research

QAnon followers may describe their conspiracy-centered life similarly. There may be anxiety, disappointment, failure, and frustration, particularly as predictions fail and prophecies do not come to pass.[15] Yet, they may contend, it is a deeply fulfilling life revolving around a grand narrative that helps them understand themselves and major portions of their seemingly chaotic world. It provides them a clear purpose as a virtuous defender of innocent children and a righteous warrior against perceived extreme injustices and human rights abuses. For them, it's a compelling, group-defining narrative that offers binding ties to a far-reaching community of fiercely loyal and passionate believers to which they belong. They have their own group markers and merchandise, bumper stickers to slap on the backs of their cars. QAnon identifies for them a major cause they see as worth fighting for, a profoundly important agenda worth advancing, one that goes well beyond their own individual interests. It makes it abundantly clear to them that regardless of whatever else may be true of the circumstances of their lives, they truly matter, their lives count for something. QAnon can possibly infuse their otherwise ordinary and overlooked lives with tremendous meaning. The QAnon life, they might insist, is a deeply meaningful life.

Of course, people can be mistaken about all kinds of things, including about whether or not their own lives are meaningful. There's no good reason to suppose that *if I believe I have a meaningful life, then my life is indeed meaningful*. There is no guarantee my judgments about which lives are meaningful and which are not are correct—just as my judgments about which actions are morally right aren't guaranteed to be correct. Consequently, there is no good reason to think people, including faithful Christians, are infallible about any of this.

Furthermore, there's no good reason to think that a fulfilling life committed to (1) a narrative that offers understanding of oneself and the world, (2) purpose, (3) belonging, (4) being a part of something larger than oneself, and (5) personal significance makes for a meaningful life. Consider, for example, the life of Robert Chambliss, "the Alabama Ku Klux Klansman

---

Center's American Trends Panel," Pew Research Center, December 4–18, 2017, https://assets.pewresearch.org/wp-content/uploads/sites/11/2018/08/28151638 /Combined-Topline.pdf.

15. For more on failed prophecies, see "How Many QAnon Predictions Have Been Wrong? All of Them. Reinstatement Day Is No Different," Fact Pac, updated December 4, 2021, https://factpac.org/how-many-qanon-predictions-have-been -wrong-all-of-them-reinstatement-day-is-no-different/.

who was convicted of murder in the 1963 bombing of a Birmingham church that killed four black girls."[16] He was "nicknamed 'Dynamite Bob' for his links to so many of the more than 40 blasts that terrorized black citizens ... in the civil rights era."[17] Chambliss, like other violent white supremacists, may have found that the KKK and its toxic ideology provided him with the ingredients for a meaningful life. Like other violent white supremacists, he may have found such a life to be deeply fulfilling, a life he embraced without reservation or regret. Even so, it should be very clear to Christians that Chambliss and other white supremacists, who tenaciously hold dear the KKK and its ideology and act upon its terrorist agenda, no matter their claims on Christianity, are not living meaningful lives. And this is so regardless of how fulfilling that life may be for them. The same thing could be said of Heinrich Himmler and the men in the SS (*Schutzstaffel*) of the Nazi Third Reich.[18] Surely no Christian ought to think that these lives count as meaningful lives, no matter how fulfilling they may have been for the people living them. After all, to say that one has a meaningful life is to offer a positive evaluation of that life, to hold it up as a model for imitation, admiration, and celebration.[19] This is not to say that a meaningful life must be a truly heroic life. Our lives need not be heroic to be worthy of imitation, admiration, and celebration or to be fulfilling.

One retort is that, while most people are loathe to say that Chambliss's and Himmler's particular lives were meaningful, some white supremacists or other Nazis would insist that they were. Or, at the very least, that they were meaningful *to* Chambliss and Himmler themselves.

16. See Obituary, "Robert E. Chambliss, Figure in '63 Bombing," *New York Times*, accessed June 8, 2022, https://www.nytimes.com/1985/10/30/us/robert-e-chambliss-figure-in-63-bombing.html.

17. See Rick Bragg, "38 Years Later, Last of Suspects Is Convicted in Church Bombing," *New York Times*, May 23, 2002, https://www.nytimes.com/2002/05/23/us/38-years-later-last-of-suspects-is-convicted-in-church-bombing.html.

18. For more on Himmler and the SS, see "Heinrich Himmler," Holocaust Encyclopedia, accessed June 8, 2022, https://encyclopedia.ushmm.org/content/en/article/heinrich-himmler, and "The SS," Holocaust Encyclopedia, accessed June 8, 2022, https://encyclopedia.ushmm.org/content/en/article/ss.

19. Thaddeus Metz notes that we can "think of happiness in terms of pleasant experiences and of meaningfulness as what merits great esteem or admiration." See Thaddeus Metz, "This Is How You Can Find Meaning in Your Life, and Still Be Happy," World Economic Forum, May 31, 2017, https://www.weforum.org/agenda/2017/05/this-is-how-you-can-find-meaning-in-your-life-and-still-be-happy/.

This is not a successful response. Just because other white supremacists and Nazis *regarded* Chambliss's and Himmler's lives as meaningful doesn't establish that their lives were *in fact* meaningful. And to say that their lives were meaningful to Chambliss and Himmler themselves is just to say that they regarded their own lives as meaningful. But again, this doesn't establish that their lives were in fact meaningful. It just shows they are mistaken about whether their own lives were meaningful.

Christians should think that there's a factual nature to which lives are meaningful and acknowledge that people can be mistaken about which ones are. Christians are accustomed to thinking that people may "do what is right in their own eyes" yet fail to do what is in fact right.[20] So, yes, perhaps Chambliss and Himmler thought that their lives were meaningful, and perhaps other white supremacists and Nazis agreed. But they're just wrong about that. As noted above, people are fallible about all kinds of things, and this is one of them.

On the other hand, one might insist that the QAnon life is a meaningful life on the grounds that it is a life that makes a noticeable social and political difference. The difference can be seen on the local, state, and national levels. School curriculum is changed, voting laws are altered, government and public health officials are targeted and threatened, public health guidelines and practices are effected, the Republican Party is refashioned, churches and religious media are transformed, pizza shops and capitol buildings are stormed.[21] As part of a difference-making social and

---

20. See Judg. 17:6; 21:25; Prov. 14:12.

21. For more, see the Southern Poverty Law Center's "What You Need to Know about QAnon," found at https://www.splcenter.org/hatewatch/2020/10/27/what -you-need-know-about-qanon. See also the Anti-Defamation League's profile on QAnon: https://www.adl.org/qanon. See also Mary Ellen Flannery, "Is QAnon Radicalizing Your School Board," National Education Association, June 2, 2021, https://www.nea.org/advocating-for-change/new-from-nea/qanon-radicalizing -your-school-board; Craig Timberg and Elizabeth Dwoskin, "With Trump Gone, QAnon Groups Focus Fury on Attacking Coronavirus Vaccines," *Washington Post*, March 11, 2021, https://www.washingtonpost.com/technology/2021/03/11/with -trump-gone-qanon-groups-focus-fury-attacking-covid-vaccines/; Marc-André Argentino, "QAnon Conspiracy Theories about the Coronavirus Pandemic Are a Public Health Threat," *Conversation*, April 8, 2020, https://theconversation.com/qanon -conspiracy-theories-about-the-coronavirus-pandemic-are-a-public-health-threat -135515; Drew Harwell et al., "QAnon Reshaped Trump's Party and Radicalized Be-

political movement, a QAnon adherent may get the sense that their life is meaningful. Yet a brief moment's reflection will show that the same could rightly be said of Chambliss and Ku Klux Klansmen as well as Himmler and the SS officers. They all had, or were parts of movements that had, a profound effect upon the social and political realities of countless people. Yet Christians ought to hold that these are not meaningful lives, regardless of their impact. *The impactful, consequential life is not the same thing as the meaningful life.* The impacts and the consequences can be disturbing, distressing, and downright demonic.

Perhaps it can be argued that QAnon followers, while experiencing fulfillment, are doing what they believe to be the right thing. They, one might charitably presume, genuinely and sincerely believe that countless children are in danger as a sinister cabal of powerful elites perpetrates gross injustices against them and otherwise ordinary citizens trying to make a life for themselves and their families. Rather than stand by, rather than compartmentalize their beliefs and behavior and live a disintegrated life, they take purposeful action built on conviction, whether that's in the voting booth, or proselytizing and rallying over the Internet or in person, or injuring and murdering those they believe to be perpetuating such atrocities.

It's reasonable, one might continue, to think that an integrated and fulfilled life spent doing what one genuinely and sincerely believes to be the right thing counts as a meaningful life. Once again, however, Christians should acknowledge that Chambliss and the Ku Klux Klansmen and Himmler and the SS officers may very well have felt fulfilled doing what they genuinely and sincerely believed was the right thing to do. But this should not alter a Christian's considered judgment that they all failed to live meaningful lives. We can assume that many of those participating in the QAnon conspiracy, Christian or not, are doing what they think is the right thing and are fulfilled by it. Yet Christians should still contend that those are not meaningful lives. Simply put, a fulfilling life spent doing what one genuinely and sincerely believes is the right thing to do is not equivalent to living a meaningful life.

---

lievers: The Capitol Siege May Just Be the Start," *Washington Post*, January 13, 2021, https://www.washingtonpost.com/technology/2021/01/13/qanon-capitol-siege -trump/; Clare Foran, "'An Existential Threat': The Republicans Calling for Their Party to Reject QAnon Conspiracy Theories," CNN, updated April 10, 2021, https:// www.cnn.com/2021/04/10/politics/qanon-republican-party-congress/index.html.

Agapē Love and True Meaning

Christians, most of whom would claim that everyone is made in the image of God, might be uncomfortable with the notion that some people didn't live, or aren't living, meaningful lives. They may wish to insist that everyone's life is meaningful, given that all people are beloved children of God, created in the image of God. This conclusion applies to saints and sinners alike, even violent domestic terrorists like Chambliss and genocidal, anti-Semitic fascists like Himmler. God loves them, and so one might suppose that their lives are indeed meaningful.

The inference is that being beloved by God makes one's life meaningful, that God's love all by itself transforms what might otherwise be meaningless into something meaningful. There's no good reason to accept this inference. It may very well be that God's love of everyone bestows worth, value, and dignity upon everyone, as Nicholas Wolterstorff has argued. *But this is not the same thing as bestowing meaning upon the life that is lived.* Humans who have such incalculable worth, value, and dignity can *still live lives with little or no meaning.*

There's no need for discomfort here. Christians ought to affirm that God loves everyone without exception. Moreover, Christians ought to affirm that everyone without exception has equal worth, value, and dignity. In addition, Christians ought to affirm that *agapē* love of oneself and one's local and global neighbors is the fitting response to that worth, value, and dignity. However, Christians need not affirm that all lives are meaningful, or meaningful to the same degree. This is *not* to say that some people count for less or that some lives are expendable. It is to say, rather, that some lives are not well lived, that they go very poorly from the moral point of view. This doesn't result in forfeited worth, value, and dignity; but, given that there is a moral dimension to meaningfulness, it does result in diminished meaning, perhaps even to the point of meaninglessness.[22]

What *does* make for a more meaningful life is finding fulfillment in living a life of *agapē* love directed toward all without exception.[23] A life marked

---

22. See Thaddeus Metz, "The Meaning of Life," *Stanford Encyclopedia of Philosophy*, substantive revision, February 9, 2021, https://plato.stanford.edu/archives/win2021/entries/life-meaning/.

23. Harvard's Study of Adult Development is "a longitudinal study that has been following two groups of men over the last 80 years" to determine, among other things, "what psychosocial variables and biological processes from earlier in life

by fully inclusive *agapē* love is a life that seeks to promote the flourishing of all, to secure a good life for all, while desiring and pursuing cooperative community, or shalom, with all. To do this is to live a life that fulfills the law, that keeps the royal law found in Scripture, that links one to the Good Samaritan in inheriting eternal life.[24] To put this *agapē* love at the center of one's life is, as Howard Thurman puts it, to practice "the religion of Jesus."[25] This life might not yield material success or generate headlines, but it will result in a meaningful life.

Finding fulfillment in living out a life of fully-inclusive *agapē* love is to reject the toxic conspiracies and culture of QAnon. Conspiracies like QAnon are a barrier to love. One's ability to love well is seriously compromised if one is in the grips of a distorting and perverse network of misinformation that caters to, perhaps even rewards, bad intellectual habits and violence in the name of a cause one believes to be righteous. One's views of, and one's dispositions toward, one's local and global neighbors are likely warped and distorted by the torrent of misinformation put forth by QAnon conspiracies. One begins to see enemies where there are none. One cultivates and feeds one's suspicions of wicked intentions, sinister agendas, and evil alliances. And one begins to direct one's energies away from addressing genuine injustices and human rights crises and toward efforts that are either ineffective at preventing and rectifying harms or, worse, that bring real harm and further entrench sociopolitical and economic inequities.[26]

---

predict health and well-being in late life." About this study, Melanie Curtin writes: "According to George Vaillant, the Harvard psychiatrist who directed the study from 1972 to 2004, there are two foundational elements to this: 'One is love. The other is finding a way of coping with life that does not push love away.'" While not specifically a study on meaningfulness, the territory covered is adjacent. See https://www.adultdevelopmentstudy.org/grantandglueckstudy, and Melanie Curtin, "This 75-Year Harvard Study Found the 1 Secret to Leading a Fulfilling Life," *Inc.*, accessed June 8, 2022, https://www.inc.com/melanie-curtin/want-a-life-of-ful fillment-a-75-year-harvard-study-says-to-prioritize-this-one-t.html.

24. See Rom. 13:8; James 2:8; Luke 10:25–37. For some additional relevant texts, see the following: Matt. 22:34–40; Mark 12:28–31; 1 Cor. 13:1–3; Gal. 5:13–14; and 1 John 4:7–12.

25. Howard Thurman, *Jesus and the Disinherited* (Boston: Beacon, 1976), 89.

26. As Paul Renfro writes: "Moral panics like QAnon work to distract from less outrageous, far more insidious sources of harm. Even worse, they contribute to punitive policies that separate and hurt families, perpetuate mass incarceration and keep people in a state of fear." See Paul M. Renfro, "QAnon Misdirects Our Atten-

Indeed, participating in QAnon leads one away from *agapē* love—the very life and teachings of Jesus—and away from a meaningful life.

References

Abrams, Zara. "What Do We Know about Conspiracy Theories?" American Psychological Association, November 18, 2020. https://www.apa.org /news/apa/2020/conspiracy-theories.

Allen, Mike. "QAnon Infects Churches." *Axios*, May 31, 2021. https://www.ax ios.com/qanon-churches-popular-religion-conspiracy-theory-c5bcce0 8-8f6e-4501-8cb2-9e38a2346c2f.html.

Argentino, Marc-André. "QAnon Conspiracy Theories about the Coronavirus Pandemic Are a Public Health Threat." *Conversation*, April 8, 2020. https://theconversation.com/qanon-conspiracy-theories-about-the-co ronavirus-pandemic-are-a-public-health-threat-135515.

Beaty, Katelyn. "QAnon: The Alternative Religion That's Coming to Your Church." Religion News Service, August 17, 2020. https://religionnews .com/2020/08/17/qanon-the-alternative-religion-thats-coming-to-your -church/.

Bethune, Brian. "The End of Neighbours: How Our Increasingly Closed-Off Lives Are Poisoning Our Politics and Endangering Our Health." *Maclean's*, August 8, 2014. https://www.macleans.ca/society/the-end-of -neighbours/.

Bragg, Rick. "38 Years Later, Last of Suspects Is Convicted in Church Bombing." *New York Times*, May 23, 2002. https://www.nytimes.com/2002/05/23/us /38-years-later-last-of-suspects-is-convicted-in-church-bombing.html.

Curtin, Melanie. "This 75-Year Harvard Study Found the 1 Secret to Leading a Fulfilling Life." *Inc.*, accessed June 8, 2022. https://www.inc.com/mela

tion Away from the Real Threats to Children," *Washington Post*, August 27, 2020, https://www.washingtonpost.com/outlook/2020/08/27/qanon-misdirects-our-at tention-away-real-threats-children/. See the following for how QAnon and conspiracies like it undermine and impede efforts against child sex trafficking specifically or, as the Polaris Project puts it, "mislead well-meaning people into doing more harm than good": "How Unproven Trafficking Stories Spread Online and Why Stopping Them Matters," *Polaris* (blog), July 22, 2022, https://polarisproject .org/blog/2020/07/how-unproven-trafficking-stories-spread-online-and-why -stopping-them-matters/; Annie Reneau, "If You Really Want to #SaveTheChildren, Stop Sharing QAnon Conspiracy Theories," Upworthy, August 13, 2020, https://www.upworthy.com/save-the-children-stop-the-qanon-conspiracies.

nie-curtin/want-a-life-of-fulfillment-a-75-year-harvard-study-says-to
-prioritize-this-one-t.html.

Flannery, Mary Ellen. "Is QAnon Radicalizing Your School Board?" National
Education Association, June 2, 2021. https://www.nea.org/advocating
-for-change/new-from-nea/qanon-radicalizing-your-school-board.

Foran, Clare. "'An Existential Threat': The Republicans Calling for Their Party
to Reject QAnon Conspiracy Theories." CNN, updated April 10, 2021.
https://www.cnn.com/2021/04/10/politics/qanon-republican-party
-congress/index.html.

Forrest, Brett. "What Is QAnon? What We Know about the Conspiracy-
Theory Group." *Wall Street Journal*, February 4, 2021. https://www.wsj
.com/articles/what-is-qanon-what-we-know-about-the-conspiracy
-theory-11597694801.

Foust, Michael. "57 Percent in U.S. Are Searching for More Meaning and Purpose to Life, Poll Shows." Christian Headlines, April 7, 2021. https://
www.christianheadlines.com/contributors/michael-foust/57-percent-in
-us-are-searching-for-more-meaning-and-purpose-to-life-poll-shows
.html.

Hahnenberg, Edward P. *Awakening Vocation: A Theology of Christian Call*. Collegeville, MN: Liturgical Press, 2010.

Harkins, Gina. "New Recruiting Ad Tells Gen Z to Ditch the Digital World
and Join the Marines." Military.com, September 20, 2020. https://www
.military.com/daily-news/2020/09/17/new-call-gen-z-escape-virtual
-world-and-join-marines.html.

Harwell, Drew, et al. "QAnon Reshaped Trump's Party and Radicalized Believers: The Capitol Siege May Just Be the Start." *Washington Post*, January 13, 2021. https://www.washingtonpost.com/technology/2021/01/13
/qanon-capitol-siege-trump/.

"Heinrich Himmler." Holocaust Encyclopedia, accessed June 8, 2022. https://
encyclopedia.ushmm.org/content/en/article/heinrich-himmler.

"How Many QAnon Predictions Have Been Wrong? All of Them. Reinstatement Day Is No Different." Fact Pac, updated December 4, 2021. https://
factpac.org/how-many-qanon-predictions-have-been-wrong-all-of
-them-reinstatement-day-is-no-different/.

"How Unproven Trafficking Stories Spread Online and Why Stopping Them
Matters." *Polaris* (blog), July 22, 2022. https://polarisproject.org/blog
/2020/07/how-unproven-trafficking-stories-spread-online-and-why
-stopping-them-matters/.

LaFrance, Adrienne. "The Prophecies of Q." *Atlantic*, June 2020. https://www

.theatlantic.com/magazine/archive/2020/06/qanon-nothing-can-stop
-what-is-coming/610567/.

Marx, Leo. "The Machine in the Garden." *New England Quarterly* 29, no. 1
(1956): 27–42. doi:10.2307/363061.

McDonald, Brody. "How QAnon Reacts to Failed Predictions." Global Network
on Extremism & Technology, March 31, 2020. https://gnet-research
.org/2021/03/31/how-qanon-reacts-to-failed-predictions/.

Metz, Thaddeus. "The Meaning of Life." *Stanford Encyclopedia of Philosophy*,
substantive revision, February 9, 2021. https://plato.stanford.edu/ar
chives/win2021/entries/life-meaning/.

———. "This Is How You Can Find Meaning in Your Life, and Still Be Happy."
World Economic Forum, May 31, 2017. https://www.weforum.org
/agenda/2017/05/this-is-how-you-can-find-meaning-in-your-life-and
-still-be-happy/.

Parker, Kim, et al. "How Urban, Suburban and Rural Residents Interact with
Their Neighbors." Pew Research Center, May 22, 2018. https://www.pew
research.org/social-trends/2018/05/22/how-urban-suburban-and-rural
-residents-interact-with-their-neighbors/. "QAnon." Anti-Defamation
League. https://www.adl.org/qanon.

"Religiosity and Conspiratorial Beliefs Linked in Baylor Religious Survey Findings." Baylor University, June 9, 2021. https://www.baylor.edu/media
communications/news.php?action=story&story=223733.

Reneau, Annie. "If You Really Want to #SaveTheChildren, Stop Sharing QAnon
Conspiracy Theories." Upworthy, August 13, 2020. https://www.upwor
thy.com/save-the-children-stop-the-qanon-conspiracies.

Renfro, Paul M. "QAnon Misdirects Our Attention Away from the Real Threats
to Children." *Washington Post*, August 27, 2020. https://www.washington
post.com/outlook/2020/08/27/qanon-misdirects-our-attention-away
-real-threats-children/.

"Robert E. Chambliss, Figure in '63 Bombing." Obituary. *New York Times*, accessed June 8, 2022. https://www.nytimes.com/1985/10/30/us/robert-e
-chambliss-figure-in-63-bombing.html.

"Speaking of Psychology: Why People Believe in Conspiracy Theories, with
Karen Douglas, PhD." American Psychological Association, accessed
June 8, 2020. https://www.apa.org/research/action/speaking-of-psychol
ogy/conspiracy-theories.

"The SS." Holocaust Encyclopedia, accessed June 8, 2022. https://encyclopedia
.ushmm.org/content/en/article/ss.

"Study of Adult Development." Harvard University, accessed June 8, 2022. https://www.adultdevelopmentstudy.org/grantandglueckstudy.

"Survey: 1-in-4 under 40 Don't Know Any Neighbors by Name." Ownerly, accessed June 8, 2022. https://www.ownerly.com/data-analysis/do-you -know-your-neighbors-survey/.

Thurman, Howard. *Jesus and the Disinherited*. Boston: Beacon, 1976.

Timberg, Craig, and Elizabeth Dwoskin. "With Trump Gone, QAnon Groups Focus Fury on Attacking Coronavirus Vaccines." *Washington Post*, March 11, 2021. https://www.washingtonpost.com/technology/2021/03/11/with -trump-gone-qanon-groups-focus-fury-attacking-covid-vaccines/.

Twenge, Jean M. "Have Smartphones Destroyed a Generation? More Comfortable Online Than Out Partying, Post-Millennials Are Safer, Physically, Than Adolescents Have Ever Been. But They're on the Brink of a Mental-Health Crisis." *Atlantic*, September 2017. http://www.postgrowth.ca/up loads/8/4/9/4/84946882/have_smartphones_destroyed_a_generation .pdf.

"2017 Pew Research Center's American Trends Panel." Pew Research Center, December 4–18, 2017. https://assets.pewresearch.org/wp-content/up loads/sites/11/2018/08/28151638/Combined-Topline.pdf.

"What You Need to Know about QAnon." Southern Poverty Law Center, October 27, 2020. https://www.splcenter.org/hatewatch/2020/10/27/what -you-need-know-about-qanon.

Wolf, Susan. *Meaning in Life and Why It Matters*. Princeton: Princeton University Press, 2010.

6

THE LOST CHRISTIAN VIRTUE
OF REASONABLENESS

David A. Horner

There's an old joke about a Scotsman who's just been discovered after being marooned on a deserted island for twenty years. His rescuers are impressed with how well he's done for himself under the circumstances, such as building a house and raising crops. But they are baffled to find two completed church buildings, erected a half mile apart. "Why did you build *two* churches?" they ask. "It's simple, laddies," he replies. "One is the church I go to. The other is the church I *don't* go to."

We understand the joke because it hits so close to home. Christians are notorious for their "splitting personalities," characterized by bickering, grumbling, nastiness, and division. And that's on our good days.

Why are Christians so unreasonable? How can we be so rigid, inflexible, and unyielding about issues that are not central to the Christian faith? Why can't we disagree agreeably over such things? These questions are particularly pressing these days, as believers increasingly attack and divide over issues such as conspiracy theories. It's time for us to recover the Christian virtue Paul commended to the church in Philippi, which was struggling with squabbles and disunity: "Let your reasonableness be known to everyone" (Phil. 4:5 ESV). The term Paul uses for "reasonableness" has a rich background in classical Greek philosophy. We'll look at Aristotle's account and fill it out with biblical insights from the rest of Paul's message to the Philippians.

Two Kinds of Reasonableness

First, let's distinguish between two sorts of "reasonableness" that are relevant to approaching conspiracy theories. *Epistemic reasonableness* (from the Greek word for knowledge) is being reasonable about which ideas you accept as true. Our focus here is on *moral reasonableness*: being reasonable in *how* you engage with other people *in relation to ideas and issues*—especially people with whom you disagree.[1] It's what we often have in mind when we say: "Please, just be reasonable about this."

It's easy to see that epistemic reasonableness is important for approaching conspiracy theories. But so is moral reasonableness—unless we're marooned on a deserted island, our thinking inevitably occurs within social contexts where we influence and are influenced by others with our beliefs. It matters not only *what* we believe and why, but also *where* and *with whom* we believe and act on our beliefs. Our context. This is particularly important in relation to conspiracy theories, where difficulties typically arise less from what someone believes and more from how that person relates to others about it.

In Psalm 73 we see an example of taking social context into account when engaging a controversial idea. Asaph, an Israelite worship leader, recounts his deep struggle with the reality of evil and suffering, coming eventually to the brink of abandoning belief in the goodness of God. He stops short of acting on this conclusion, however, in view of its likely effect on others in his community. "If I had spoken out like that," Asaph says to God, "I would have betrayed your children" (Ps. 73:15).[2] Waiting, rather than immediately "posting" his initial thoughts and conclusions, was an act of caring for his social context. But it also opened up some needed space in which he could continue to think and evaluate. Eventually Asaph reaches a fuller understanding and embraces God's goodness as a deep personal conviction.

Moral reasonableness is about considering and relating appropriately to our social context as we engage and evaluate ideas and issues. As we'll see, this sort of reasonableness lies behind Paul's use of the term. (In what follows, unless I specify otherwise, "reasonableness" refers to moral reasonableness.)

1. Thanks to the editors for suggesting these labels.
2. Unless otherwise stated, all Scripture citations in this chapter are from the New International Version.

Reasons for Unreasonableness

Unreasonableness has both intellectual and relational elements. On the *intellectual* side, it involves mistaking the importance or centrality of an idea or issue—these are contextually dependent upon the community or practice in view. Affirming the deity of Jesus Christ is central and deeply important to the Christian community, but it's peripheral and unimportant to the game of golf. When we say, "Just be reasonable about this," we often mean: "This is not the sort of issue we should be fighting over. It's not important in this context." The unreasonable person confuses something secondary (peripheral, negotiable) with what is primary (central, nonnegotiable)—an intellectual mistake. While epistemic reasonableness is also concerned with avoiding intellectual mistakes, its focus is on whether or not an idea is *true*. The focus here is on the *importance* of the idea in its proper context.

On the *relational* side, unreasonableness involves failing to treat people appropriately with regard to an idea or issue, typically by being overly rigid, unyielding, or dogmatic—not relational inappropriateness in general, but specifically with regard to the idea or issue at stake. When we say, "Be reasonable about this," we often mean something like: "Don't be so inflexible. Can't we agree to disagree on this?"

I knew a seminary student (not where I teach!) whose final paper for a class was due at a certain time on a certain date. The professor's rule was that papers not submitted by then would not be accepted. Early the morning of the due date the student's wife went into labor and gave birth about the time the paper was due. Once mother and child had been settled adequately, the student rushed to campus with his paper. But it was now late, and the professor would not accept it, given the rule.

I hope you agree that the professor was being unreasonable. His response would have been appropriate if the student had been a slacker or had deliberately ignored the rules, but that was not the case. The professor wrongly assessed the importance and stringency of the rule in relation to the class and this situation (an intellectual mistake), and he failed to treat the student appropriately in light of the rule's actual importance (a relational failure). The two are related. The professor's distorted grasp of the rule's importance likely fueled his relational insensitivity. But it's also likely he had relational deficits, perhaps feeling threatened by students, or he possessed an excessive desire for control, which distorted his grasp of the rule's importance. In any case, we (again, I hope!) want to say to the professor, "Come on, please be reasonable about this. Yes, the rules you've laid down are important. But *in this case*, the reasonable thing to do is to relax them out of concern for the student and his specific circumstances."

Reasons for Christian Unreasonableness

Unreasonableness is certainly not unique to Christian believers. But our failures in this area are particularly tragic, in light of Jesus's words: "By this everyone will know that you are my disciples, if you love one another" (John 13:35). And devout Christian believers do seem particularly prone to rigidity and inflexibility in their beliefs and commitments. This tendency, I suggest, is a dark side of something good, which is their desire to remain faithful to Christian beliefs and commitments.

Put most simply: Christians are and ought to be people of strong conviction. However, the "conviction dial" of many believers has only one setting: maximum strength. Because followers of Jesus are a minority community defined by core beliefs and value commitments often at odds with their surrounding culture, sustaining these beliefs and commitments over time requires holding them as strong, unyielding convictions—standing firm, being steadfast and immovable (1 Cor. 15:58). Faithfulness to Jesus means having hills we're willing to die on. No yielding, no compromise.

But not all hills are ones to die (much less kill!) on, and not all yielding is wrong. It's simply not true that "compromise anywhere" leads inevitably to "compromise everywhere." Yielding and compromise may be exactly what's called for in situations where truly essential matters are not at issue. In such cases, *failing* to yield or compromise—refusing to back off and give room for nuance and disagreement, insisting that everyone must agree with me—is a form of *un*faithfulness.

Losing our convictions—allowing nonnegotiable and central commitments to drift and become negotiable and peripheral—is not the only threat to Christian faithfulness. So also is *confusing our convictions*—allowing secondary beliefs, opinions, and preferences to creep into primary status where they dilute and obscure what is truly essential. Moreover, while false tolerance and compromise—the notions that no ideas are any truer than any other and that all convictions are negotiable—are clearly incompatible with holding faithfully to Christian convictions, this doesn't mean we should reject all tolerance and compromise. These are distortions. *True* tolerance respects and values others even when rejecting their views. *Proper* compromise invites appropriate give-and-take in secondary matters but is fully compatible with unwavering conviction in what is primary. Both are necessary for social well-being.

Holding strong convictions about what is truly essential and nonnegotiable is a matter of Christian faithfulness. But so is recognizing when ideas and issues such as conspiracy theories are secondary and negotiable, and treating folks with respect and grace even when we disagree about them. Of course, distinguishing between primary and secondary matters is not always obvious, nor is knowing when to hold a point and when to back off and leave room for difference. We need wisdom. We need the virtue of reasonableness.

The Virtue of Reasonableness

Like us, the believers in Philippi had "splitting personalities." They struggled with dissension, disagreement, and disunity among themselves (Phil. 1:27; 2:3-4, 12-16; 3:15). Their relational squabbles were so serious that Paul, in an unusual move, singles out two influential women in the church at odds with each other: "I plead with Euodia and I plead with Syntyche to be of the same mind in the Lord" (4:2). It's instructive that Paul doesn't address the specific issue about which they disagree, nor does he identify either woman's view as mistaken—only their inability to get along. Nor does he demand that they come to the same conclusion. Rather, he exhorts them to agree ("be of the same mind") *in the Lord*. That's what's primary, a common space for disagreeing agreeably over secondary things. This is the context where, three verses later, Paul exhorts *all* the Philippians, "Let your reasonableness be known to everyone" (4:5 ESV).

The Greek term for "reasonableness" here is *epieikeia*, rendered in the New Testament in terms such as "gentleness," "consideration," "forbearance," "moderation," and "kindness."[3] No single English word adequately conveys the full scope of *epieikeia*, as it carries resonances of all these terms. Matthew Arnold termed it "sweet reasonableness," arguing that it was the chief attribute of Jesus and his early followers. The relational aspect of *epieikeia* is obvious in the English terms above, but its intellectual element comes into clearer view when we consider the Greek philosophical tradition that forms the term's background context. Aristotle's treatment of *epieikeia* was the most influential.[4]

---

3. *Epieikeia* also appears in Acts 4:24; 2 Cor. 10:1; 1 Tim. 3:3; Titus 3:2; James 3:17; and 1 Pet. 2:18.

4. We have no evidence that Paul had read Aristotle or was directly influenced

Aristotle and *Epieikeia*

According to Aristotle, *epieikeia* is a virtue—a character trait formed by habitual practice. Virtues are developed capacities and dispositions to see things in certain ways, care about and be motivated in certain ways, and feel and act in certain ways.[5] A kind person, for example, cares about others and recognizes their needs, discerns how best to meet those needs, and acts appropriately to do so.

Aristotle identifies *epieikeia* (often translated as "equity") as a form of justice. Justice is a virtue that disposes one to discern correctly what is "due" to each person and motivates one to make sure the person receives it. *Epieikeia* is a subsidiary virtue that enables one to adapt and flex in exceptional cases in order to preserve true justice grounded in the common good.

Aristotle illustrates with two cases calling for *epieikeia*. The first is of a judge tasked with determining legal justice in a court of law, rendering punishments and rewards according to legal statutes and stipulations. Yet exceptional cases sometimes arise where strictly adhering to a law's requirement would conflict with the common good and thus not actually preserve justice. Strict justice and true justice can come apart, according to Aristotle, because "law is always a general statement, yet there are cases which it is not possible to cover in a general statement." The "equitable" judge is able to discern when to make an exception to a statute, "deciding as the lawgiver would himself decide if he were present on the occasion."[6] Doing so is not unjust, Aristotle stresses, even though it does not follow the letter of the law. Rather, it preserves what is *truly* just in this case.[7] The best judges are those with the wisdom—*epieikeia*—to discern such cases and decide appropriately.

As we saw with the seminary professor, judges are not the only ones faced with determining how best to apply rules and procedures to exceptional situations. What he lacked, according to Aristotle, is *epieikeia*.

---

by him. But indirect influence is highly likely, given the general influence of Aristotle's account of *epieikeia* on subsequent philosophers, including the Stoics, with whom Paul was certainly familiar (Acts 17:18-20).

5. For Paul's understanding of virtue, see N. T. Wright, *After You Believe: Why Christian Character Matters* (New York: HarperOne, 2010).

6. Aristotle, *The Nicomachean Ethics*, trans. H. Rackham, Loeb Classical Library (Cambridge, MA: Harvard University Press, 1934), 1137b12-23.

7. Thomas Aquinas is blunt: To follow the letter of the law when it ought not to be followed is a sin. *Summa theologiae* IIaIIae.120.1. ad 1.

The second case Aristotle mentions extends more generally to situations where people have a legitimate right to something (having rights is also a matter of justice) but in certain cases choose not to demand that right, when they discern that it's better not to. "And from this it is clear what the equitable man is: he is the one who by choice and habit does what is equitable, and who does not stand on his rights unduly, but is content to receive a smaller share although he has the law on his side. And the disposition described is Equity."[8]

Aristotle's *epieikeia* has both intellectual and relational components. It involves grasping what's truly at stake in a situation related to justice, whether a matter of rules or personal rights and privileges, discerning whether it calls for pushing and insisting or else making an exception or settling for less—and caring enough for the well-being of others to be willing to do so. *Epieikeia* is moral reasonableness.

The Christian Virtue of Reasonableness

Aristotle provides a helpful framework of *epieikeia*. Paul is likely to have at least that in mind when he exhorts the Philippians to let their reasonableness be evident to everyone. But he surely has more in mind as well, as his conception is further informed and transformed by his Christian understanding. Let's conclude by filling out our picture of *Christian* reasonableness with four suggestions that emerge from the rest of Paul's letter to the Philippians.

First, keep first things first and second things second. For Paul, unity in the body of Christ is a first thing—not unity simply for its own sake, but for the sake of the gospel: "Whatever happens, conduct yourselves in a manner worthy of the gospel of Christ. . . . Stand firm in the one Spirit, striving together as one for the faith of the gospel" (1:27). Pursuing a common mission binds us together. Our frequent dissensions over secondary matters usually indicate that we've lost track of our common purpose.

Second, pray for loving discernment. Paul prays that "your love may abound more and more in knowledge and depth of insight, so that you may be able to discern what is best" (1:9-10). He's concerned that the Philippians grow in their ability to grasp what truly matters, but it's their *love* he prays would grow in this way—the impetus and driving motivation for Christian

---

8. Aristotle, *Nicomachean Ethics* 1137b33–1138a4.

discernment is love for each other. Our pervasive confusions of primary and secondary matters suggest that our motivation is elsewhere.

Third, surrender your rights and preferences out of concern for the good of others and the progress of the gospel. Paul celebrates that the gospel is proclaimed, even when the proclaimers treat him shamefully. While he has every right as an apostle to be respected and treated fairly, he makes no demands. His sole concern is that Jesus be proclaimed (1:12–15). The supreme example is Jesus, who humbled himself and set aside his divine prerogatives to give his life for us (2:6–8)—a model we are to follow: "In your relationships with one another, have the same mindset as Christ Jesus" (2:5). How often are struggles over disputed matters about protecting our own rights, privileges, or reputation? Of course, we should be quick to defend the legal rights of vulnerable people, and sometimes to defend our own (see Acts 25:1–12). We need wisdom to know when this is appropriate. But few divisions among Christians are over such issues. "Do nothing out of selfish ambition or vain conceit. Rather, in humility value others above yourselves, not looking to your own interests but each of you to the interests of the others" (Phil. 2:3–4).

Finally, trust God and his timing. Secondary agendas are often fear-driven compulsions to control, correct, and protect our circumstances and concerns. But that's ultimately up to God, not us. "Our citizenship is in heaven. And we eagerly await a Savior from there, the Lord Jesus Christ" (3:20)—he's the one who will ultimately make things right. We know Paul has this in mind when he exhorts the Philippians to be reasonable, for his next words are: "The Lord is near" (4:5). It's because the Lord is near—coming again to put things right but also present to us now by his Spirit—that we can afford to be reasonable. We can back off, allow room for differences, and let go of our own rights and privileges and interests for the sake of the gospel and the good of others, because Jesus will take care of our concerns in his time. He's God and we're not.

So let our reasonableness be evident to everyone.

References

Aristotle. *The Nicomachean Ethics*. Translated by H. Rackham. Loeb Classical Library. Cambridge, MA: Harvard University Press, 1934.

Arnold, Matthew. *St. Paul and Protestantism with an Essay on Puritanism and the Church of England*. London: Smith, Elder, & Co., 1875.

Dodson, Joseph R., and David E. Briones, eds. *Paul and the Giants of Philoso-*

phy: Reading the Apostle in Greco-Roman Context. Downers Grove, IL: IVP Academic, 2019.

Thomas Aquinas. *Summa theologiae* IIaIIae.120.1. ad 1.

Virt, Günter. "Moral Norms and the Forgotten Virtue of *Epikeia* in the Pastoral Care of the Divorced and Remarried." *Melita Theologica* 63 (2013): 17–34.

Willard, Dallas. *The Allure of Gentleness: Defending the Faith in the Manner of Jesus*. San Francisco: HarperCollins, 2015.

Wright, N. T. *After You Believe: Why Christian Character Matters*. New York: HarperOne, 2010.

7

A FAILURE OF HUMBLE PROPORTIONS

Michael W. Austin

There are child trafficking tunnels under the White House. Hillary Clinton, Joe Biden, Oprah Winfrey, and Tom Hanks are all pedophiles. Donald Trump won the 2020 election, and "you gotta smoke a lot of dope in your momma's basement not to believe that fact." Every one of these claims, all of which are consistent with the beliefs spread by QAnon, was made *in a single sermon* by Greg Locke, pastor of Global Vision Bible Church near Nashville.[1] Now, I don't live in my parents' basement, and I don't smoke a lot of dope—or any dope, for that matter—but I don't believe any of the claims made by Locke. I just don't think there is good evidence for them. As we'll see, how we approach evidence is both an intellectual and moral issue that has vital importance for followers of Jesus of Nazareth.

Sadly, however, belief in false and even outlandish conspiracy theories—the types of conspiracy theories that are the focus of this chapter—is all too common among Christians. Consider a recent survey in which 49 percent of Protestant pastors agreed with the statement "I frequently hear members of my congregation repeating conspiracy theories they have heard about why something is happening in our country."[2] Significant numbers

1. David Gilbert, "Evangelical Pastors Are Secretly Spreading the Gospel of QAnon on YouTube," *Vice*, September 8, 2021, https://www.vice.com/en/article/k78jwx/qanon-pastors-spreading-conspiracies-youtube.

2. Aaron Earls, "Half of U.S. Protestant Pastors Hear Conspiracy Theories in Their Churches," Lifeway Research, January 26, 2021, https://lifewayresearch

of Christians in America believe at least some of the claims of QAnon.[3] Over half of white evangelicals believe there is a "deep state" at work in America. Half of white evangelicals believe that Antifa was behind the January 6 insurrection in Washington, DC, rather than supporters of Donald Trump. Thirty-six percent of white Catholics, 35 percent of Hispanic Catholics, and 25 percent of Black Protestants believe this as well, compared to only 19 percent of non-Christians. Many Christians also believe conspiracy theories related to the 2020 presidential election, the coronavirus pandemic, mask wearing, vaccines, the media, and the perceived threat of a global government.[4]

There is a lot behind this phenomenon, including a variety of psychological, spiritual, moral, sociological, and historical reasons. In this chapter I want to focus on how humility is an antidote to belief in such conspiracy theories, and how belief in them can involve a failure of humility.

Intellectual Humility

A friend of mine and I have had some back-and-forth over the past year or so about what I take to be false conspiracy theories related to the 2020 presidential election. He has challenged me to think more about these things than I would have otherwise and to look at sources I was not aware of, which I appreciate. He is also guilty of a mistake, a point which I've raised with him, that is relevant here. In John 16:13 Jesus speaks of the Holy Spirit coming and guiding his disciples "into all the truth." We make a mistake, however, if we think that this means we can find out the truth *about anything we want to know.* My friend has prayed that God will lead him into the truth about the 2020 election. But why do we think God will lead us into truth about the 2020 election, even if we fervently and persistently ask him to do so? We could pray that God would lead us into the truth about many

.com/2021/01/26/half-of-u-s-protestant-pastors-hear-conspiracy-theories-in-their -churches/.

3. Jack Jenkins, "QAnon Conspiracies Sway Faith Groups, Including 1 in 4 White Evangelicals," *Christianity Today*, February 11, 2021, https://www.christianitytoday .com/news/2021/february/white-evangelicals-qanon-election-conspiracy-trump -aei.html.

4. Daniel Burke, "How QAnon Uses Religion to Lure Unsuspecting Christians," CNN, October 15, 2020, https://www.cnn.com/2020/10/15/us/qanon-religion -churches/index.html.

things, prayers that he is not bound to answer as we want, by his character or his promises, including the 2020 election. I might ask God to show me who will win the World Series, who shot JFK, if a deep state exists, whether the moon landing was faked, if Hillary Clinton is a pedophile, or whether the Russians have been blackmailing Donald Trump. There are truths about all these things, but that doesn't mean God will lead me to know any of those truths. One reason is that we humans are, well, human. We are limited, dependent, finite creatures, all of which is relevant to our quest for truth. I think my friend is actually pretty humble, but in this particular case he is not fully appreciating his limited access to the truth about the 2020 election. So what follows is not directed at him. Rather, it is directed at all of us because we can all forget, or at least fail to fully appreciate, our nature as limited, finite, dependent creatures. But this forgetting poses special problems with respect to belief in conspiracy theories.

This leads us to an important Christian virtue, the intellectual virtue of humility. This is a virtue, or excellence, of the mind. As human beings, we have limits, including limits related to what we can know, and related to what we should seek to know. Intellectual humility instructs us to accept those limits. Intellectual humility has a few central components.[5] First, the intellectually humble person has an appropriate level of awareness of her intellectual weaknesses and limits. She's not obsessed with them, but neither does she ignore them. Second, such a person accurately (or reasonably, at least) assesses what her intellectual weaknesses and limitations are. Third, the intellectually humble person seeks to own her intellectual weaknesses and limitations.

Christians who believe the moon landings were faked, that the 2020 election was stolen from Trump, that "the Left" is using the pandemic to figure out who they can and cannot control, that the COVID vaccines magnetize people who get them, that there are child-trafficking tunnels under the White House, or that "the Marxist globalist Satanists"[6] are pushing for all of us to wear masks, are all exhibiting failures of intellectual humility.

How so?

---

5. Nathan L. King, *The Excellent Mind: Intellectual Virtues for Everyday Life* (New York: Oxford University Press, 2020), 106–30. I've added the language about limits, though I think it is consistent with the definition offered here.

6. Kyle Mantyla, "DeAnna Lorraine Claims That 'God Does Not Want Us Wearing Masks,'" *Right Wing Watch*, July 17, 2020, https://www.rightwingwatch.org/post /deanna-lorraine-claims-that-god-does-not-want-us-wearing-masks/.

They are failing to appropriately appreciate their intellectual limits and to accurately assess what those limits are. Think about the past two years. There are people who suddenly knew the truth about all of the following, contrary to the consensus—sometimes an overwhelming consensus—of the relevant experts and participants in these events: the results of the 2020 election, the laws of several state constitutions related to election procedures, the efficacy of face masks in limiting the spread of the coronavirus during a global pandemic, immunology, virology, public health, international relations, the nature and role of government, computer technology related to voting machines, 5G wireless technology, a variety of issues related to race and racism, and global climate change. It is one thing to have *opinions* about these things, even, in some cases, highly informed opinions. But when a single person has deep convictions about some, most, or all of these issues, something is wrong.

Consider just one of these, the 2020 election. It doesn't matter how much "research" you do by watching YouTube videos, engaging with alternative news sources, and scouring the Internet, it is a safe bet that you (and I) simply don't have either the investigative skills or access to enough of the relevant true information to make a reliable and informed judgment that the 2020 election was stolen based on that research. This is compounded by the problem that so much misinformation and disinformation is out there. Many think, "I can do my own research." But this often involves an overreach related to both our abilities and expertise. Engaging in such overreach is a failure of intellectual humility, as it involves a failure to appropriately appreciate and accurately assess our intellectual weaknesses and limits.

Also, many who believe and then propagate false conspiracy theories are failing to own their intellectual weaknesses and limits. One aspect of this is that we must learn to accept our intellectual limitations. For example, as another friend of mine recently and rightly pointed out to me, those who believe in a minority view in a particular field (e.g., climate change) or who believe in one or more conspiracy theories (e.g., the COVID vaccines are designed to allow the government to track our movements) ought to question why they, as laypersons, are intellectually capable of discerning that some outliers in a particular field are correct, rather than the overwhelming consensus of experts. This is yet another failure of intellectual humility because it is a failure to accept that one is simply not sufficiently equipped to make these kinds of judgments, at least in a reliable manner.

One good question to ask is this: Do all the conspiracy theories I believe (or that I am at least drawn to believing) reflect and reinforce my own political, ethical, and religious beliefs? If so, that's a solid piece of evidence that something may have gone wrong. If so, my belief in all these conspiracies is reflective of my liberal or conservative biases, rather than a humble and passionate concern for the truth. This is one way to own our intellectual limits and weaknesses that can help us correct them.

Moral Humility

In a recent CBS News documentary, Greg Locke preached the following to his congregation: "These bunch of sex trafficking mongrels are about to be exposed. These bunch of pedophiles in Hollywood are gonna be exposed for who they are. I don't care what you think about fraudulent Sleepy Joe, he's a sex trafficking demon possessed mongrel, he's on the Left."[7] It would be nice to dismiss Locke as a fringe figure, and in some senses he is. Yet he has over 2.2 million followers on Facebook and a large online platform and is an active traveling speaker. He's published two books (both published by Locke Media Group). He is influential, he's reflective of what a lot of people believe, and that's a big problem. There are failures of intellectual humility in the above claims that we've discussed already. But there is another failure here, related to the moral virtue of humility. This is a virtue of the whole person, not merely the mind, and includes a disposition to speak and act in certain ways that reflect the humble speech, actions, and character of Jesus.

What is the moral virtue of humility?[8] To understand this, as a Christian virtue, we must look to Christ. One of the best descriptions of the humility of Christ is found in Philippians 2:1–11 (NRSV):

> [1]If then there is any encouragement in Christ, any consolation from love, any sharing in the Spirit, any compassion and sympathy, [2]make my joy complete: be of the same mind, having the same love, being in full accord and of one mind. [3]Do nothing from selfish ambition or conceit, but in humility regard others as better than yourselves. [4]Let each of you look not to your own interests, but to the interests of others. [5]Let the same mind be in you that was in Christ Jesus,

7. "An (Un)Civil War: The Evangelical Divide," CBS News, October 21, 2021, https://www.youtube.com/watch?v=KnsrTroXwEg.

8. Michael W. Austin, *Humility and Human Flourishing* (New York: Oxford University Press, 2018), chap. 2.

⁶who, though he was in the form of God,
did not regard equality with God
as something to be exploited,
⁷but emptied himself,
taking the form of a slave,
being born in human likeness.
And being found in human form,
⁸he humbled himself
and became obedient to the point of death—
even death on a cross.
⁹Therefore God also highly exalted him
and gave him the name
that is above every name,
¹⁰so that at the name of Jesus
every knee should bend,
in heaven and on earth and under the earth,
¹¹and every tongue should confess
that Jesus Christ is Lord,
to the glory of God the Father.

In verses 1–4, Paul urges the Philippians to be united for the sake of the gospel. To do so, they must humbly value the interests of others rather than their own honor and interests. Rather than trying to climb up the social ladder, the norm in Greco-Roman society, Paul challenges members of the Philippian church to step down that ladder in humble and loving service to others.[9] He goes on in verses 5–11 to encourage them to imitate the humility exemplified by Christ in his incarnation and crucifixion.

Several things will be true about the humble person. She will tend to engage in self-sacrificial actions for the good of others. She will not seek honor or social status, at least not for its own sake. Moreover, she will not think of human beings in a hierarchical manner, regardless of their wealth, fame, influence, or power. She will relate to them all in light of their equal inherent dignity and worth as image-bearers of God. The insults from Greg Locke ("Sleepy Joe") and what is really nothing more than outright slander and defamation, including the use of a racist term ("he's a sex trafficking demon possessed mongrel"), reveal a failure of humility.

9. Ben Witherington III, *Paul's Letter to the Philippians: A Socio-Rhetorical Commentary* (Grand Rapids: Eerdmans, 2011), 31–32.

We all fail with respect to humility, to be sure. Arrogance and pride are relentless aspects of human nature. Change is possible, but it is often slow. We can come to reflect the humility of Christ, by God's grace, over time. My concern here with many who advocate these types of conspiracy theories is that they actually see nothing wrong with how they are speaking about others, not only to denigrate them but also to prop up both themselves and their precious platforms. Joe Biden and Donald Trump are both image-bearers of God. They should be treated and spoken about as such. It's all too easy to demonize people who are part of another political tribe. It's all too easy to demonize people in Hollywood. And apparently, it is all too easy for people who profess to be followers of Jesus to demonize Anthony Fauci; Francis Collins; the Centers for Disease Control and Prevention (CDC); public health officials at the national, state, and local levels; school boards; Marxists; critical race theorists; and on and on it goes.

According to Jesus, what we say reveals what is in our hearts (Matt. 12:33–37). And if malice, slander, and demonization are present in our speech, then that is a warning sign about what is going on in our hearts. As a remedy to this, we must seek to imitate Christ, to engage in the spiritual practices he did, to seek to be humble as he was humble, to refuse when we are reviled to revile in return (1 Pet. 2:23). It isn't easy, but this is the Way (Acts 9:2; 19:9, 23; 22:4; 24:14).

The "Foolishness" of the Cross and the Foolishness of Conspiracy Theories

The Way of Jesus also includes a certain form of foolishness, but not the kind many immediately think of in this context. Parts of 1 Corinthians are both often misunderstood and misapplied, in my experience. Paul tells the Corinthian church that the wisdom of the world has been made foolish by God (1:20). Many take this as a justification for believing false and outlandish things, such as many of the conspiracy theories discussed in this book. But that is not the point Paul is making. Indeed, it is far from his point. What is it, though, that is foolish in the eyes of the world, according to Paul? *It is the cross of Christ* (1:23). The Greeks desire wisdom; they and other gentiles see the cross as foolishness (1:22–23). They fail to realize that Christ is the very embodiment of truth and wisdom (Col. 2:3). If Christians are to be thought of as fools, it ought to be because of our belief in Christ, and in the message and meaning of the cross, rather than some deeply misguided belief in false conspiracy theories.

This leads us back to where we began this chapter, with Pastor Greg Locke. In the CBS News documentary, in response to a question about whether people will just say he's "a crazy conspiracy theorist," Locke says that "Christians have always believed things that the world thought *that is nuts, these people are crazy, you know, they're absolutely crazy* . . . at the end of the day I'm just willing to look crazy." I agree that we should be willing to look like we are foolish, but not because we believe and spread conspiracy theories. Rather, it should be because we believe and spread the love that is at the heart of the gospel of Christ, demonstrated by him in so many ways, including his death on the cross.

Locke's willingness to be called "crazy" is at best based on a serious misunderstanding, and is at worst nothing more than grifting. His reply to a question about his responsibility *for giving evidence* that there are pedophile rings, that COVID vaccines are sugar water, and that the election was fraudulent, is telling.[10] He says, "For the most part I'm preaching to a pretty one-sided crowd, that's why they're flying here, driving here, taking a bicycle or a cruise ship here because they like what I say, because I'm saying what they feel, I'm scratching their itch type of deal." He doesn't think any of these claims will come back on him, but he also says that he hopes that they do. Why? Because then the evidence will come to the surface. But it's hard to see why he doesn't *just give the evidence now*, unless he in fact doesn't have it. It's also hard not to immediately think of the words in 2 Timothy 4:3-4, "For the time is coming when people will not put up with sound doctrine, but having itching ears, they will accumulate for themselves teachers to suit their own desires, and will turn away from listening to the truth and wander away to myths" (NRSV).

Only God knows the heart of those who flock to Locke and his teaching. But as far as Locke himself is concerned, we get a glimpse into what is going on there. As one of my former (conservative) pastors put it after watching the documentary, "Greg Locke literally admits he's just grifting from the pulpit. He calls other ministers cowards, but his supposed courage is in fact a form of cowardice to scratch the itching ears of far-right consumers."[11]

Many of us wrongly think that we are following Christ when in fact we've been discipled by political pundits, politicians, and politically oriented pas-

10. "An (Un)Civil War."

11. Robert Cunningham, Twitter post, October 27, 2021, https://twitter.com/tcp crobert/status/1453339038132359179.

tors on the right and the left. This should not be. We should be followers of the Way, not of People for the American Way. Our heritage is found in Christ, not the Heritage Foundation. If we are going to be seen as fools, let it be because we are imitating Christ and his sacrificial love on the cross, because we are seeking Christ and his kingdom, rather than because we are pursuing a larger social media following, money, or political power.

In short, if we are to be thought of as fools, let it be for humbly following the crucified Christ, rather than QAnon.

References

Austin, Michael W. *Humility and Human Flourishing*. New York: Oxford University Press, 2018.

Burke, Daniel. "How QAnon Uses Religion to Lure Unsuspecting Christians." CNN, October 15, 2020. https://www.cnn.com/2020/10/15/us/qanon-religion-churches/index.html.

Earls, Aaron. "Half of U.S. Protestant Pastors Hear Conspiracy Theories in Their Churches." Lifeway Research, January 26, 2021. https://lifeway research.com/2021/01/26/half-of-u-s-protestant-pastors-hear-conspir acy-theories-in-their-churches/.

Gilbert, David. "Evangelical Pastors Are Secretly Spreading the Gospel of QAnon on YouTube." *Vice*, September 8, 2021. https://www.vice.com /en/article/k78jwx/qanon-pastors-spreading-conspiracies-youtube.

Jenkins, Jack. "QAnon Conspiracies Sway Faith Groups, Including 1 in 4 White Evangelicals." *Christianity Today*, February 11, 2021. https://www.chris tianitytoday.com/news/2021/february/white-evangelicals-qanon -election-conspiracy-trump-aei.html

King, Nathan L. *The Excellent Mind: Intellectual Virtues for Everyday Life*. New York: Oxford University Press, 2020.

Mantyla, Kyle. "DeAnna Lorraine Claims That 'God Does Not Want Us Wearing Masks.'" *Right Wing Watch*, July 17, 2020. https://www.rightwing watch.org/post/deanna-lorraine-claims-that-god-does-not-want-us -wearing-masks/.

"An (Un)Civil War: The Evangelical Divide." CBS News, October 21, 2021. https://www.youtube.com/watch?v=KnsrTroXwEg.

Witherington, Ben, III. *Paul's Letter to the Philippians: A Socio-Rhetorical Commentary*. Grand Rapids: Eerdmans, 2011.

8

GETTING ANGRY

Gregory L. Bock

There's nothing wrong with getting angry. Jesus got angry with the money changers in the temple (John 2:13–17), and God gets angry at human sinfulness (Isa. 30:27). What matters is how angry we get, what we get angry at, and what we do with our anger. James offers good advice about the matter: "Know this, my beloved brothers: let every person be quick to hear, slow to speak, slow to anger; for the anger of man does not produce the righteousness of God" (James 1:19–20).[1] In short, we must keep our anger under control and use it as God intended (Eph. 4:26). This chapter explores whether some Christian conspiracy theorists have an anger problem and whether those on the other side might, too.

How Angry We Get

Let's assume for the moment that some of the worst conspiracy theories are true. For example, vaccines contain tracking devices, contrails are really chemtrails, and the 2020 US presidential election was rigged. If these were true, then anger would be appropriate, right? But how angry should we get?

Joseph Butler, an eighteenth-century Anglican bishop, defends anger, calling it a "generous movement of the mind" and a God-given passion that helps us respond appropriately to sin.[2] He also thinks anger deters crime

---

1. Scripture quotations in this chapter come from the English Standard Version.
2. *Joseph Butler: Fifteen Sermons Preached at the Rolls Chapel and Other Writings*

because potential criminals fear the wrath of the community in the form of punishment. If anger is indeed given by God for these reasons, then it makes sense to call it "righteous anger," at least sometimes. So, when is it not righteous?

Butler describes several types of sinful anger, which he calls "abuses." One of these is excessive anger.[3] For example, consider when someone cuts you off in traffic. Responding with anger is understandable and appropriate because reckless driving is dangerous. But "road rage" would be inappropriate. In other words, it would be wrong to tailgate someone at high speed for ten miles while yelling obscenities. Imagine if someone cut Jesus off when he was driving. How would he respond?

Butler says anger is excessive when it interferes with our ability to love one another. Remember that the most important moral command, according to Jesus, is to love our neighbors and our enemies (Matt. 22:39; 5:44). Let's call this The Love Condition:

> *The Love Condition: anger shouldn't interfere with loving one's neighbors or one's enemies.*

Anger violates this condition when it causes us to disrespect others or lose sight of the fact that God loves every single person. For example, anger that springs from a belief in a conspiracy theory might prevent us from acting kindly toward government workers who enforce a vaccine mandate or a clerk at a grocery store who enforces a mask mandate. This anger, if not contained, might also hurt those closest to us.

Butler tries to help us see how we can distinguish between normal and excessive anger. He says the intensity of anger we feel should never exceed the anger we might feel when we hear of someone we don't know being wronged. We might get angry for a time. We might even speak out publicly on behalf of the victim. However, our anger on behalf of a stranger is muted and contained, and the feelings pass relatively quickly. But when we are the victims, the anger is much more intense. We often take it personally, and our anger can get the best of us. For Butler, the anger we feel for someone we don't know is instructive for how we ought to feel when we ourselves are the victims, even if it's hard. When anger consumes us, we ought to forgive,

---

on Ethics, ed. David McNaughton (New York: Oxford University Press, 2017), sermons 8-9, pp. 68-83.

3. *Joseph Butler*, 72.

which means to commit to overcoming our anger and resume following Jesus's command to love.[4]

Some might claim that Jesus doesn't really care how we feel or how angry we get as long as we don't harm anyone. What matters, they say, is that we do the right thing, but we can't help how we feel. This view seems to take discipleship to be a matter of strict obedience and not one that involves the heart. Consider the popular Christian song lyric "Love is a verb" and the sometimes-heard expression "You have to love them, not like them." While duty and actions are important, to stress them at the expense of the emotions is a Kantian idea, not a Christian one. (Kant is famous for an account of ethics that stressed acting for the sake of the moral law as a matter of duty, not feeling.) Can you imagine Jesus saying to a married man, "It's okay if you hate your wife; just as long as you fulfill your obligations to her." Such an ethics misses the point of the Sermon on the Mount, which is that following the law isn't just an external matter but is also an internal one. Christian love is about actions and the heart, and it involves our whole (redeemed) being—heart, soul, and mind (Matt. 22:37). Of course, loving feelings don't always come easy, and from time to time our sense of duty may be all that keeps us from saying or doing something we regret. Love is, *at minimum*, commitment and obligation. But perfect love includes feelings, too. As Paul says in 1 Corinthians 13:3, "If I give away all I have, and if I deliver up my body to be burned, but have not love, I gain nothing." What Paul is saying here is that he could do the most charitable thing, but if his heart isn't in it, then his actions are worthless. So, we ought to guard our hearts.

Do conspiracy theorists have a more serious anger problem than others? I don't think so. You see plenty of angry politicians and pundits on mainstream channels. Why some conspiracy theorists feel so strongly is something I can only speculate about here. Perhaps it's because of some personal tragedy, for which they blame the government. Perhaps they think their rights are being violated by an evil cabal. Perhaps it's the angry rhetoric on social media that alleges elite members of society are in league with the devil. Whatever the reason or source, Christians should be careful that their beliefs about the world don't interfere with their ability to love others.

We need to guard our hearts. One way we can do this is by monitoring our daily news and social media intake. If what we listen to each day leaves us angry and unpleasant to be around, we can try fasting from these inputs for a week or a month and see if we notice a difference. Another way to guard our

---

4. *Joseph Butler*, 78.

hearts is to focus on the truths of Scripture and remember where our hope lies—not in political power or in winning the so-called culture war but in the coming resurrection and return of Jesus when all things will be set right. As 1 Peter 1:3–4 says, "He has caused us to be born again to a living hope through the resurrection of Jesus Christ from the dead, to an inheritance that is imperishable, undefiled, and unfading, kept in heaven for you." We can count on trouble in this world (John 16:33), and, like many Christians throughout history, we may even be persecuted and killed. If we respond to persecution by hating our enemies, then we have surely lost our way—*and our witness*. Remember that we should be known for our love (John 13:35).

What We Get Angry At

Our anger should be directed at sin. For example, Jesus got angry at the money changers in the temple (John 2:13–17). He got angry at people who misled little children (Luke 17:2). He got angry at the Pharisees and called them "whitewashed tombs" (Matt. 23:27). And he got angry with Peter for trying to interfere with God's plans (Matt. 16:23).

If people were spraying poisonous chemicals on the population from airplanes or spreading COVID-19 via 5G networks, I'm sure he'd get angry at them, too, but Jesus got angry at *true* sin. By "true" I'm not talking about how serious it is. I mean it was *real*. When Jesus got angry, his judgment was accurate and indisputable. He didn't get angry at something that he mistakenly thought was a sin. For instance, he never had to apologize to the Pharisees and say, "I'm sorry. I shouldn't have gotten so angry with you. I thought you were acting self-righteously, but now I see that I simply misjudged you." Of course not!

Our judgment, on the other hand, is fallible. "To err is human," right? In fact, this is one of the "abuses" in Butler's list: "We imagine an injury done us, when there is none."[5] Given this epistemic weakness on our part, we ought to be careful with our judgments, especially when what we believe could have dramatic consequences. We don't want to be caught imagining a conspiracy "when there is none," as Butler might say. For example, believing that the COVID-19 vaccine campaign is just an elaborate conspiracy to implant chips in people will cause some people to forgo the shot, risking their own health and the lives of those around them. We should investigate such claims carefully before accepting them, which we can do by practicing

5. *Joseph Butler*, 72.

critical thinking. This involves looking carefully at the evidence, staying alert for logical fallacies, and recognizing our own cognitive biases (see the appendix for some critical thinking tools relevant to assessing conspiracy theories). Tip: ask conspiracy theorists what kind of evidence they would need to change their minds.

Our fallibleness also requires that we cultivate humility. Someone who is mistaken and proud is unlikely to ever recognize the fact. On the other hand, those who acknowledge how little they actually know and admit they could be wrong about what they claim to know are more likely to avoid mistakes. A humble person is also open-minded and listens carefully to other perspectives, even those of enemies. As Thomas Merton writes, "Are we willing to learn something from [our adversaries]? . . . If we are obviously unwilling to accept any truth that we have not first discovered and declared ourselves, we show by that very fact that we are interested not in the truth so much as in 'being right.'"[6] Tip: ask conspiracy theorists whether they think it's possible that they're wrong.

Humble people don't get angry very quickly because they don't rush to judgment too quickly. They spend time examining the evidence and listening to different points of view. The slower we are to get angry, the more likely we are to discover our mistake before we do something we regret. For once our anger spills out, it may be impossible to repair the damage, which I take to be one of the reasons behind the command to be slow to anger (James 1:19).

What We Do with Our Anger

Consider the actions of Edgar Maddison Welch, the guy who walked into a pizzeria in Washington, DC, on December 4, 2016, with a loaded AR-15 because he believed that elite Satan-worshiping Democrats held young children as sex slaves in the pizzeria's basement. It should be obvious that walking into a crowded family restaurant and discharging a firearm is an inappropriate way to express anger. Welch's actions were horrific and put many people in danger.

There are many ideas (especially political ones) that lead people to commit acts of violence, but this is not the way of the Jesus. Consider what Jesus says to Peter when he pulls out a sword to fight the soldiers who came

6. *Thomas Merton: Essential Writings*, ed. Christine M. Bochen (Maryknoll, NY: Orbis, 2000), 131.

to arrest them: "Put your sword back into its place. For all who take the sword will perish by the sword" (Matt. 26:52). Although Peter had followed Jesus for some time, he didn't fully understand his teachings until after the cross. Remember, when Jesus predicted his death and resurrection, Peter rebuked him, saying that he shouldn't have to die. Then Jesus rebuked him, saying, "Get behind me, Satan! For you are not setting your mind on the things of God, but on the things of man" (Mark 8:33). The Bible calls us to love our enemies. It says, "If your enemy is hungry, feed him; if he is thirsty, give him something to drink; for by so doing you will heap [metaphorical] coals on his head" (Rom. 12:20). Let's heap metaphorical coals on our enemies' heads, not real ones.

Does this mean that Jesus wants us to be doormats, ignoring injustice and evil in the world? No. But it's possible to express our anger in a way that doesn't increase the amount of suffering in the world. Consider Martha Nussbaum's suggestions in her book *Anger and Forgiveness*. She argues for what she calls "transition anger," which means redirecting our anger into things that can bring about positive change, such as joining a peaceful protest or a victim's advocacy group.[7] Anger directed in these ways can actually be an expression of love for others. For one, it can bring social awareness and prevent future instances of wrongdoing, protecting other would-be victims. Also, transition anger might be useful in the transformation and rehabilitation of wrongdoers, giving them an opportunity to make amends for what they've done.

In the middle of the Cold War and the upheaval of the sixties, Merton wrote an essay explaining how Jesus's teachings on meekness in the Sermon on the Mount apply to problems of the day and how Christians can resist evil and promote peace. He writes, "[The meek] seek justice in the power of truth and of God, not by the power of man. . . . [Meekness] refrains from self-assertion and from violent aggression because it sees all things in the light of the great judgment. . . . The Beatitudes indeed convey a profound existential understanding of the dynamic of the Kingdom of God. . . . This is a dynamism of patient and secret growth, in belief that out of the smallest, weakest, and most insignificant seed the greatest tree will come."[8] His point is that the way of a Christian is not the way of violence.

---

7. Martha Nussbaum, *Anger and Forgiveness: Resentment, Generosity, and Justice* (New York: Oxford University Press, 2016), 35.

8. *Thomas Merton*, 126.

Neither is it the way of typical political power if politics requires compromising the virtues found in the Sermon on the Mount.

By the time Peter wrote his first epistle to the church in Asia Minor, he had come to better understand Jesus's teachings. In the letter, he addresses persecuted believers and instructs them to act honorably in ways that would be perceived by others as "good" (1 Pet. 2:12). This clearly rules out attacking a local pizza establishment with an automatic weapon, right? He also writes, "Be subject for the Lord's sake to every human institution, whether it be to the emperor as supreme, or to governors as sent by him to punish those who do evil and praise those who do good" (2:13–14). But what if these powerful people are rigging elections and injecting us with tracking devices? I don't see that Peter's message to us would be any different: "Honor everyone. Love the brotherhood. Fear God. Honor the emperor" (2:17). Anyway, there are ways to protest without using violence. Consider Martin Luther King Jr.'s strategy of civil disobedience as a prime example.[9]

Then is the way of Jesus the way of pacifism? Perhaps. I don't have the space here to wade into these waters. I would point interested readers to Michael W. Austin's *God and Guns* for a good starting point.[10] But whether or not force is ever justified, Jesus clearly teaches that we must always love our enemies and not hate them.

Anger, Contempt, and Unity

As I say above, anger issues aren't unique to conspiracy theorists. Non-conspiracy theorists in the church also need to check their anger. They might get angry at conspiracy theorists for associating the gospel with what appears to be an irrational belief. They might get angry at them for tying the gospel to politics. Also, they might get angry at them for misleading other Christians. Of course, the object of our anger might be justified, but then what matters is how we deal with it. Do we let this anger divide us? Some might say, "Yes! We must put the truth first!" I say, however, let's not sacrifice *either* truth *or* love, but put love first!

Many non-conspiracy theorists I've talked to in the church openly express their disdain for conspiracy theorists. They call them "crazy" and "deceived" and make little effort to hear them out or talk to them. I think this demonstrates a lack of respect. Respect doesn't mean you have to agree

---

9. Nussbaum, *Anger and Forgiveness*, 31.
10. Michael W. Austin, *God and Guns in America* (Grand Rapids: Eerdmans, 2020).

with them, but it does mean that you value them as persons and take their views seriously (even if you disagree), just as you would want someone to do with your views. I don't think this lack of respect is a form of anger but something else. Nussbaum calls it contempt. She defines anger as an emotional response to an *action*, whereas contempt is a response to something deeper, such as the other's personality or character.[11] Contempt patronizes the other and despises the other, viewing the other as less-than. This isn't loving; it's hateful. It's also divisive, and division is bad if it's for anything other than the main issue of concern, the love of Jesus. There is room in the church for Republicans and Democrats, Calvinists and Arminians, creationists and evolutionists. There is even room for both flat-earthers and round-earthers. But there is no room for contempt.

I'd like to end this chapter with an appeal to grace and unity. Jesus prayed that we would be one (John 17:21). What binds us together as a body of believers is our shared love of Jesus and his love for us, so let's cultivate this love in our hearts. Love builds up (1 Cor. 8:1); it is patient, kind, and long-suffering (1 Cor. 13). Excessive anger destroys this love. So does contempt. Whether you believe in conspiracy theories or not, don't stop loving one another.[12]

References

Austin, Michael W. *God and Guns in America*. Grand Rapids: Eerdmans, 2020.

Butler, Joseph. *Joseph Butler: Fifteen Sermons Preached at the Rolls Chapel and Other Writings on Ethics*. Edited by David McNaughton. New York: Oxford University Press, 2017.

Merton, Thomas. *Thomas Merton: Essential Writings*. Edited by Christine M. Bochen. Maryknoll, NY: Orbis, 2000.

Nussbaum, Martha. *Anger and Forgiveness: Resentment, Generosity, and Justice*. New York: Oxford University Press, 2016.

11. Nussbaum, *Anger and Forgiveness*, 50.

12. Thanks to Michael W. Austin, Jason Cook, and Heather Bock for helpful feedback on an earlier draft of this chapter.

IT'S MUCH WORSE THAN YOU THINK

J. Aaron Simmons and Kevin Carnahan

A recent study by the Survey Center on American Life presents a stagger-ing reality.[1] White evangelical Republicans in the United States[2] are far more likely to believe that "there was widespread voter fraud in the 2020 presidential election" than nonevangelical Republicans (74 percent versus 54 percent). Moreover, the study shows that evangelicals are also more likely than nonevangelical Republicans to believe that there was a "deep state" working to undermine the Trump administration (67 percent versus 52 percent), that Antifa was "mostly responsible" for the January 6 riots at the Capitol (60 percent versus 42 percent), and that "Donald Trump has been secretly fighting a group of child sex traffickers that include promi-nent Democrats and Hollywood elites" (31 percent versus 25 percent). If this is not bad enough, a recent survey published in the *Economist* shows that evangelicals are more likely than "everyone else" to believe that the COVID vaccine is being used to microchip the population, that vaccines cause autism, and even that NASA staged the moon landing.[3]

1. Daniel A. Cox, "Rise of Conspiracies Reveals an Evangelical Divide in the GOP," Survey Center on American Life, February 12, 2021, https://www.american surveycenter.org/rise-of-conspiracies-reveal-an-evangelical-divide-in-the-gop/.

2. Unless specifically stated, all subsequent mentions of "evangelicals" will refer to white evangelicals in the United States.

3. "What Drives Belief in Conspiracy Theories, a Lack of Religion or Too Much?" *Economist*, July 27, 2021, https://www.economist.com/graphic-detail/2021/07/27 /what-drives-belief-in-conspiracy-theories-a-lack-of-religion-or-too-much.

Such data on evangelicals and conspiracy theories makes it paramount that we figure out what could possibly explain how so many within this group are so committed to patently false claims—and doing so while claiming that their beliefs are not only rational but strongly supported by evidence. To try to offer an epistemic diagnosis of this situation and why it is so dangerous for our society, we will suggest that such evangelicals are guilty of what we term an *epistemology of ignorance*. To make this case, we will first distinguish the sort of epistemological failure occurring with evangelicals from other alternatives within conspiracy theory more broadly. To that end, we will discuss three ideal types of conspiracist: (1) the psychologically disposed individual conspiracist, (2) the social conspiracist, and (3) the cultic conspiracist. Evangelical conspiracists, we will argue, are instances of the second type.

The problem in dealing with social conspiracism is that the kinds of errors involved in it invert so much of the believer's epistemology that it is hard, and maybe increasingly impossible, to gain a foothold for criticism from any alternative position. Worse than simply being isolated in their own self-protective epistemic communities, they end up engaging in what we will call *Teflon hermeneutics* whereby no criticism can stick because they have refused the shared social context in which reasonable discourse must occur. Thus, while evangelical conspiracists may not be immediately irrational concerning their ability to draw conclusions, many of them are, quite regrettably, no longer reasonable participants in critical social dialogue.

Complicated Definitions

It is necessary to address some problems with language when discussing conspiracy theories. The first concerns the term "conspiracist." We use this term to refer to a person who believes in a conspiracy theory, as opposed to a "conspirator," who participates in a conspiracy. But to that we add one proviso: we are using the term to designate people whose belief in a conspiracy is grounded in some kind of epistemic error.[4] There are, of course, *true* conspiracies. If one is, all things considered, justified in believing that a conspiracy exists, one is not, in our terms, a conspiracist. There are senses in which conspiracists may be more or less justified in believing in a conspiracy. They may be justified internal to their community (which is, itself, epistemically flawed), or justified internal to a particular set of sources (which are epistem-

---

4. Our distinction is related to Quassin Cassam's distinction between "conspiracy theories" and "Conspiracy Theories." Q. Cassam, *Conspiracy Theories* (Medford, MA: Polity, 2019).

ically unreliable, etc.). But as we are using the term, the conspiracist can only be justified relative to something *short of* all things considered. We believe that in the cases at stake with contemporary white evangelicalism (viz., QAnon, the microchip-vaccine theory, etc.), the situation is clear enough to allow nonconspiracists to recognize conspiracists, even if the conspiracists would continue to challenge their categorization.[5]

Not only is the concept of "conspiracist" complicated, but also the category of "evangelical." There are theological definitions (e.g., Protestants who affirm conversionism, biblicism, crucicentrism, activism),[6] historical definitions (e.g., people affiliated with traditional denominations associated with "evangelical" organizations such as the National Association of Evangelicals in the United States),[7] sociological definitions (e.g., social conservatives who appeal to Christianity to justify their political stances), or even definitions attending to personal identity (e.g., one who describes oneself as "evangelical"). All these definitions are slippery because they also are "idealized" in ways that tend to isolate one's political orientation from one's theological commitments and one's historical context. In practice, though, such aspects of one's identity are not so easily separable from each other. Accordingly, exactly who counts as an evangelical is a matter of legitimate debate. Famously, George Marsden acknowledged the complexity of finding a rigorously stable definition when he said in the 1950s that an evangelical was "anyone who likes Billy Graham."[8]

5. This is a particularly complicated issue for philosophers because one of the requirements of responsible philosophical argumentation is to show dialogical charity to one's interlocutors. That means that the philosopher should at least attempt to describe those of whom one is critical in ways that would allow those people to recognize themselves in the critique. Otherwise, one risks engaging in straw-man fallacies. However, one of the common characteristics of conspiracists is their belief that they are the "truly" or "ultimately" rational members of society. As such, to describe them as already epistemically irresponsible in some sense is a description that they are, undoubtedly, going to resist. Yet, in order to take seriously the epistemic stakes of the current varieties of conspiracism, such a description is an important qualifier from the outset.

6. See David W. Bebbington, *Evangelicalism in Modern Britain: A History from the 1730s to the 1980s* (London: Unwin Hyman, 1989).

7. See George Marsden, *Understanding Fundamentalism and Evangelicalism* (Grand Rapids: Eerdmans, 1991).

8. Jonathan Merritt, "Defining *Evangelical*," *Atlantic*, December 7, 2015, https://www.theatlantic.com/politics/archive/2015/12/evangelical-christian/418236/.

Determining who counts as an evangelical is even more difficult because evangelicalism in the United States is quite different in social manifestation from that in the United Kingdom or in South Africa, say. Finally, making sense of evangelicalism in the United States requires attending to the theological and political distinctions between predominantly white evangelicals and nonwhite evangelicals.[9]

Despite these difficulties, we will be thinking particularly about white evangelicalism in the United States and will operate with a broadly conjunctive definition: people who usually identify as evangelical Christians, who are usually socially conservative, who are generally associated with historically "evangelical" denominations, and who hold theological commitments of activism, crucicentrism, conversionism, and biblicism. Neither with conspiracists nor with evangelicals are we able to be extremely precise, but these general definitions are adequate for the diagnosis that we are offering here.

Three Ideal Types of Conspiracist

Karl Popper once posited that conspiracism is born from a wrongheaded background tendency: that all events must have been intended by someone.[10] Popper's analysis obviously falls well short of providing an account of all conspiracism. But it is an example of conspiracism born of an individual's psychological dispositions.

Multiple psychological mechanisms have been suggested as contributing to the belief in conspiracies.[11] Humans, it turns out, are predisposed

---

9. See Eliza Griswold, "Evangelicals of Color Fight Back against the Religious Right," *New Yorker*, December 26, 2018, https://www.newyorker.com/news/on-religion/evangelicals-of-color-fight-back-against-the-religious-right; and Michael O. Emerson and Christian Smith, *Divided by Faith: Evangelical Religion and the Problem of Race in America* (Oxford: Oxford University Press, 2001).

10. Karl Popper, "The Conspiracy Theory of Society," in *Conspiracy Theories: The Philosophical Debate*, ed. David Coady (New York: Routledge, 2019).

11. J. van Prooijen and K. Douglas, "Belief in Conspiracy Theories: Basic Principles of an Emerging Research Domain," *European Journal of Social Psychology* 48, no. 7 (2018): 1–12; J. van Prooijen and K. Douglas, "Connecting the Dots: Illusory Pattern Perception Predicts Belief in Conspiracies and the Supernatural," *European Journal of Social Psychology* 48, no. 3 (2017): 320–35; J. van Prooijen and M. van Vugt, "Conspiracy Theories: Evolved Functions and Psychological Mechanisms," *Perspectives on Psychological Science* 13, no. 6 (2018): 770–88.

to find patterns, and often do so even when faced with a random series of events. We are also inclined to attribute intentionality where it does not exist. Confirmation bias makes us more likely to pay attention to evidence that supports our preconceptions. Hindsight bias makes us think that contingent occurrences were more foreseeable than they really were. These dispositions and biases vary depending on the individual. Some psychologists suggest that dispositions like these can be tied to particular personality types or traits. Thus, it is possible to posit the existence of some people with a "conspiracy mind-set" regardless of their specific beliefs.[12] Accordingly, the psychologically disposed individual conspiracy theorist operates according to what we will term *an epistemology of irrationality*. Simply put, the person's dispositions facilitate an embrace of biases, rather than an attempt to overcome them. The person is "irrational" in the sense that relevant epistemic mechanisms are not sufficiently aimed at tracking truth. Ultimately, he or she fails to draw appropriate conclusions from well-supported premises.

The second kind of conspiracism offers a more social explanation directly relevant to evangelical conspiracism. We do not doubt that nonrational psychological functions must be involved in the tendencies of evangelical conspiracism, but other factors must play a more central role due to the way the conspiracies get facilitated and affirmed within sociotheological communities of discourse in particular ways. Thankfully, research on information systems provides very good accounts of the different set of factors at play in evangelicalism. Cailin O'Connor and James Weatherall's recent book *The Misinformation Age* (2019) traces out how social systems of information work; how they can lead to truth and how they can fail. O'Connor and Weatherall set out to show how even the most relatively rational participants (a system of ideal scientists) in an information system can be misled. As they point out, most of us are confused about the way science works. We think there is *an* experiment somewhere that proves or disproves a thesis. In reality, scientists extremely rarely deal with such clear-cut conclusions. There is no such thing as a perfect experiment, but even if one had a perfect experiment, it is rare that any one experiment could either prove or disprove a thesis. Even the simplest experiment will often be testing multiple variables that have different probabilities of producing particular conclusions. Anyone who has flipped a coin a few times knows that a small sample of flips would likely give massively misleading data on how likely

12. R. Imhoff and M. Bruder, "Speaking (Un-)Truth to Power: Conspiracy Mentality as a Generalized Political Attitude," *European Journal of Personality* 28 (2014): 25-43.

the coin was to produce heads or tails. This means that coming to conclusions takes more than *one* study. Indeed, it takes whole cadres of scientists doing different studies and then stepping back to take in the breadth of the information produced in order to arrive at conclusions that can be supported by, or at least account for, all the data that has been generated.[13]

In this process, it makes a significant difference to whom one is listening as authoritative in a specific area. If one listens only to a small number of colleagues, one is much more likely to get things wrong. If one listens only to other scientists who use the same methodology for their experiments as he or she does, this more likely leads to errors. Unfortunately, the information system in real-life science includes all sorts of conditions that might lead to such situations. Academic journals are more likely to publish novel findings, less likely to publish findings that repeat earlier experiments, and less likely to publish findings that confirm long-held conclusions.

Thus, even under the best of circumstances, largely rational individuals can be led to incorrect conclusions by the information systems in which they work. Things get worse when we introduce "propagandists" into the mix. Propagandists are interested contributors to the information system. They may fabricate data, but they usually don't need to. Because information systems are inherently fragile, they need only to publicize the minority findings that fit with their interests. Doing this can prolong the time it takes for the system to come to consensus, and in some cases can lead to a wrong consensus.

If this is a problem for scientists, it is an even bigger problem for those uneducated in how to deal with scientific data. The scientist will more easily be able to discern when a contributor to the information system is a propagandist, and thus, will be more able to sort out the information from that contributor. However, for someone unfamiliar with the inherent complexity operating in the system, distinguishing propagandists from legitimate scientists is extremely difficult. When faced with such a daunting epistemic task, it can be tempting for such nonexperts either to refer to "science" as a monolith or to grow increasingly skeptical of "science" because scientists disagree. Rather than trusting the process with its very messy but self-critical and self-correcting aspects, it is easier simply to believe those voices (usually propagandists) who are affirming what they already think.

13. For more on the way in which science and objectivity are particular narratives operating in relation to social goals and discursive communities, see Brandon Inabinet and J. Aaron Simmons, "Retooling the Discourse of Objectivity: Epistemic Postmodernism as Shared Public Life," *Public Culture* 30, no. 2 (2018): 221–43.

It is at this point that we run into an irony in the rationality of information systems. Contrary to the popular idea of a "marketplace of ideas" where every idea should be welcome, it often becomes most rational to ignore information from some sources. Sometimes listening to *all* the sources is more likely to lead to wrong conclusions than to right ones. The idea is that once we distinguish between legitimate scientists and propagandists, we should ignore the latter. It is an epistemically superior position, all things considered, to protect oneself against the influence of propagandists.

But what happens if you make a mistake on this level? What if your worldview leads you to conclude that the propagandists are properly functioning sources of knowledge, and that properly functioning sources of knowledge are the propagandists? If there is an error at this point, it will appear rational to you to insulate yourself against properly functioning sources of knowledge. A conspiracy by propagandists will lead you to believe that properly functioning knowledge sources are the real conspirators. Here we reach the situation of the social conspiracist who falls into an *epistemology of ignorance*.

The final kind of conspiracist, the cultic conspiracist, is also caught in a social-epistemic trap, but the trap works much more directly on the conspiracist's rationality. Cults are, not by accident, often built upon narratives of an evil conspiracy in the outside world and a safe haven within the cult itself. As Alexandrea Stein suggests, cults are "totalist" communities in the sense that they seek to dominate all parts of the individual cultist's life.[14] This allows the cult to function as the epistemic authority and source of value for the cultist. The cult leader functions as the central authority and caregiver for followers. Cults then expose members to a disorienting regimen of training in which they are conditioned both to fear and to depend wholly upon the cult—often at the cost of abandoning their own self-trust.[15] The psychological result, as Stein puts it, is something akin to dissociation. One's rational thought is short-circuited by the need for approval from the community and the cult leader. Whenever infallibilism is attributed to one's central epistemic authority, problems follow for responsible social life.[16] Due to the way that such cultic conspiracism functions

14. Alexandrea Stein, *Love, Terror, and Brainwashing* (New York: Routledge, 2021).

15. See Linda T. Zagzebski, *Epistemic Authority: A Theory of Trust, Authority, and Autonomy in Belief* (Oxford: Oxford University Press, 2012).

16. This is tricky business because the line dividing cultic conspiracism and responsible obstinacy in belief is not always clear. For example, internal to personal

to bring all of one's life into the gravity of a central authority, it operates according to what we will term an *epistemology of insularity*.

With these three ideal types of conspiracism in place, and the three different epistemologies that underwrite each of them, we will now turn to the specific way in which social conspiracy shows up in evangelicalism.

Evangelicals and Social Conspiracy

No doubt, some evangelicals have individual conspiratorial psychological tendencies. Some evangelical communities also exhibit cult-like tendencies. But as a movement, evangelicalism is much closer to social conspiracism. Evangelicals affirm a view of the world in which they are a persecuted minority, in a society marked by a massive, coordinated project by liberal propagandists to undermine the truth.[17] They then consider it not only rational but also morally required to oppose such propagandists.

The problem, of course, is that their worldview is inverted. As Christians, evangelicals are among the most religiously privileged members of American society. American culture is constructed around Christian holidays. American coinage claims that "In God We Trust," a phrase that was first proposed as an explicitly Christian theological claim.[18] The pledge to the American flag still includes the claim that America is "one nation under God," a phrase added during the (often explicitly anticommunist) evangelical revivalism of the 1950s. But evangelicals perceive themselves as among the most oppressed groups in the country. One poll shows that the majority of white evangelicals believe Christians face more discrimina-

relationships, it might make sense to believe something at odds with evidence in particular cases (see C. S. Lewis, "On Obstinacy in Belief," *Sewanee Review* 63, no. 4 [October–December 1955]: 525–38). However, the big difference is that responsible obstinacy does not relocate the epistemic authority on an external social leader, but instead locates it internal to lived relationships of trust. That said, cultists are quite likely to see what they are doing as merely a version of such responsible relationality. Again, though, here we are attempting to offer true descriptions even if those being described would bristle at the account.

17. Jack Jenkins, "Survey: Faith Groups Showcase Media Divide," Religious News Service, May 14, 2021, https://religionnews.com/2021/05/14/survey-white -evangelicals-trust-fox-news-black-protestants-look-to-mainstream-networks/.

18. David Mislin, "The Complex History of 'In God We Trust,'" *Conversation*, February 2, 2018, https://theconversation.com/the-complex-history-of-in-god-we -trust-91117.

tion in the United States than do Muslims.[19] Rather than identifying *with* the oppressed, contemporary white evangelicals identify *as* the oppressed. Among their oppressors they include the institutions of mainstream media and science. Thus, they make fundamental mistakes about how to distinguish propagandists from relatively reliable sources of truth.

Why would evangelicals be disposed toward such social conspiracism? There are several reasons. First, Christianity itself has narrative roots that provide potential fertile ground for social conspiracism. After all, Jesus was identified for crucifixion in what amounts to a conspiracy among Romans, Pharisees, and one of his own disciples. And Christianity has repeatedly manifested tendencies to speak, for instance, in terms of a dualism between the "church" and the "world," echoing the language of the Gospel of John, which probably reflected a sectarian community that felt rejected by a social conspiracy.[20]

But not *all* Christians are conspiratorial, so a sufficient explanation requires more than this. A partial further explanation may be provided by looking at eschatological beliefs that are specific to particular evangelical communities. Some believe in a coming end-times vision that builds upon the dualism noted above. All one need do is review the *Left Behind* novels of the early twenty-first century to find a worldview capable of supporting all manner of conspiracy theories about the outside world as really just part of the satanic plan to deceive and then to dominate.[21]

Probably the most significant reason that evangelicals believe in a world set against them is that such a belief isn't entirely wrong. White American evangelicalism, especially as it has been influenced by fundamentalism, has deep ties to biblical literalism and white supremacist culture,[22] two elements of culture that have been under attack for the last century in the United States. The tricky part is that these things *should* be attacked in the

19. E. Green, "White Evangelicals Believe They Face More Discrimination Than Muslims," *Atlantic*, March 10, 2017, https://www.theatlantic.com/politics/archive/2017/03/perceptions-discrimination-muslims-christians/519135/.

20. Jaime Clark-Soles, *Scripture Cannot Be Broken: The Social Function of the Use of Scripture in the Fourth Gospel* (Boston: Brill, 2003).

21. For a classical consideration of evangelicals and eschatology, see D. N. Hempton, "Evangelicals and Eschatology," *Journal of Ecclesiastical History* 31, no. 2 (April 1980): 179–94.

22. Mark Noll, *The Civil War as a Theological Crisis* (Chapel Hill: University of North Carolina Press, 2015); and Randall Balmer, *Bad Faith* (Grand Rapids: Eerdmans, 2021).

name of moral decency and epistemic responsibility. Rather than see the "worldly" critique as an opportunity for righteous correction, evangelicals far too often dismiss it out of hand because it doesn't square with their narrative of their own correctness.

Social Conspiracism and Teflon Hermeneutics

Each form of conspiracism noted above comes with its own self-reinforcing mechanisms. For the individual conspiracist, these are built into the *irrational* psychological makeup of the individual. For the cultist conspiracist, they are enforced directly by the *insular* community under the command of the cult leader. Social conspiracism, however, relies on a more diffuse mechanism for self-support: the *ignorant* worldview of the conspiracist itself.

The basic formula for such social conspiracists is that if my oppressed community thinks X, then everyone who holds non-X is obviously wrong, probably an oppressor, and should be not only ignored but also defeated in what evangelicals often consider a "battle for the soul." When non-X is the view held by scientists, then science gets viewed as a threat, rather than a resource. When non-X is held by members of one's political party, then those people come to be seen as traitors (e.g., Republican members of Congress who voted to impeach Trump are labeled "Pelosi Republicans"). When non-X is held by members of one's church, then they are wolves to be cast out in the name of protecting the sheep.

The result of such an epistemology of ignorance is a *Teflon hermeneutics* whereby all criticism just slides off. Nothing can stick because it is not a matter of needing more information. It is, instead, a matter of not being able to adjudicate between legitimate evidence and self-defensive narratives meant to reinforce the power of those who benefit from the furtherance of propaganda. As such, no amount of information can be sufficient to transform belief because accommodating such information/evidence is tantamount to violating the foundational commitments of their own worldview.

William James explains that what we hold at the center of our "web of belief" is much harder to dislodge because it requires rethinking one's very social identity. This is the case for evangelical conspiracists. It is not possible that they could have been wrong about something that they held deeply because it means there might be other things they have gotten wrong as well about God, themselves, and the world. Instead, they believe, it is better to double down on the belief and reinforce their self-conception. What is truly insidious about such ignorance is that it is cloaked in theological justifications and anchored in what John Sanders terms an "authoritative" conception of God.[23] Such a God is not interested in partnership and collaboration, but in dominance and superiority. It is not a stretch then to see the attraction of so many evangelicals to Trump's bravado, narcissism, and misogyny.[24] Trump represents what they take to be true of themselves and God: they are all strong enough to stand up to the evil propagandists.

Following on this framework, for example, claims about the need for masks during the pandemic are presented as a failure to trust God's providence. Evidence about Trump's loss in 2020 is reframed as a test of faith. And so on. It is one thing to oppose the man who brags about sexual assault, but it is something very different when that man is presented as God's chosen leader.[25] Teflon hermeneutics is frustrating in all circumstances, but it is especially vicious when reinforced by bad theology.

Conclusion

We have argued that white evangelicals in the United States are closest to social conspiracists. In some senses this makes them, however ironically, more rational than other kinds of conspiracists. The fundamental error in their rationality is not found in failing to draw appropriate conclusions from evidence (*epistemology of irrationality*), or even in recognizing reliable sources within their worldview due to the irresistible gravity and infallibility of a central authority figure (*epistemology of isolation*). The problem lies *within* their worldview itself. Evangelicals believe that they live in an antagonistic world full of propagandists that are trying to mislead them. In short, conspiracism is not the errant conclusion of evangelical reasoning, but rather one of the background beliefs about the world they hold before

23. John Sanders, *Embracing Prodigals: Overcoming Authoritative Religion by Embodying Jesus' Nurturing Grace* (Eugene, OR: Cascade, 2020).

24. See Sarah Posner, *Unholy: Why White Evangelicals Worship at the Altar of Donald Trump* (New York: Random House, 2020); John Fea, *Believe Me: The Evangelical Road to Donald Trump* (Grand Rapids: Eerdmans, 2018).

25. Eugene Scott, "Comparing Trump to Jesus, and Why Some Evangelicals Believe Trump Is God's Chosen One," *Washington Post*, December 18, 2019, https://www.washingtonpost.com/politics/2019/11/25/why-evangelicals-like-rick-perry-believe-that-trump-is-gods-chosen-one/.

they even start to draw particular conclusions. This is why we have termed their view an *epistemology of ignorance*.

The problem, though, is that they don't just need more education or knowledge. Instead, they are already predisposed toward being unable to recognize such education as legitimate (e.g., consider the widespread narrative of colleges as indoctrinating Christian kids). The problem is much more difficult to address because it requires undermining the very conditions by which evangelicals begin the process of belief formation. Their epistemological well is poisoned from the outset, and there is no way to fix things without digging a new well and rerouting the water.

The fact that evangelicals are not tinfoil-hat-wearing conspiracists might at first appear promising for the prospect of dialogue. But it is not clear that the error of the social conspiracists is actually more fragile than the individual believer. In fact, it may be much stronger because it is *self-supporting*. If there is a conspiracy of liberal propagandists out to mislead you, then you are going to sort out any sources that advocate for views of the situation that are alternatives to your own. The system is closed along with any possibility for dialogue. They operate according to *a Teflon hermeneutics* whereby all criticism slides right off as simply another example of the propaganda they are right to resist. Although the social conspiracism that we have described here is certainly not limited to evangelicals (indeed, increasingly it is becoming the default setting for being on the political right in the United States), given the outsized influence that white evangelicals continue to have in American political life, evangelical conspiracism, in particular, is more than a threat to discourse—*it is a threat to democracy.*

Evangelicals are not only becoming unreasonable members of society,[26] but they are a threat to the very possibility of a reasonable society. Things are not just bad; they are *much* worse than you think.

References

Balmer, Randall. *Bad Faith*. Grand Rapids: Eerdmans, 2021.

Bebbington, David W. *Evangelicalism in Modern Britain: A History from the 1730s to the 1980s*. London: Unwin Hyman, 1989.

Cassam, Q. *Conspiracy Theories*. Medford, MA: Polity, 2019.

26. See John Rawls, *Political Liberalism*, expanded ed. (New York: Columbia University Press, 2005).

Clark-Soles, Jaime. *Scripture Cannot Be Broken: The Social Function of the Use of Scripture in the Fourth Gospel*. Boston: Brill, 2003.

Cox, Daniel A. "Rise of Conspiracies Reveals an Evangelical Divide in the GOP." Survey Center on American Life, February 12, 2021. https://www.americansurveycenter.org/rise-of-conspiracies-reveal-an-evangelical-divide-in-the-gop/.

Emerson, Michael O., and Christian Smith. *Divided by Faith: Evangelical Religion and the Problem of Race in America*. Oxford: Oxford University Press, 2001.

Fea, John. *Believe Me: The Evangelical Road to Donald Trump*. Grand Rapids: Eerdmans, 2018.

Green, E. "White Evangelicals Believe They Face More Discrimination Than Muslims." *Atlantic*, March 10, 2017. https://www.theatlantic.com/politics/archive/2017/03/perceptions-discrimination-muslims-christians/519135/.

Griswold, Eliza. "Evangelicals of Color Fight Back against the Religious Right." *New Yorker*, December 26, 2018. https://www.newyorker.com/news/on-religion/evangelicals-of-color-fight-back-against-the-religious-right.

Hempton, D. N. "Evangelicals and Eschatology." *Journal of Ecclesiastical History* 31, no. 2 (April 1980): 179–94.

Imhoff, R., and M. Bruder. "Speaking (Un-)Truth to Power: Conspiracy Mentality as a Generalized Political Attitude." *European Journal of Personality* 28 (2014): 25–43.

Inabinet, Brandon, and J. Aaron Simmons. "Retooling the Discourse of Objectivity: Epistemic Postmodernism as Shared Public Life." *Public Culture* 30, no. 2 (2018): 221–43.

Jenkins, Jack. "Survey: Faith Groups Showcase Media Divide." Religious News Service, May 14, 2021. https://religionnews.com/2021/05/14/survey-white-evangelicals-trust-fox-news-black-protestants-look-to-mainstream-networks/.

Lewis, C. S. "On Obstinacy in Belief." *Sewanee Review* 63, no. 4 (October–December 1955): 525–38.

Marsden, George. *Understanding Fundamentalism and Evangelicalism*. Grand Rapids: Eerdmans, 1991.

Merritt, Jonathan. "Defining *Evangelical*." *Atlantic*, December 7, 2015. https://www.theatlantic.com/politics/archive/2015/12/evangelical-christian/418236/.

Mislin, David. "The Complex History of 'In God We Trust.'" *Conversation*, February 2, 2018. https://theconversation.com/the-complex-history-of-in-god-we-trust-91117.

Noll, Mark. *The Civil War as a Theological Crisis*. Chapel Hill: University of North Carolina Press, 2015.

O'Connor, C., and J. O. Weatherall. *The Misinformation Age: How False Beliefs Spread*. New Haven: Yale University Press, 2019.

Popper, K. "The Conspiracy Theory of Society." In *Conspiracy Theories: The Philosophical Debate*, edited by David Coady. New York: Routledge, 2019.

Posner, Sarah. *Unholy: Why White Evangelicals Worship at the Altar of Donald Trump*. New York: Random House, 2020.

Prooijen, J. van, and K. Douglas. "Belief in Conspiracy Theories: Basic Principles of an Emerging Research Domain." *European Journal of Social Psychology* 48, no. 7 (2018): 1–12.

———. "Connecting the Dots: Illusory Pattern Perception Predicts Belief in Conspiracies and the Supernatural." *European Journal of Social Psychology* 48, no. 3 (2017): 320–35.

Prooijen, J. van, and M. van Vugt. "Conspiracy Theories: Evolved Functions and Psychological Mechanisms." *Perspectives on Psychological Science* 13, no. 6 (2018): 770–88.

Rawls, John. *Political Liberalism*. Expanded ed. New York: Columbia University Press, 2005.

Sanders, John. *Embracing Prodigals: Overcoming Authoritative Religion by Embodying Jesus' Nurturing Grace*. Eugene, OR: Cascade, 2020.

Scott, Eugene. "Comparing Trump to Jesus, and Why Some Evangelicals Believe Trump Is God's Chosen One." *Washington Post*, December 18, 2019. https://www.washingtonpost.com/politics/2019/11/25/why-evangelicals-like-rick-perry-believe-that-trump-is-gods-chosen-one/.

Stein, Alexandrea. *Love, Terror, and Brainwashing*. New York: Routledge, 2021.

"What Drives Belief in Conspiracy Theories, a Lack of Religion or Too Much?" *Economist*, July 27, 2021. https://www.economist.com/graphic-detail/2021/07/27/what-drives-belief-in-conspiracy-theories-a-lack-of-religion-or-too-much.

Zagzebski, Linda T. *Epistemic Authority: A Theory of Trust, Authority, and Autonomy in Belief*. Oxford: Oxford University Press, 2012.

10

ALL CHRISTIANS
ARE CONSPIRACY THEORISTS

Christian B. Miller

To call someone a "conspiracy theorist" these days is usually not meant to be a compliment. The term has negative connotations, implying that the person is being irrational or in some other way irresponsible in his or her thinking.[1]

But as I will argue here, all Christians are conspiracy theorists. And, as a Christian myself, I am therefore a conspiracy theorist. Yet as I will also suggest, this does not make me irrational.

We shall proceed as follows. The first section presents one of the leading definitions of a conspiracy theory and explains how Christian belief would meet this definition. Section 2 considers some additional criteria that have been offered for conspiracy theories, which are also satisfied by Christian belief. Section 3 expands the discussion by showing that many (although not all) Christians actually accept *multiple* conspiracy theories. Section 4

---

1. As the philosopher Charles Pigden writes, "to call someone 'a conspiracy theorist' is to suggest that he is irrational, paranoid, or perverse" ("Conspiracy Theories and the Conventional Wisdom," *Episteme* 4 [2007]: 219). Similarly, Jovan Byford writes that the label "conspiracy theory" "is a way of branding an explanation untrue or insinuating that it is based on insufficient evidence, superstition, or prejudice" (*Conspiracy Theories: A Critical Introduction* [London: Palgrave Macmillan, 2015], 21). Or take Rob Brotherton, "Calling something a conspiracy theory is often used to summarily dismiss a claim as ludicrous" (*Suspicious Minds: Why We Believe Conspiracy Theories* [London: Bloomsbury, 2015], 79). Finally, as Quassim Cassam notes, "Conspiracy theorists get a seriously bad press. Gullible, irresponsible, paranoid, stupid. These are some of the politer labels applied to them" (*Conspiracy Theories* [Cambridge: Polity, 2019], 1).

notes some criteria for a conspiracy theory that are not satisfied by Christian belief but points out that they are not very plausible as criteria anyway. Finally, the paper concludes by considering why any of this matters.

A Leading Definition of a Conspiracy Theory

In his paper "On Conspiracy Theories," the philosopher Brian Keeley writes, "A conspiracy theory is a proposed explanation of some historical event (or events) in terms of the significant causal agency of a relatively small group of persons—the conspirators—acting in secret."[2] What I want to highlight from Keeley's definition is that a conspiracy theory provides an *explanation* of events, it involves a *small group* of persons,[3] and there is an element of *secrecy*. Thus, claiming that 9/11 was really the result of a secret plot by a few members of the Bush administration would count as a conspiracy theory.

Christianity does too. The key point is that, according to Christianity, God is a trinity, and so in some sense is or consists of multiple persons. These persons—the Father, Son, and Holy Spirit—have already each played a significant role in this universe. They are also playing various roles in this universe right now, and will continue to do so in the future.

The Father, for instance, played a causal role in creating the universe and is actively involved in sustaining the universe. The Son became a human being and atoned for sin. The Spirit inspired the prophets and sanctifies believers. These and other events are meant to be explained, from a Christian perspective, by the significant causal agency of a small group of persons acting in secret. Hence we have a conspiracy theory, at least according to Keeley's definition.

The "secret" part should be clarified a bit more. The activities of all three persons have been a secret to many people throughout human history, since they require divine revelation to grasp, and that revelation has not been available to a lot of people. The very existence of the Trinity is unknowable to human beings when left to our own devices, and the same goes for the specific actions performed by each of the persons of the Trinity, such as the fact that the Spirit is sanctifying the redeemed. Even with the aid of divine

---

2. Brian Keeley, "Of Conspiracy Theories," *Journal of Philosophy* 96 (1999): 109–26. See also Brian Keeley, "God as the Ultimate Conspiracy Theory," *Episteme* 4 (2007): 135–49; Pigden, "Conspiracy Theories," 222; and Cassam, *Conspiracy Theories*, 3.

3. In a later paper, Keeley weakens this requirement by allowing an omnipotent being by itself to be the conspirator (Keeley, "God as the Ultimate Conspiracy Theory," 140).

revelation, there is much concerning the workings of the persons of the Trinity that we still do not grasp. Thus we do not typically know why the persons act as they do, or why they allow events to unfold a certain way, or what their plans are for the future. Perhaps most of this is simply beyond our capacity to understand. Other pieces of knowledge we can grasp with our mental faculties, but the knowledge is kept from us, at least in this life.[4]

Hence, because of their views about God as a trinity, Christians accept a conspiracy theory. Note that my claim is a very strong one. It is that *all* Christians are conspiracy theorists, not just some. Why do I say that?

This follows so long as we accept that there are orthodox beliefs all Christians must accept to count as Christian. These are true, central claims of Christianity the rejection of any one of which would mean that one does not count as a Christian.[5] They make up what C. S. Lewis called "mere Christianity."

Examples of such beliefs include the very existence of God in the first place, as well as the specifically Christian doctrine of the incarnation, whereby Jesus was one person with a divine nature and a human nature. There are other orthodox Christian beliefs as well, but the belief that concerns us here is about the doctrine of the Trinity, the claim that there is one God who is three persons, Father, Son, and Holy Spirit. This is one of the essential commitments of Christianity.

So in order to be a Christian, at least doctrinally, one must accept the doctrine of the Trinity. But that doctrine commits the Christian to believing in a conspiracy theory. Therefore, *all* Christians are indeed conspiracy theorists.[6]

Other Proposed Requirements for Conspiracy Theories

Maybe this conclusion follows just because of how Keeley defined conspiracy theories. Perhaps his definition is idiosyncratic, and on other proposals Christianity would not count as a conspiracy theory.

---

4. In his 2007 paper, Keeley allows that being inscrutable is an acceptable feature of a conspiracy theory as opposed to being secretive ("God as the Ultimate Conspiracy Theory," 141). See also the discussion of secrecy in Byford, *Conspiracy Theories*, 79-81.

5. For a very helpful discussion of what orthodox belief involves, see Eleonore Stump, "Orthodoxy and Heresy," *Faith and Philosophy* 16 (1999): 147-63.

6. The closest parallel to my view that I have found in the conspiracy theory literature is Keeley, "God as the Ultimate Conspiracy Theory," although he never focuses on Christianity or the Trinity specifically.

There isn't space here to go through all the proposals that have been made in the conspiracy theory literature. I will have to be content with just mentioning a few claims about conspiracy theories that are not a part of the passage we quoted from Keeley. Some of these claims are contestable, but we won't consider here whether they are plausible or not. Instead, we will only see what would follow with respect to Christianity if we accept them.

Premodern worldview. One claim discussed later in Keeley's article is that conspiracy theorists are committed to a premodern worldview. As he writes, "The conspiratorial world view offers us the comfort of knowing that while tragic events occur, they at least occur for a reason, and that the greater the event, the greater and more significant the reason. Our contemporary world view, which the conspiracy theorist refuses to accept, is one in which nobody—not God, not us, not even *some* of us—is in control."[7] Clearly, Christianity meets this requirement, and so let's move on.

Contrarian. Another alleged feature of conspiracy theories is that they are contrarian. As Quassim Cassam clarifies this idea, "The thing that Conspiracy Theories are contrary to is *appearances* or the *obvious* explanation of events. . . . The starting point of a Conspiracy Theory is that things aren't as they seem."[8]

We can accept that Christianity is contrarian in this sense. It is not obvious that what created the universe or what sustains the universe in existence is a perfect divine being. But even if a Christian were to say that God is the obvious explanation for various events, what is certainly *not* obvious is that the *Trinity*, three divine persons acting in harmony, is what explains these events. That is not as things seem to be, apart from divine revelation.

I am not claiming that Christianity will count as a conspiracy theory according to all the requirements that have been offered by writers on the subject. In fact, in section 4 we will run into some problematic requirements. But at least with respect to these additional requirements of a

---

7. Keeley, "Of Conspiracy Theories," 124. See also Glenn Bezalel, "Conspiracy Theories and Religion: Reframing Conspiracy Theories as *Bliks*," *Episteme* 16 (2019): 3; and Brotherton, *Suspicious Minds*, 70–71.

8. Cassam, *Conspiracy Theories*, 20. See also Keeley, "Of Conspiracy Theories," 116–17; Brotherton, *Suspicious Minds*, 67–69; and Bezalel, "Conspiracy Theories and Religion," 3.

premodern worldview and being contrarian, my claim still holds that all Christians are conspiracy theorists.[9]

More Conspiracies for Christians

Before turning to the more problematic requirements, I want to extend my claim even further, to say that all Christians accept one conspiracy theory, and many Christians accept *multiple* conspiracy theories. This last part follows if a Christian maintains that the devil or devils are real and are involved in this world in some way. This is a common belief in the history of Christianity, and it meets all the requirements we have outlined above. In particular, certain events are going to be produced by a small group of agents operating in secret, and this explanation will be both contrarian and premodern.

One potential sticking point is the requirement of a "small group." The devil is not a trinity of persons, and if the devil is working alone, then we don't have a small group. But the devil *isn't* always depicted as working alone. He has his minions who can work with him (Mark 3:22, Luke 11:15), just as God has angels who can work with him. In the case of the devils, we would thereby have a group (although to be fair, it may not be clear whether it counts as a "small" group).

So Christians who accept this picture of the demonic are conspiracy theorists twice over. But we need not stop there. For if the devil has his devils, God has his angels. And when a couple of angels work in secret (from humans, not from God) to accomplish something, that would meet the requirements of a conspiracy theory. Hence, some Christians are conspiracy theorists three times over.

I have been careful in this section to say only "some" Christians. Unlike the Trinity, it is not essential to Christian belief that one accept the real existence of the devil and devils. Many Christians—perhaps the vast

---

9. I will just assert that the same holds for additional requirements such as that there be a unified explanation provided with explanatory reach (Keeley, "Of Conspiracy Theories," 119), that the theory have an "esoteric feel" (Cassam, *Conspiracy Theories*, 22), that the subject matter not be "a petty and obvious plot" (Byford, *Conspiracy Theories*, 21), and that the theories "purport to reveal hitherto undiscovered plots in the hopes of persuading the as yet unalerted masses" (Brotherton, *Suspicious Minds*, 66), and that conspiracy theories have a "comprehensive and all-encompassing character" (Byford, *Conspiracy Theories*, 34 [emphasis removed]).

majority throughout history—have accepted their real existence. But some Christians, especially today, may hold that the devil is only fictional or metaphorical. In that case, as Christians, they still are committed to at least one conspiracy theory. But perhaps not more.

Some Additional Requirements

Let's leave aside devils and angels and return to God understood as a trinity of three persons. Thus far I have made it seem like it is fairly straightforward to apply the requirements of a conspiracy theory to the Christian conception of God. But there are some alleged requirements that would block my conclusion.

Here I will present three of them. In each case, my response will be that while the proposed requirement might hold in *many* cases of conspiracy theories, it isn't a *necessary condition* that must be met in all cases. And so Christianity will still be able to count as a conspiracy theory even if it does not satisfy any of these proposals.

An evil purpose. The most obvious source of trouble for my argument is the claim made by some writers that the small group of conspiring agents must be up to no good. Keeley, for instance, writes that "The true intentions behind the conspiracy are invariably nefarious."[10] And Cassam claims that the conspirators must "work together in secret to do something illegal or harmful."[11] Rob Brotherton puts it succinctly: "We are up against Evil Incarnate."[12]

Obviously, a Christian will not accept that the persons of the Trinity are evil or have wicked plans in secret. So if this really is a requirement for all conspiracy theories, then some Christians might still count as conspiracy theorists because of their views about the devil. But not all Christians would automatically count in virtue of accepting the Trinity.

The thing to say here, I think, is that having an evil purpose is *not* a requirement for all conspiracy theories. Keeley, for instance, just applies it to what he calls *unwarranted* conspiracy theories.[13] And consider examples like this:

10. Keeley, "Of Conspiracy Theories," 117. In a later paper, Keeley weakens this to just requiring that the conspiracies be "morally suspect" ("God as the Ultimate Conspiracy Theory," 141).

11. Cassam, *Conspiracy Theories*, 3.

12. Brotherton, *Suspicious Minds*, 71–73. See also Byford, *Conspiracy Theories*, 21.

13. Keeley, "Of Conspiracy Theories," 117. Similarly, Brotherton admits that "Conspiracy can be necessary and benign" (*Suspicious Minds*, 72).

The Aliens. An asteroid is on a collision course with Earth, potentially killing millions of people. When it gets to Earth's atmosphere, it disintegrates. There is a widely accepted scientific explanation for what happened to the asteroid. But some people believe instead that benevolent aliens used an invisible laser to destroy the asteroid and thereby save human lives.

Surely, if anything is going to count as a conspiracy theory, this alien explanation does. But the aliens' intentions were compassionate, not evil. Thus, having an evil purpose is not required for there to be a conspiracy theory.[14]

Falsity. One might think that conspiracy theories can't be *true*. As Jovan Byford writes, "A casual account is unlikely to be labelled a 'conspiracy theory' if it is believed to be true . . . it is a way of branding an explanation untrue."[15] But naturally Christians hold it is true that God is a trinity, and that the persons of the Trinity bring about various changes in the world. Therefore, *as Christians*, they can't count as conspiracy theorists, although perhaps non-Christians who think that Christian commitments are false could still count Christians as conspiracy theorists.

But the problem here is with the requirement. It is not a plausible requirement to be a conspiracy theorist that one believe the proposed explanatory theory to be false. There are plenty of examples of conspiracy theories throughout history that were believed to be true, *and* were indeed true. Examples include Watergate, the CIA's plans to kill Castro, Iran-Contra, and Enron.[16] Christianity can be in this group as well.

Unfalsifiability. Another much-discussed requirement is that conspiracy theories be unfalsifiable. Byford, for instance, writes that "they are by their very nature irrefutable. Logical contradictions, disconfirming evidence, even the complete absence of proof have no bearing on the conspiratorial explanation because they can always be accounted for in terms of the conspiracy."[17]

This feature of unfalsifiability seems to apply in our alien example. Someone might point out that there was no laser beam visible at the time the asteroid disintegrated. But the conspiracy theorist can reply that the la-

---

14. For additional examples, see Keeley, "Of Conspiracy Theories," 118.

15. Byford, *Conspiracy Theories*, 21. For additional examples of this kind of claim, see Brotherton, *Suspicious Minds*, 64.

16. See Byford, *Conspiracy Theories*, 24, 32.

17. Byford, *Conspiracy Theories*, 36. See also Keeley, "Of Conspiracy Theories," 121–23; Brotherton, *Suspicious Minds*, 75–77; and Bezalel, "Conspiracy Theories and Religion," 7.

ser was invisible. Then it is pointed out that there were no aircraft detected near our planet that might have fired the laser. But the conspiracy theorist replies that the laser was fired from a faraway planet. And so it goes.

Some Christians might claim that Christianity is unfalsifiable as well, or that certain elements of Christianity are, such as the doctrine of the Trinity. If so, then so much the better for my position, since that means Christianity meets this requirement for a conspiracy theory as well. My main argument would be unaffected.

But other Christians might not agree that Christianity is unfalsifiable. For example, they might acknowledge that if the doctrine of the Trinity can be shown to be logically contradictory, then that would falsify it. Or if compelling evidence emerges for the unreliability of the biblical texts, thereby undermining our basis from divine revelation for thinking that God is a trinity, then that would also falsify the doctrine in a different way.

I do not need to get into any of these discussions here. Suppose—just for the sake of discussion—that the Trinitarian conception of God is falsifiable. The thing to say at that point would be that unfalsifiability is not a requirement for a conspiracy theory. Here is a simple example to show this:

The Birthday. During the course of the day, a number of surprising events happen to Jones. He finds a fifty-dollar bill outside his front door. There is a box of candy in his mailbox. A DVD of his favorite movie is sitting on the hood of his car. Today is Jones's birthday, and he surmises that these events were caused by his siblings, who planted the gifts for him personally. Unbeknownst to Jones, it turns out that his siblings were not involved at all. They have been playing golf in the Bahamas for the past week, but never told Jones.

Jones holds a conspiracy theory about what explains the money, candy, and DVD. Furthermore, it is clearly falsifiable. He can get plenty of evidence that shows that his siblings have not been in town for several days. Plus the video from the door cam reveals that it was actually Jones's best friend who left the gifts.

Jones clearly believes a conspiracy theory is true, even if it concerns a relatively minor matter and the goal of the alleged conspirators would be to benefit Jones and not to bring about evil in the world. But that theory is falsifiable.

So unfalsifiability is not a requirement for conspiracy theories. Neither are falsity and having an evil purpose genuine requirements of conspiracy theories.[18] Hence none of them threatens my claim about Christianity and conspiracy theories.

Conclusion—So What?

I have argued that all Christians accept at least one conspiracy theory about the activities of the divine persons, and that if you add angels and devils, then many Christians actually believe multiple conspiracy theories.

Suppose I am right about this. So what? you might say. What follows?

Answering this important question would take far more space than I have here. But let me briefly suggest three things, each of which will be stated from within my perspective as a Christian.

The first implication is that something can be a conspiracy theory and still be *true*. From a Christian perspective, many conspiracy theories are clearly false. But the most important conspiracy theory there ever has been is a theory about the existence of God as three divine persons who are responsible for so many different features of our world. That theory is a conspiracy theory. And it is true.

Second, believing in a conspiracy theory can also be rational and justified.[19] I started the chapter by noting that conspiracy theories often have a bad name these days. And when it comes to theories about, say, Holocaust denial or 9/11 being the work of the Bush administration, this negative view is certainly warranted.

But not in all cases. To take an example from American history, the theory that explains the Watergate break-in as the work of Nixon and his aides is a conspiracy theory. But it is rational to believe as well, given the evidence that has been produced for it over the years. Other examples include theories about Iran-Contra and CIA plots to kill Castro. So, some conspiracy theories can be rational and justified. From a Christian perspective, that includes a Trinitarian theory about the work of the persons of the Trinity.

Finally, Christians are of course free to label various theories "conspiracy theories." But that should be intended as a merely descriptive label. Christians should not intend "conspiracy theory" to be an expression of

18. Nor is the claim that the theory is "amateurish" a genuine requirement (Cassam, *Conspiracy Theories*, 23–25).

19. For very helpful discussion here, see Pigden, "Conspiracy Theories and the Conventional Wisdom."

derision, with the implication being that because it is a conspiracy theory it is automatically defective or problematic in some way. Unless, that is, Christians are willing for the same negativity to apply to themselves as well. Otherwise they would be guilty of hypocrisy.

Christians should be labeled "conspiracy theorists," and they should willingly accept that label so long as it is not used as a term of derision. It is, instead, just a reflection of who they are.[20]

References

Bezalel, Glenn. "Conspiracy Theories and Religion: Reframing Conspiracy Theories as *Bliks*." *Episteme* 16 (2019): 1–19.

Brotherton, Rob. *Suspicious Minds: Why We Believe Conspiracy Theories*. London: Bloomsbury, 2015.

Byford, Jovan. *Conspiracy Theories: A Critical Introduction*. London: Palgrave Macmillan, 2015.

Cassam, Quassim. *Conspiracy Theories*. Cambridge: Polity, 2019.

Keeley, Brian. "God as the Ultimate Conspiracy Theory." *Episteme* 4 (2007): 135–49.

———. "Of Conspiracy Theories." *Journal of Philosophy* 96 (1999): 109–26.

Pigden, Charles. "Conspiracy Theories and the Conventional Wisdom." *Episteme* 4 (2007): 219–32.

Stump, Eleonore. "Orthodoxy and Heresy." *Faith and Philosophy* 16 (1999): 147–63.

20. I am grateful to Mike Austin and Greg Bock for inviting me to be a part of this volume.

11

CHRISTIANITY, CONSPIRACY THEORIES, AND INTELLECTUAL CHARACTER

Nathan L. King and Keith D. Wyma

"You just put a pedophile in the White House." That was the first thing one of us read on social media on November 7, 2020—the day after the US presidential election was called for Joe Biden. The poster, an employee of our Christian university, thereby referred to the widely held conspiracy theory that Democrats were secretly running a child-trafficking ring. Such remarks—and the conspiracy theories they involve—are a commonplace. Here are some others:

- "There was a massive conspiracy to steal the election for Joe Biden. Both election officials and voting machine companies are in on it."
- "Antifa was behind the January 6 attack on the US Capitol."
- "Don't trust the mainstream media. They're part of a liberal conspiracy to brainwash America into getting the COVID-19 vaccine."

Many people believe such conspiracy theories. The rest of us stand amazed, struggling to explain how such seemingly improbable theories could gain so much traction. Are conspiracy theorists mentally unstable? Are they unreasonable? Or intellectually vicious? Or something else?

We begin by noting, straightaway, that belief in conspiracy theories is not always unreasonable, much less a sign of mental instability or stupidity. Indeed, almost everyone thinks that *some* conspiracies have occurred (e.g., Watergate).

Nevertheless, it is very often irrational to believe conspiracy theories. Further, we will argue that accepting a conspiracy theory often involves a failure of intellectual virtue—for example, a lack of carefulness, humility, or fair-mindedness. It might be tempting to infer that many of those who believe in conspiracy theories have intellectual vices like carelessness, arrogance, or unfairness. However, we urge caution in making that inference. To lack a virtue is not always to have its corresponding vice, and intellectual charity to conspiracy theorists demands that we consider other possibilities. Thus, taking our cue from Thomas Aquinas, we explore the possibility that conspiracy theorists suffer from a condition that places them between intellectual virtue and vice—namely, an intellectual kind of *weakness of will*.

Our Intellectual Character Matters to God

Intellectual virtues are the character traits of excellent thinkers—curiosity, intellectual carefulness, intellectual autonomy, intellectual humility, open-mindedness, fair-mindedness, and so on.[1] These virtues often consist in a mean between two extremes, called *vices*. For example, intellectual humility stands between the vice of arrogance (a deficient awareness of or owning of our intellectual limitations) and self-deprecation (an excessive focus on or exaggeration of our limitations):[2]

Area of Activity	Vice (Deficiency)	Virtue	Vice (Excess)
Managing our intellectual limitations	Arrogance	Humility	Self-deprecation

The various intellectual virtues differ from each other because they involve different areas of activity. Curiosity concerns how we manage our

1. For a more thorough introduction to intellectual virtues, see Nathan L. King, *The Excellent Mind: Intellectual Virtues for Everyday Life* (New York: Oxford University Press, 2021). For an introduction designed explicitly for Christian readers, see Philip Dow, *Virtuous Minds: Intellectual Character Development* (Downers Grove, IL: InterVarsity Press, 2013).

2. Our account of intellectual humility follows that of Dennis Whitcomb et al., "Intellectual Humility: Owning Our Limitations," *Philosophy and Phenomenological Research* 94, no. 3 (2017): 509–39.

appetite for knowledge; carefulness concerns our habits when it comes to making inferences from complex bodies of evidence; humility concerns the way we interact with our intellectual limitations; open-mindedness concerns our interaction with new and challenging ideas; and so on. However, all intellectual virtues have these facets in common: a stable, consistent motivation to gain, keep, and share things like truth and knowledge—and to avoid falsehood and ignorance.

To have the motivations characteristic of intellectual virtue is *not* the same as a devotion to holding our own beliefs come what may. Rather, intellectually virtuous people are dedicated to seeking, speaking, and living the truth, even when it conflicts with their other desires and loves or requires them to change their beliefs. To be any other way is to risk constructing a false reality in one's own image. To put the point in distinctively Christian terms, it is to construct an *idol*.

To paint a fuller picture of the relationship between Christian discipleship and intellectual character, we can start with Jesus's summary of the Old Testament law: "'Love the Lord your God with all your heart and with all your soul and with all your mind.' This is the first and greatest commandment. And the second is like it: 'Love your neighbor as yourself.' All the Law and the Prophets hang on these two commandments" (Matt. 22:37-40 NIV). A striking feature of these commands is that they are not meant to apply just to one-off, singular actions. No—they summarize the *dispositions* that God-fearing, neighbor-loving people are to have. They tell us that we are to have a loving *character*. Moreover, this kind of character involves all of our being. It concerns not just our passions or emotions but also our *minds*.[3] As C. S. Lewis puts it, "God is no fonder of intellectual slackers than of any other slackers."[4]

How does this connect to the idea of intellectual character? Start with our love of God. On the Judeo-Christian view, our minds are a wonderful gift from God. An important way to express gratitude to God for this gift is to use our minds well. To do so, must exhibit such intellectual virtues as carefulness, humility, honesty, open-mindedness, and fairness. The command to love God with our minds, then, demands that we pursue such virtues.[5]

---

3. We can make this point only briefly here. For further development, see Dow, *Virtuous Minds*, chaps. 10 and 11, and James Sire, *Habits of the Mind: Intellectual Life as a Christian Calling* (Downers Grove, IL: InterVarsity Press, 2000).

4. C. S. Lewis, *Mere Christianity* (New York: Touchstone, 1996), 75.

5. Thanks to Daniel Howard-Snyder for helpful discussion here.

What about Jesus's second command? Loving actions toward others—as opposed to mere warm feelings—often require virtuous thinking and oppose intellectual vice. Philip Dow lays down the challenge starkly: "If you are . . . tempted to think that intellectual character has little to do with practical Christian living, try loving your neighbor as yourself while practicing intellectual hastiness. It can't be done."[6] Dow's point generalizes: it is impossible to love others well if our thinking about them displays intellectual arrogance, dishonesty, closed-mindedness, unfairness, and their like.

Here's the point. Our intellectual character—whether virtuous, vicious, or somewhere in between—affects what we believe. What we believe affects what we do. Our actions in turn affect other people—for good or ill. Thus, our intellectual character affects other people. If this is right, then loving others well requires that we attend to our intellectual character.

Beliefs in Conspiracy Theories as Failures of Intellectual Virtue

Let's apply what we have learned to discussions of conspiracy theories.[7]

We'll start with intellectual carefulness. This virtue is centrally a matter of seeking to avoid falsehood and irrational belief in cases where they are realistic threats. Careful thinkers find a mean between the deficiency vice of *carelessness*—roughly, insufficient attention to the threats of falsehood and irrationality—and the excess vice of *scrupulousness*. Consider the following case:

Careless Carl: Carl is often quite careful about his decisions. He buys a car only after thorough consideration of the comparative prices, options, capabilities, etc., of different vehicle makes. Sadly, in other areas, Carl is not so careful. He thinks that Antifa was behind the January 6 attack on the US Capitol. When asked why he thinks this, he says, "Antifa's soldiers are so evil that they will do *anything* to make Trump and his supporters

---

6. Dow, *Virtuous Minds*, 37.

7. To clarify: we do not claim that our illustrations are typical of all conspiracy theorists. Further, some people who *deny* conspiracy theories can and do fail to exemplify intellectual virtues. Our focus on the faults of conspiracy theorists stems from our sense that within evangelical circles, the problems with believing these theories are not being taken seriously enough. Our account is intended as a corrective to current trends and a prompt for reflection. All the cases we discuss are based on actual interactions, though we have changed the names.

look bad. An attack on the Capitol is just the kind of thing those slime-balls would think up. Think about it. It's the *only* good explanation!"

We submit that Carl's thinking fails to exhibit intellectual carefulness. First, Carl displays a penchant for the complicated over the simple. Consider one key fact to be explained: that people dressed in Trumpist apparel, waving Trump flags, and chanting Trumpist slogans stormed the Capitol building. (We take it that this much is beyond dispute.) Now, how to explain this fact? A standard explanation is that the appearances match reality: it *was* Trump supporters who stormed the Capitol. The conspiracy theorist admits this appearance but insists that the appearance is deceiving because a large group of anti-Trump people conspired to (1) put on Trumpist clothing; (2) travel to a specific area within Washington, DC; (3) launch a coordinated attack that *appeared* to be in response to Donald Trump's command to "fight like hell" at the Capitol; and (4) do all this for the purpose of making Trump and his supporters look bad. Carl's explanation of the events includes the appearance of a Trumpist insurrection but *adds* a great deal more. This is a major disadvantage of the theory—one that makes it, other things being equal, less likely to be true than its competitors. Carl ignores this and thereby fails to think in the way a careful person would.

Now, it can be reasonable to embrace a very complicated theory—especially if simpler theories cannot explain important parts of our evidence. If investigators uncovered emails including plans for the attack that circulated among known Antifa members, or discovered Antifa paraphernalia among those arrested during the attacks—*then* the careful thinker might embrace the Antifa theory over the standard theory. But as it stands, there is no such evidence. Carl thus embraces a theory that has the cost of being very complicated without the benefit of being able to explain anything that the simpler theory cannot explain—again, a failure of carefulness.

But perhaps we are being too hard on Carl. After all, maybe Carl is simply not trained in the rules of thought needed to make a good inference from the data. If so, *that*, by itself, wouldn't be a mark of carelessness. This is a fair point. But notice: even those who lack technical training can ask whether there are any alternative explanations, besides theirs, that fit the data. And Carl clearly fails to do this—he says that the Antifa explanation is the *only* explanation. In making this move, he jumps to conclusions. He not only fails to consider all the alternatives to his theory—he fails to consider even the alternative that seems most obvious.

We can avoid thinking like Carl does by asking one simple question: What alternatives to my theory might explain the facts in question? If we make a list of such theories and at least ask what each has going for it, we'll thereby slow down enough to take a small step toward intellectual carefulness.

Let's examine another intellectual virtue—humility. This virtue stands between the vices of arrogance and self-deprecation. Consider the following case:

Bold Brandi: Brandi doesn't wholesale reject the beliefs of experts. In fact, she relies upon them continually in trusting that electricians have wired her house correctly, that engineers have designed her automotive brakes to maximize safety, etc. However, while Brandi is not a doctor and has no formal medical training, this does not keep her from holding firm opinions about a range of medical issues. In her view, sunscreen is totally unnecessary—"It's unnatural. It wasn't part of God's original creation, and Adam and Eve didn't need it—so why should we?" In her view, the "military-industrial sunscreen complex" has foisted upon the public the lie that sunscreen is important for healthy, cancer-free skin. On other matters, she is no less bold. Though she believes that COVID-19 is a real phenomenon, she is convinced that instead of wearing masks and getting vaccines, citizens should continue life as normal. As part of her weekly Twitter posting, she says, "We need a lot of people to get exposed to the disease in order to reach herd immunity, you fools! Don't drink the vaccine Kool-Aid!" When commenters ask why she is so confident in her medical opinions, she tweets back, "Because I did my own research."[8]

Brandi falls short of intellectual humility. Now, it is in general good to do our own research. Indeed, this is part of what it is to be a virtuous inquirer—to seek to know things "for oneself." However, when we conduct such research, we are wise to consider how fit we are to do it, especially relative to those who have been studying a topic for their whole lives. When we are not experts, experts are more likely to get to the truth than we are, for two reasons. First, because they have been studying for longer than we have, they usually have more relevant evidence than we do. Thus, they are less

---

8. For an insightful treatment of the phrase "Do your own research," see Nathan Ballantyne, Jared Celniker, and David Dunning, "Do Your Own Research" (unpublished manuscript, September 2021).

likely than we are to form their views based on a small or biased sample of the available evidence. Second, they have more training than we do in the relevant methods of reasoning from the evidence.[9] They are thus less likely than we are to make mistakes in evaluating that evidence.

Of course, none of this guarantees that the experts are always right; and for our own lack of expertise, we *might* be right. However, the betting person should usually bet with the experts, and against us, when the two conflict. If, like Brandi, we usually bet on ourselves instead, we fail to own our limitations—and thereby fail to exhibit humility. To keep ourselves from veering in the direction of arrogance, we might ask ourselves questions like these: Do I think that experts are usually wrong in areas of their expertise—even when they have reached consensus? If so, why do I think this? What reasons can I give for thinking the experts are wrong, given that I am not an expert myself, or given that I lack relevant training? If I think that I'm right and the experts are wrong in a given case, what makes me so special? What makes me an exception?

Here is one more case:

Uneven Evan: Evan is a Christian apologist and blogger. He spends much of his time arguing for Jesus's resurrection. His specialty is refuting conspiracy theories surrounding the start of Christianity. "There's simply no way the disciples could have stolen Jesus's body," he writes. "A conspiracy on that scale would have been 'found out' immediately. It would have been too hard to pull off, and at least one of the disciples would have 'squealed' under the threat of torture from authorities." When Evan isn't defending the resurrection, he's usually commenting on politics or bashing the mainstream media. He believes that the 2020 US presidential election was rigged in favor of Joe Biden, that the rigging took place via dishonestly programmed voting machines, and that local election officials in several locations were in on the conspiracy. Further, when the mainstream media reports that there is no evidence of a conspiracy of the sort that could change the results of the election, Evan claims that this is just evidence of "liberal bias." He wholly disregards mainstream sources, opting instead for exclusively right-wing

9. For a brief, helpful discussion of medical expertise in the COVID era, see Nathan Ballantyne and David Dunning, "Which Experts Should You Listen to during the Pandemic?" *Scientific American*, June 8, 2020, https://blogs.scientificamerican .com/observations/which-experts-should-you-listen-to-during-the-pandemic/.

news, which he takes as the unvarnished truth despite acknowledging that it is biased, too.

Evan fails to exhibit the virtue of *intellectual fairness*. In particular, Evan fails to be *evenhanded* in his standards of evidence and in his treatment of sources of information. When it comes to his standards of evidence, Evan quickly dismisses resurrection conspiracy theories because, in his words, they would be too hard to "pull off." However, he studiously ignores the fact that the conspiracy theories he believes involve many, many more people than the resurrection conspiracy theories do, and would also (given modern technology) be easier to detect.[10] Further, when he dismisses mainstream reports related to election conspiracy theories, he ignores them because, as he says, they have a "liberal bias." But Evan fails to address the right-wing bias his own favored sources exhibit. In all of this, Evan applies different standards of evidence to his own views than he applies to those of his dissenters—a clear failure of evenhandedness and therefore fairness.

Sadly, we might very well find ourselves taking steps like Evan's. No one, regardless of religious or political persuasion, is immune from such mistakes (we, the authors, include ourselves). To keep ourselves from taking such steps, it can help to stop and ask some questions: When I criticize others for what I take to be an intellectual mistake, do I note and criticize the same mistake when I make it? If I accuse others of bias, do I recognize my own bias? Am I consistent and evenhanded in the ways I handle arguments, objections, news sources, and so on? In my intellectual exchanges with others, do I heed Jesus's warning: "With the measure you use, it will be measured to you" (Matt. 7:2 NIV)?

Again, the cases we discuss—though based on real people—do not represent the only ways in which conspiracy theorists reason. We claim merely that the sort of thinking discussed in these cases is fairly common, and that it is seriously damaging when it does occur. After all, people make decisions based on conspiracy thinking. The belief that the 2020 election was rigged actually led American citizens to attack the Capitol. Conspiracy-based beliefs about COVID vaccines have led many people not to get vaccinated—with deadly results. The claim that Antifa was behind the January 6 attacks might lead someone to join the Proud Boys; and so on.

10. For highlighting the kind of inconsistency Evan displays here, we are indebted to Nancy Casady.

Aquinas's Insight into Weakness of Will

When conspiracy theorists' thoughts and behaviors do harm others, it is natural for those harmed to respond in anger. Injured parties might be tempted to call conspiracy theorists "fools," or accuse them of having intellectual vices. Without dismissing the possibility of righteous anger, we urge caution and charity here.

First, there is a difference between those who start and perpetuate conspiracy theories (on the one hand) and those who fall prey to them (on the other). The former deserve our ire—or perhaps our neglect. The latter need our correction and our sympathy.

Second, while those in both groups often fail to exhibit intellectual *virtue*, we should not for that reason regard them as having intellectual *vices* like carelessness, arrogance, or unfairness. (More on this shortly.)

Finally, all conspiracy theorists need our charity. For the Christian, that is not negotiable. Part of that charity involves *hoping* that others do not have intellectual vices, and being eager to think as well of them as we reasonably can. Intellectual charity requires that we work imaginatively (but not irrationally) to see ways in which others may not be as intellectually bad as we think. In light of this, and with the help of Thomas Aquinas, let's explore the idea that conspiracy theorists might suffer from something that falls short of intellectual vice—namely, weakness of will.

Aquinas crafted a conceptually rich and fruitful framework for analyzing intentional actions, including how those actions can go astray through weakness of will.[11] This notion carves out space that allows us to see how a person could fail to have a given virtue without thereby having its corresponding vices. Just as important, Aquinas's particular account of weak-willed actions sheds light on exactly *how* today's social and political climate can make conspiracy beliefs (and the intellectual acts that lead to them) so tempting.

Before we can explore how weakness of will applies to conspiracy beliefs, though, we need to see Aquinas's framework for action, both in its *pieces* and in its *process*. First the pieces: Aquinas joins many other philosophers and psychologists in explaining our intentional actions in terms of our beliefs and our desires. In other words, our actions come partly from a cognitive piece and partly from a motivational piece.

11. This section draws on an account of Aquinas originally presented in Keith D. Wyma, *Crucible of Reason: Intentional Action, Practical Rationality, and Weakness of Will* (Lanham, MD: Rowman & Littlefield, 2004).

Aquinas assigns the cognitive direction to our faculty of reason.[12] As a Christian, Aquinas believes our nature has an ultimate good, to know and love God.[13] And it's reason's job to measure all of our actions in terms of not just *a* good we might want in the moment, but in terms of this *ultimate* good, of whether a given action leads us toward or away from God.[14] In coming to know and love God, we also come to know what God loves and to love that as well, content expressed concisely in the first and second greatest commandments, which Aquinas identifies as *charity*.[15] So reason's task is to guide action in light of charity's goal—which, as we've discussed, requires pursuing intellectual virtue—and to identify and recommend specific actions that serve this goal. Reason's charitable standard encompasses everything we can intentionally do, including how we investigate claims, assess evidence, and other factors related to whether we believe conspiracy theories.[16]

The second piece of action mechanics is the will. Aquinas identifies the will as the psychological faculty that enables us both to choose whether to act and to execute actions through motive force the will provides.[17] Will is closely aligned with reason, so that the appetite—the motivation toward acting—in the will is keyed to the conceptions of good that reason considers.[18] However, because our free agency rests centrally in the will, the will can accept or reject individual goods—goals or actions—reason proposes.[19] No good, even God, is so complete and perfect *as human reason can conceive it* that it simply compels the will's acceptance.[20] We might think of reason as a projectionist, putting images—conceptions of goods—on a screen in front of an audience of one, the will. Will responds to the images either with "Yes, more of this!" or "No, try something else!" Reason then changes the slide accordingly.

Unfortunately, though, human action emerges from a broken mechanism that allows a third piece into the mix: passions. For Aquinas, "passion" in-

---

12. Aquinas, *Summa theologiae (ST)* I q. 82, a. 4, rep. 3; II-I q. 14, a. 6, resp.; q. 17, a. 1, resp.

13. Aquinas, *ST* II-I q. 3, a. 8, resp.

14. Aquinas, *ST* I-II q. 77, a. 8, resp.

15. Aquinas, *ST* II-I q. 4, a. 4, resp.

16. Aquinas, *ST* II-I q. 1, a. 3, resp; q. 18, a. 9, rep. 3.

17. Aquinas, *ST* II-I q. 14, a. 1, rep. 1; q. 15, a. 3, resp.; q. 16, a. 2, resp.

18. Aquinas, *ST* II-I q. 8, a. 1, resp.

19. Aquinas, *ST* I q. 82, a. 2, rep. 2; a. 4, resp.; II-I q. 1, a. 7, rep. 1.

20. Aquinas, *ST* I q. 82, a. 2, resp.; II-I q. 5, a. 8, resp.

cludes a range of psychological motivations and effects, including emotions (like anger or fear) and desires (like hunger or a feeling of loyalty to a person or group). Passions create motive force to act, and they also can affect the body's—and thus the *mind*'s—functioning.[21] It's as if passion hijacks reason's projection booth and changes the slide, presented to will, into a "good" of satisfying the passion, whether that's rational or not. Passion provides a rival goal to reason's, and the bodily effects of passion can virtually nail attention to an action that achieves the new goal.[22] That introduces a big problem into our action mechanics: now we can end up choosing and acting on goals that are against our better reason—which we call "*weakness of will.*"

To see how weakness of will occurs, we need to examine the second aspect of intentional action: its process, the "dance" between reason and will (and passion, which "cuts in") that generates action. Aquinas identifies a series of subacts by reason and will, each nudging forward to produce an intentional action. For this chapter's purposes, we're going to condense this process and focus on three reason subacts. Action starts in reason by recognizing some good and presenting it to will as a general *judgment* about action—a "slide" with a principle to act on.[23] With will's approval, reason then runs through possibilities of available action and means-end assessments of whether they would satisfy the principle; this process is *deliberation*.[24] It reaches a conclusion identifying a specific action to take.[25] Reason can then present a new "slide," called *discretive judgment*, to express the conclusion.[26] That completes the belief piece of intentional action, and through the will's choice, motive force is now applied to complete the desire piece and to perform the action.

Here's why all this matters: Aquinas delineates the reason subacts because he realizes they're *points where actions can break down*. In particular, *the interference of passions can derail action at these points, which is what happens in weak-willed actions*.[27]

---

21. Aquinas, *ST* II-I q. 33, a. 3, resp.; q. 77, a. 2.
22. Aquinas, *ST* II-I q. 77, a. 1.
23. Aquinas, *ST* II-I q. 9, a. 1, resp.
24. Aquinas, *ST* II-I q. 14, a. 1, resp. and rep. 1; a. 6, resp.
25. Aquinas, *ST* II-I q. 14, a. 5, resp.
26. Aquinas, *ST* II-I q. 13, a. 1, rep. 2; q. 14, a. 6, resp. The identifier "discretive" comes from commentator John Driscoll, "On Human Acts," in *Summa Theologica*, vol. 3 (San Francisco: Benziger Brothers, 1948), 3201-19.
27. Aquinas, *ST* II-I, q. 17, a. 4, rep. 2. This is made quite clear in both Alan Dona-

Applying Aquinas's Account

We believe that when Christians accept conspiracy theories, often this is because the actions they would normally agree to (and even normally take), because of their commitment to truth in relation to belief formation and investigation, are being disrupted by passions, thus turning their acceptance into weakness of will against intellectual virtue, rather than outright intellectual vice. We'll now explore how the identified reason-acts may have broken down, in our conspiracy-theorist examples, through the weak-willed allowance of passions affecting them.

First, we have to recognize that if our conspiracy-theorists experience strong passions, that's in part due to how others, especially news sources, present the situations to them. Whether journalists and pundits are themselves victims of these passions, or whether they callously use them to sell their brand, is another issue; but either way, the rest of us—including our example conspiracy theorists—find our attempts to stay informed clouded by passions raised.

In light of that, consider Careless Carl. We've seen that he fails to act with the virtue of intellectual carefulness, but that doesn't mean he's intellectually vicious; rather, he seems weak-willed about carefulness. After all, he usually decides carefully. When it comes to conspiracy theories, though, Carl's action starts to derail at the judgment stage, with a rival principle—about accepting a view if it "exposes treachery against my just cause!"—emerging from a passion like indignation, and really goes off the rails at the deliberation stage because of passion's potential to nail Carl's attention to its agenda, so that a complete crash occurs in the discretive judgment. This leads to Carl's acceptance of the conspiracy theory as "the only view that makes sense." Aquinas sometimes labels this kind of failure *thoughtlessness*, because it centers in deliberation gone awry.[28]

Next consider Bold Brandi. She fails to be intellectually humble, but she doesn't seem simply intellectually arrogant, either. After all, Brandi usually *does* value the judgments of experts in fields where she's ignorant. But in

---

gan, "Thomas Aquinas on Human Action," in *The Cambridge History of Later Medieval Philosophy: From the Rediscovery of Aristotle to the Disintegration of Scholasticism, 100-1600,* ed. Norman Kretzmann et al. (Cambridge: Cambridge University Press, 1982), 642-54, here 654; and Ralph McInerny, *Aquinas on Human Action: A Theory of Practice* (Washington, DC: Catholic University of America Press, 1992), 179.

28. Aquinas, *On Evil* q. 15, a. 4, resp.

these medical areas, especially about COVID, she sees expert consensus as undermining her political ideology, bringing up strong passions in her that damagingly intrude at the early stage of *judgment*. Brandi's intellectual humility is pushed out of the "slideshow" from the start. Aquinas would call this a *blindness of mind* about matters that threaten her ideology.[29] Her passions prompt virtually no *deliberation* and a quick *discretive judgment* to rely on "her own research." Brandi is similar to what Aristotle called *impetuously* weak-willed people: passion gets ahold of their decision making before deliberation and skips right over it to action.[30]

Finally, consider Uneven Evan. Evan not only has training in logic and reasoning; he regularly uses it, as shown in his apologetic work. At the level of *judgment*, he's strongly committed to reason's principle on intellectual fairness. But because he's strongly impassioned about his political loyalties and the election, he's got a rival judgment "slide" from passion that accepts the "right" bias in news gathering. Now, Evan is too well trained for his *deliberation* to be wholly skewed; at some level he realizes the inconsistency in his treatment of the evidence, since he acknowledges bias in his unquestioned sources. And that's Evan's problem: he can't hold onto his *discretive judgment* to weigh those biases, even in his preferred sources. He passionately wants so much for the vote *not* to have been accurate, he just can't bring himself to apply his intellectual fairness to the claim that the vote was fraudulent. Aristotle called this the paradigm *weakness* because it wavers at the point of acting; Aquinas agrees and also sometimes calls it *inconstancy*.[31]

Conclusion

That brings us back to our main point: it's clear that belief in the kinds of conspiracy theories in our examples—for the types of "reasons" in the examples—fails to be intellectually virtuous. However, that doesn't mean such conspiracy believers are intellectually vicious. It's quite plausible that they may instead be weak-willed in these areas. Aquinas gives us an insightful account of how that might work. Beyond its successful explanatory power, we have two additional reasons to explore the application of

29. Aquinas, *On Evil* q. 15, a. 4, resp.

30. Aristotle, *Nicomachean Ethics* 1150b20-22, 1152a19. Aquinas agrees in his *Commentary on the Nicomachean Ethics*, at VII.L.7: C1419.

31. Aristotle, *Nicomachean Ethics* 1150b20-22, 1152a18-29; Aquinas, *Commentary on the Nicomachean Ethics* VII.L.7: C1419; *On Evil* q. 15, a. 4, resp.

Aquinas's account in the matter of conspiracy beliefs. First, it allows us to be more intellectually charitable—allows us to better meet God's command to love others—than assuming intellectual vice in Carl, Brandi, Evan, and their fellows. And second, it offers us a more constructive way to discuss their beliefs with them. As Aristotle pointed out, a vicious person can't even perceive the possibility of correction, but a weak-willed person—since she or he accepts reason's principle at least in general—can.[32] Instead of simply berating or confronting conspiracy believers, we might ask them questions like these: "What are some things about how your political position is treated that make you angry?" Or, "What fears do you have regarding these issues?" And, "Do you see any ways those passions may have influenced your decision in this matter?" There's no guarantee such an approach will work, but it's more charitable as a starting point than the alternative. It surely has a better success outlook than starting from condemnation of foolishness, irrationality, and intellectual vice.

References

Aristotle. *Nicomachean Ethics*. Translated by Terence Irwin. Indianapolis: Hackett, 1985.

Ballantyne, Nathan, Jared Celniker, and David Dunning. "Do Your Own Research." Unpublished manuscript, September 2021.

Ballantyne, Nathan, and David Dunning. "Which Experts Should You Listen to during the Pandemic?" *Scientific American*, June 8, 2020. https://blogs.scientificamerican.com/observations/which-experts-should-you-listen-to-during-the-pandemic/.

Donagan, Alan. "Thomas Aquinas on Human Action." In *The Cambridge History of Later Medieval Philosophy: From the Rediscovery of Aristotle to the Disintegration of Scholasticism, 100-1600*, edited by Norman Kretzmann et al. Cambridge: Cambridge University Press, 1982.

Dow, Philip. *Virtuous Minds: Intellectual Character Development*. Downers Grove, IL: InterVarsity Press, 2013.

Driscoll, John. "On Human Acts." In *Summa Theologica*, 3:3201–19. San Francisco: Benziger Brothers, 1948.

King, Nathan L. *The Excellent Mind: Intellectual Virtues for Everyday Life*. New York: Oxford University Press, 2021.

Lewis, C. S. *Mere Christianity*. New York: Touchstone, 1996.

32. Aristotle, *Nicomachean Ethics* 1150b35.

McInerny, Ralph. *Aquinas on Human Action: A Theory of Practice*. Washington, DC: Catholic University of America Press, 1992.

Sire, James. *Habits of the Mind: Intellectual Life as a Christian Calling*. Downers Grove, IL: InterVarsity Press, 2000.

Thomas Aquinas. *Commentary on the Nicomachean Ethics*. Translated by C. I. Litzinger, OP. Chicago: Henry Regnery Co., 1964.

———. *On Evil*. Translated by Jean Oesterle. Notre Dame, IN: University of Notre Dame Press, 1995.

———. *Summa Theologica*. San Francisco: Benziger Brothers, 1948.

Whitcomb, Dennis, Heather Battaly, Jason Baehr, and Daniel Howard-Snyder. "Intellectual Humility: Owning Our Limitations." *Philosophy and Phenomenological Research* 94, no. 3 (2017): 509-39.

Wyma, Keith D. *Crucible of Reason: Intentional Action, Practical Rationality, and Weakness of Will*. Lanham, MD: Rowman & Littlefield, 2004.

12

HOW SHALL WE THEN THINK? BIBLICAL INSIGHTS ON CONSPIRACY

Dru Johnson

Conspiracy theories are not new.[1] Though they run rampant on YouTube, 8Chan, and anywhere that fast and lazy information can be shared. Such hearsay and speculation mixed ruinously in antiquity too. Conspiracies have a long and reckless pedigree, with which even our Lord and Savior had to deal. So too did the early church. Some of the tortures and executions they suffered were directly rooted in rumors about their secret worship meetings. Our sisters and brothers supposedly conspired about incest, infanticide, and cannibalism.[2] Why else would they have been so secretive if they weren't up to no-good, so the thinking went.

More than mere gossip, conspiracies still stir up persecution against Christians around the world. Such dangers make sense of why the Old Testament authors and even Jesus confronted conspiracies head-on, but not in the way we might expect. The obvious dangers of conspiracies also make us wonder why Christian communities today, of all places, have harbored fugitive ideas that fuel bad thinking and irresponsible citizenship to the empire of God that Jesus built.

1. A shorter version of this chapter appeared in *Christianity Today* as "Jesus Cares about Your Conspiracy," November 22, 2019, https://www.christianitytoday.com/ct/2019/december/jesus-cares-about-your-conspiracy-theory.html/.

2. Bart Wagemakers, "Incest, Infanticide, and Cannibalism: Anti-Christian Imputations in the Roman Empire," *Greece & Rome*, 2nd ser., 57, no. 2 (2010): 337–54.

We might be able to understand why most Russian citizens doubt that America ever went to the moon.[3] We can even make some sense of that old-turned-new flat-earth sensation on YouTube.[4] The deep satisfaction and sense of empowerment fostered by seeing through a conspiracy is, quite simply, intoxicating. It's not difficult to understand the emotional power of believing that we've cracked a secret society. After all, who wants to be just another one of the *sheeple*?

People who feel like they are losing social or political power can find themselves leaning into conspiracy mind-sets to regain a sense of control. Dementia and the loss of memory commonly fires up imagined conspiracies. In her final years of life, my mother was convinced on several conspiracies to steal her medicine or food. But as one friend of mine used to quip, "Just because you're paranoid doesn't mean that they're not out to get you!" So, how can we ever know?

I used to work on a secret U.S. government ploy to capture and destroy cocaine before it left South America. Based upon my own experience working in covert counternarcotics operations in Colombia throughout the 1990s, I process the idea of government conspiracies through a different lens. Specifically, I find the notion of government-orchestrated conspiracies to be the least plausible of all. Members of the US government can certainly be mischievous, inept, or immoral. However, the actuality of a cross-agency government scheme to deceive the masses, that also requires a sustained and coordinated effort with 100 percent buy-in from everyone involved, is extremely thin. The probability of such conspiracies wanders into unicorn land for me. But for those without such on-the-ground experiences, I get it. Conspiracies always have a veneer of "reasonableness," and they usually play off of some kernel of truth.

As Christians, we need to grapple with the direct things Scripture has to say about conspiracy thinking. Guided by Scripture's thinking, we should be naturally inoculated against naïve consumption of conspiracy theories. More importantly, we need to believe and act upon the conspiracies that the Scriptures highlight (more on this later).

The biblical authors consistently argue that there are better and worse ways of knowing. They consistently warn against headstrong beliefs that

---

3. Russian Public Opinion Research Center, "Science and Society: Prestige and Trust," press release No. 2089, https://wciom.com/index.php?id=61&uid=1561/.

4. Glenn Branch and Craig A. Foster, "Yes, Flat-Earthers Really Do Exist," *Scientific American*, October 24, 2018, https://blogs.scientificamerican.com/observa tions/yes-flat-earthers-really-do-exist/.

cannot be changed by evidence.[5] By portraying a God who reasons with his people and people who must be reasoned with, the Scriptures want us to consider the ethics of knowing. How we come to know what we know is a theological issue that the biblical authors talk about vigorously—including conspiracies.

Bible Illiteracy Makes It Worse

With rising Bible illiteracy, we are seeing the expected confusions about the meaning of Christian community. A weak understanding of Scripture's reasoning spins out into other problems such as wild ideas about Christian calling, spiritualism devoid of biblical guidance, an inability to distinguish cultural cues from biblical principles, and so on. But by understanding the intellectual traditions in Scripture, from Torah to Gospels, we should be able to discern the patterns of God's empire in the glut of information that grows faster than we can integrate it.

Conspiracies are not new, but they seem to have more forcefulness and reach than ever before. As postmodernism gave way to a flood of data and search tools, questions about "the truth" or who controls the story about truth fell by the wayside. By the 1990s, some scholars were already predicting the rise of "supermodernism," also called "hypermodernism." Supermodernism is signaled by folks giving up on questions about either what-is-true (modernism) or who has the right to tell the correct story (postmodernism). Rather, due to the proliferation of data, algorithms, sources, and experts, we supermoderns worry most about whom we can trust to guide us through the morass of information in which we are daily mired.[6] When you're drowning in data, any coherent and authoritative-sounding pattern-maker can save you.

Enter conspiracy theories.

Conspiracy thinking injects itself into our venal lusts at this exact point. Who will guide me? The conspiracist answers: "*I will!* I, the one who knows, will peel back the corner of the tarp of history and reveal to you all its secret inner workings. You will have a view from nowhere. No longer will you need to trust 'what they want you to believe.' You are not one of the *sheeple*. You are an independent thinker who can see it for yourself." That's the tawdry promise of conspiracy.

---

5. Dru Johnson, *Scripture's Knowing: A Companion to Biblical Epistemology* (Eugene, OR: Cascade, 2015).

6. Gilles Lipovetsky, *Hypermodern Times* (New York: Wiley, 2005).

The proliferation of conspiracies among today's Christians is perplexing at first. But if Christians grow illiterate regarding the Bible's intellectual world—how it reasons about reality—then our illiteracy might better indicate whether we will bite or balk at conspiracies.

What does this look like? Illiterate Christians will ask: "But where in the Bible does it say not to believe in conspiracies?" Their failure to adopt the wisdom of the Bible's intellectual traditions funds such questions. The Bible's "intellectual traditions" emerge in long-form discussions of how to know and understand the world around us, even political conspiracies. What the biblical authors are laying down cannot be picked up through here-and-there contact with Scripture. Being hip to that discussion requires sustained attention to threads of biblical teaching sewn across Scripture. Following and submitting to those threads mean not reducing the biblical literature to moralistic fables or "the Bible says X so therefore Y" platitudes. Jesus was surrounded with folks who treated Scripture that way, and as we will see, he loathed such simplistic thinking—whether found in farmers, scribes, or Pharisees.

We discover the intellectual world of the Bible by studying beyond the words and stories to the thought patterns of Scripture. This is a literacy that, over time, can confidently assess: *Here's what I think the biblical authors would say about transhumanism, the viability of democracy, legalizing drugs, meritocracy mindset, and more.* So what does Scripture have to say about conspiracies?

Scripture's Take on Conspiracies

Jesus warns us that people will come and solicit his followers with conspiracies of his return (Luke 17:22–23). These folks will believe that they have figured it all out: "Look here, look there." Or, maybe they want to exploit the pretense of knowing for their own purposes. They will claim to be able to peel back the tarp of history to warn of Jesus's imminent return. This is expected and largely uninteresting. What is interesting? Jesus flatly instructs his disciples: do not listen to them!

Why "do not listen"? Why not, "Here's the real story" instead? Jesus and the New Testament authors all operate from the intellectual world of the Bible (Hebrew Scriptures for them). Hence, they know something many of us do not about conspiracy thinking because we are not as literate in biblical thinking as they were. Jesus had to deal with these conspiracies throughout his life, his death, his resurrection, and his ascension. Many contemporaries of Jesus wrongly thought they had pieced together why he came and what he was about to do. His own disciples had their own skewed theories, even after his death and resurrection (Acts 1:6). They seemed to think that all the pieces added up to a major and not-so-well-hidden agenda to restore the empire to Israel.

Jesus's reply to these expectations intends to chill them: "It is not for you to know" (Acts 1:7 NRSV). Notice he didn't give them the correct conspiracy; he chided them about what they can and cannot know. Jesus's reaction to conspiring minds is instructive for how we think, in general, but specifically for how we think about the proliferating conspiracies that we encounter. This is what it means to be formed by the intellectual world of the Bible.

Unlike other topics of our day that Scripture doesn't directly address—think: incarceration, democracy, crypto-currency, and so on—we do not have to go deep into the philosophies of Scripture to see its thinking on grand conspiracies. Jesus tackles this topic head-on.

Prior to his death, Jesus sternly warned his disciples against buying into the various conspiracy theories that would inevitably float around. Jesus fore-scolded them, "You will hear of wars and rumors of wars," but again, his counsel is revealing: "See to it that no one leads you astray," for "many will come in my name . . . and they will lead many astray" (Matt. 24:4-5 NRSV). Notice that, for Jesus, the conspiracies themselves lead people away from true understanding.

Conversely, Jesus tapped deep into the biblical instruction on how to think about such things. Going back to Moses's instruction to the children of Israel, God makes clear that we cannot domesticate the facts of our world. For Scripture, knowledge is a process in which we participate; it is not entirely under our command. Yet, we are responsible for what God shows us: "The hidden things belong to Yahweh our God, but the revealed things belong to us and to our children forever, that we may do all the words of this instruction" (Deut. 29:29, author's translation).

The writer of Ecclesiastes pushes this line even further. He is a man with the intellect, the finances, the time, and the passion to figure out the entire system running the universe—to get behind the curtain (Eccles. 8:16). Yet he ends up in a satisfied restraint about what is possible to understand. "Even though those who are wise claim to know, they cannot find it out" (Eccles. 8:17 NRSV). In Deuteronomy, as in Jesus's instructions, notice his happy resolve to claim that no one can see how everything works: "As you do not know [how a child grows in the womb] . . . , so you do not know the work of God" (Eccles. 11:5 NRSV) And, "beware of anything beyond these. Of making many books there is no end, and much study is a weariness of the flesh" (Eccles. 12:12 ESV).

By reducing the Bible to moralistic oracles, merely rules to be kept, or broad theological principles like "salvation," we can fail to be shaped intellectually (or "spiritually," as the New Testament authors would call it). Conspiracies are products of theological habits, for good or ill. They are often attempts to see from God's perspective. God occasionally invites us to see things from his perspective, but he most often implores us to see what the prophets (including Jesus) are trying to show us.

Yes, but what if these conspiracies are true? In most cases, it doesn't even matter. Let's ask a better question: Is it wise to hold beliefs that cannot be defeated by reason or evidence? The loud answer from across the Scriptures is, "No!"

What if we painted a different picture of spirituality that included biblical intellectualism? What if Christians, by dint of habit, stopped and asked first, "How does Scripture itself think about this concept?" Does God even care about how we know things and in whom we place our trust? Through understanding the intellectual world of the Bible—its coherent, sustained, and rigorous thinking on both abstract and concrete matters—we can see something beyond mere stories, poetry, and legal instruction. We see the biblical authors making a conscientious argument against such mentalities, developed across the Scriptures.

What's more, biblical authors regularly portray a demand for beliefs that can be supported or defeated by evidence (even eyewitness evidence).[7] People who engage in practices that could support or defeat their beliefs are commended for participating in the undramatic backbone of what biblical writers call "trust" or "devotion" (often translated as "faith," which has a decidedly different meaning in modern English).[8] Conversely, those

---

7. For example: Gen. 3:1–7; 15:7–21; Exod. 5:2; Judg. 6:36–40; Luke 1:1–4; John 20:19–31.

8. For more on "faith" as trust, allegiance, and devotion, see: Matthew W. Bates, *Salvation by Allegiance Alone: Rethinking Faith, Works, and the Gospel of Jesus the King* (Grand Rapids: Baker Academic, 2017); Christoper Seglenieks, *Johannine Belief and Greco-Roman Devotion* (Tübingen: Mohr Siebeck, 2020); Dru Johnson, *Biblical Philosophy: A Hebraic Approach to the Old and New Testaments* (New York: Cambridge University Press, 2021).

who merely seek confirmation of their views or desires are condemned by their own search.[9]

Recall that God regularly provides evidence when people ask him, "How can I know?" When Abram asked, "How am I to know," God responded with a covenant and the words, "knowing-ly you shall know" (cf. Gen. 15:8, 13, author's translation). Moses challenged God with his certainty that the Hebrews would not listen to his voice. God responded with signs and wonders that convinced Moses, then Aaron, then the elders, then Israel, and then many of the Egyptians (cf. Exod. 4:1–9, 28–31; 9:20). And the same goes for Israel in Egypt (Exod. 14:30–31), the children of Israel who would conquer Canaan (Josh. 1–4), the judge Gideon (Judg. 6:11–40), the people of Israel regarding the prophet Samuel (1 Sam. 3:19–21), Second Temple Israel in a Roman Galilee (Matt. 4:23), Jews in the diaspora (Acts 17:1–15), and gentiles in the Roman Empire (Acts 16).

Across Scripture, God rarely, *if ever*, peels back the curtain to reveal the whole conspired circumstance of a present reality. Rather, God offers evidence to convince people that he and the guidance of his prophets are trustworthy and good. Only then does he ask those same folks to trust him in order to become the kind of community through which "all the families of the earth shall be blessed" (Gen. 12:3 NRSV).

The Right Conspiracies

The Bible's authors also knew that some conspiracies turn out to be true. Scripture is centrally concerned with how to see the world truly. For example, when God himself heard of a citywide conspiracy to exploit and assault foreigners, what did God do? He went and investigated. When God heard a report of injustice, he is depicted as sending messengers (angels) to determine whether it was true (Gen. 18:21). Setting aside the question of God's all-knowing powers, the biblical authors were not afraid to depict God investigating to see if the report was true. For the sake of justice, God committed to finding out, and to risk all that confirmation entails.

God expected the same of Israel. His instructions to Israel required that they confirm reports of exploitative practices against the vulnerable. If idolatry—one such exploitative practice—is reported in an Israelite vil-

---

9. 1 Kings 21–22 offers a sophisticated narrative argument against the unchecked desire of things (Naboth's vineyard) and affirmation-seeking (yea-saying prophets).

lage, Deuteronomy demands, "You must inquire, probe, and investigate it thoroughly. And if it is true and it has been proved . . ." (13:14, author's translation). This rare piling up of three different words for "investigate" has made this passage a staple in ancient rabbinic discussions. For the sake of justice, God demands diligent investigation *as a process that should support or discredit reports that we've heard*—just as God came down to investigate at Babel and Sodom.

But biblical authors also commend a particular kind of conspiracy monitoring throughout. Repeatedly, the prophets (including Jesus) push us to investigate cover-ups and conspiracies wherever injustices batter vulnerable populations. Many ordinary conspiracies of this variety lurk in the tucked-away corners of our communities, in the form of harassed minorities and immigrants, exploited children, trafficked men and women, and overlooked elders. The abuse of power against our modern-day "widows, orphans, and foreigners" does not distinguish by country or socioeconomic status. Even Peter assumes that ordinary sinfulness can cause elders to conspire circumstances favorable for them to spiritually abuse their flock. Instead, he reminds them not to lord over their flocks because the Chief Shepherd is coming back to hold them accountable (1 Pet. 5:1-2).

In investigating and accounting for conspiracies such as these, God will use us to help others see his empire that has come and is still coming in the ordinary lives of overlooked people in our communities. But that also means there are other conspiracies—*ones that prey on our sinful desires*—that will compete and distract us from where God is trying to focus our efforts.

If we're busy carrying out the mission of the coming empire of God, we will not have much time or energy for tawdry conspiracy theories meant to tickle our ears and sate our desires for control through knowledge. And, pretending we can pull back the curtains of history to discern the exact signs of the King's coming will seem frivolous at best. The mother and father of Proverbs 1-9 don't coach their children to discern the conspiratorial signs of the times. Rather, they plead: *listen my child, incline your ear, Lady Folly desires to have, to hold, and to kill you* (Prov. 7:25-27, author's paraphrase). But the deep structures of thinking across Scripture can guide us well here.

How Shall We Then Think?

Scripture talks a lot about how we were designed to know our world—from the knowledge of Eden (Gen. 2-3) to the mysteries of the kingdom of God (Mark 4:11). Today, the best examples of knowing something accurately usually happen in science class, music training, or some other high-skill learning environment. The biblical authors filled their accounts with method and did not shy away from offering portraits of error where Hebrews got it wrong in a big way (Exod. 1–14; Num. 16; Mark 8; etc.). These were all concerned with how we can know, how trust is earned, and warnings about naïvely thinking we have figured out what's going on behind the curtain. The Bible contains instructions about our intellectual world, and failing to heed the Bible's conceptual guidance, even for Jesus's disciples, always produces a thin or naïve understanding of our world. In the guise of understanding, conspiracies can actually make us numb and dumb to reality.

Bottom line: Christians should reinvest in the intellectual world of the church by asking, "Who has been leading us to understand the nature of reality?" "How am I sinfully tempted toward certain explanations?" And key for all: "Have my beliefs become resistant to evidence or reasoning?" If God is willing to use evidence to establish his own credibility and reason with his people, then we should look for the same throughout all of our intellectual/spiritual life.

References

Bates, Matthew W. *Salvation by Allegiance Alone: Rethinking Faith, Works, and the Gospel of Jesus the King.* Grand Rapids: Baker Academic, 2017.

Branch, Glenn, and Craig A. Foster. "Yes, Flat-Earthers Really Do Exist." *Scientific American,* October 24, 2018. https://blogs.scientificamerican.com/observations/yes-flat-earthers-really-do-exist/.

Johnson, Dru. *Biblical Philosophy: A Hebraic Approach to the Old and New Testaments.* New York: Cambridge University Press, 2021.

———. *Scripture's Knowing: A Companion to Biblical Epistemology.* Eugene, OR: Cascade, 2015.

Lipovetsky, Gilles. *Hypermodern Times.* New York: Wiley, 2005.

Seglenieks, Christoper. *Johannine Belief and Greco-Roman Devotion.* Tübingen: Mohr Siebeck, 2020.

Wagemakers, Bart. "Incest, Infanticide, and Cannibalism: Anti-Christian Imputations in the Roman Empire." *Greece & Rome,* 2nd ser., 57, no. 2 (2010): 337–54.

13

FAITH, REASON, AND CONSPIRACY THEORIES

Domonique Turnipseed

Prioritizing the harmonization of faith and reason, following Thomas Aquinas, is crucial for helping Christians avoid falling victim to some of the most recent conspiracy theories within American Christianity. The counterposition is one of faith only, for Christians who are caught in the web of conspiracy theories often think they are faithful to Christ by taking this position; if the conclusions of faith and reason show that the conspiracy theory is wrong, then that conclusion must be a liberal ploy.

However, a faith that fails to interact with reason limits not only one's trust in scientific authorities but also one's ability to understand more nuanced interpretations of biblical texts and unnecessarily commits one to blind faith, enabling conspiracies to thrive. This is counter to what one would expect from Christians who claim to believe in Christ as the *logos*. In this chapter I hope to emphasize how an approach that honors both faith and reason is the best way for Christians to avoid the traps of conspiratorial thinking.

The Harmony of Faith and Reason

One thing that has increased the likelihood of modern-day American Christians to believe in conspiracy theories is the tendency to disbelieve scientific authorities to demonstrate their faith. This results in a skeptical attitude toward science, seeing faith and science as having a disjunctive relationship; the belief that one cannot be a faithful believer in the former while still holding onto the latter. On the other hand, this polarity has been propagated on some level in the mainstream culture due to misunderstandings of Christianity, which has resulted in attempts to relegate Christianity to the level of private opinion. The influential Christian scholastic philosopher Saint Thomas Aquinas attempts to resolve this tension between faith and science by putting forward the thesis that both operate harmoniously.[1] Aquinas, being a believer in the senses and natural world, holds that reason (broadly speaking, the understanding of the world without reference to religious faith) studies reality according to scientific and philosophical principles, which can even establish a general proof for the existence of God.[2] However, no principle in the natural sciences will explain how Christ is the Son of God and the second member of the Trinity; no principle can provide a general knowledge for humanity's salvation.[3] Here is where faith comes in. Faith operates on different principles than science, such as those written in the Bible and the sacraments of the church.

While faith and science are different, they both argue from their respective principles to their conclusions, and therefore, both have the status of an official branch of knowledge, that which Aristotle calls a "science." Because faith deals with things in the heavenly realm, it is the higher science, whereas reason operates according to principles in the non-heavenly realm, and thus is the lower science. Yet, both are equally valuable to humanity's ability to know the world. While faith and reason describe the world according to different principles, apparent contradictions between the two are only apparent, for if truth is really truth, then it cannot contradict itself. Instead, Aquinas concludes that with time and more study, contradictions will become resolved, or God will fully resolve that which is not yet resolved on earth. Either there is a misunderstanding of one's interpretation of faith, there is a misunderstanding of the science in question, or it is a mystery that God has yet to reveal to us, but contradictions cannot be both true and not true without canceling each other out.

Because all truth is God's truth, Aquinas is not afraid of truth claims in other scientific fields, for faith as the higher science is strong enough to

---

1. Thomas Aquinas, *Summa contra Gentiles* 1.7.1.

2. Thomas Aquinas, *Summa theologiae*, trans. Fathers of the English Dominican Province, 5 vols., Christian Classics (New York: Benziger Brothers, 1948), 1 q. 2, a. 2 (hereafter *ST*).

3. Aquinas, *ST* I q. 1, a. 1.

withstand the critiques of the world.[4] All the different branches of knowledge within the natural world have to submit to the truths of logic, but Christ, who is the embodiment of truth itself and also fully divine, does not break the truths of logic, nor is he limited to them. Rather, the truths of logic are revealed to us as expressions of God's nature, and we experience the knowledge of these truths in incomplete ways due to our human finitude. Because Christ is God in the flesh, he exceeds the limitations of the natural world's sciences uniquely. We understand him through faith using the laws of logic, which are expressions of himself.

Christ, being God in the flesh and embodying all truth in his nature, voluntarily submits to the world as its savior, but the world also submits to Christ as its maker. Yet, similar to the observation that the rules of logic transcend the existence of the world in a way such that if the world stopped existing today then the truth of the law of noncontradiction, for example, would continue, the non-created status of the rules of logic can only be such if they are part of the nature of God, who is non-created as well. The logical truths receive their eternal status in virtue of their being a part of God's eternal nature.[5]

These are powerful points to keep in mind because Aquinas believes that God so permeates the world that nothing escapes being affected by

---

4. Aquinas, *Summa contra Gentiles* 1.7.1.

5. Aquinas, *ST* I q. 84, a. 6. This is all part of a larger discussion that recognizes three of Aquinas's views: his moderate realism, his divine simplicity, and his affirmation of Christ as the third member of the Trinity. The moderate realism part comes from the fact that Aquinas follows Aristotle in locating the intelligible content, that is, the forms, in things, instead of in an abstract realm. When humanity comes into contact with another being, the form of humanity abstracts the form from that which it has come into contact with, and thus creates concepts of things in the world; humanity creates concepts of objects and things it comes into contact with. However, humanity's act of having concepts in the mind imitates God, of whom his concepts are those such as logic and numbers; for God, universals are his concepts, which belong to his nature, and as such have an eternal status. Furthermore, these concepts that are a part of God's nature do not result in God having parts or being constructed, by which one now questions the doctrine of divine simplicity (*ST* I q. 3, a. 3). Rather, these concepts exist in God's nature with a status equivalent to that of God's attributes, such as his benevolence, omnipotence, etc. God does not participate in his attributes as humans participate in theirs, but rather God is his nature, purely, and humanity participates in his nature as beings who serve as the effects of God's causal act. Lastly, with Christ being the third member of the Trinity, that which is said of God's essence is applied to Christ equally (*ST* I, q. 39, a. 1).

him. To understand as much of the truth as one can is to better understand something about the nature of God. If this were not the case, then one could reasonably say that all truth does not lead back to God somehow, unlike anything that Aquinas wants to say. In the background to Aquinas's understanding of faith and reason's harmonious relationship, one finds the company of many affirming voices in both biblical and philosophical history.

Christ as the *Logos*

We begin our analysis of how Aquinas grounds his claims that there is no true conflict between faith and reason by looking at the Gospel of John. John begins his gospel by identifying Christ as the Word who was with God and the Word who *was* God (1:1-6). This is a bit of a metaphysical difficulty because, were this description applied to anything or anyone else, we'd be suspicious of textual error on the part of the author, for this introduces an issue of proximity versus identification; that is, either Christ was with God *or* he was God, but it seems logically impossible for him to be both. Furthermore, to the American ear, to call God the "Word" can seem a bit vague. However, both of these metaphysical and linguistic difficulties meet at the crossroads of Christ.

The English usage of the term "word" is thin in comparison to the original term that John uses in Koine Greek, *logos*. On top of the meaning of "word/term," the Greek philosophical word *logos* had a deeper meaning: "reason" or "discourse."[6] Furthermore, under Greek philosopher Heraclitus, the definition of the term takes on the principle of order and knowledge. Plato, another Greek philosopher, then appears and merges his metaphysics with the term *logos* through a hierarchy of existence, in which those at the top have a status as the most real things, while those at the bottom have the lowest status of existence; they are the least real. At the top of this hierarchy are entities called forms, from which all other beings proceed. The forms are eternal and unchangeable, and therefore they possess more reality than beings within the material world that are changeable and noneternal. The Greek philosopher, Plotinus (Greek philosopher number three), furthers Plato's theory by stating that the One is the being that emanates all things from itself, firstly emanating Being, which then emanates the world of the forms, and finally emanates the material world.[7]

6. Christopher Stead, "Logos," in *The Routledge Encyclopedia of Philosophy* (1998), accessed September 11, 2021, doi:10.4324/9780415249126-A065-1.

7. Eyjólfur Kjalar Emilsson, "Plotinus (AD 204/5-70)," in *The Routledge Ency-*

All of that said, Augustine of Hippo, arguably the most notable "Christian Platonist," uses Plato's idea of emanation and Plotinus's idea of the One as the principal source for all of creation in order to follow the apostle John's assessment of Christ as "the divine word." Augustine argues that if words are simply verbal and written signs of invisible concepts and knowledge within humanity, then Christ as God is the physical and visible sign of concepts and knowledge within God.[8] In Platonic language, Christ is not just the truth, but he is the source of truth from which all other truths emanate; he is the emanation and the source of the emanation itself; hence, we return to Christ as the *logos*

By identifying Christ as the *logos*, the first principle of all reason and knowledge, we begin to see that all who exist only participate in the truth as much as they receive truth from Christ himself, regardless of whether they are aware of doing so. Equivalent to one who walks into a well-lit room while ignorant of the room's light source, people can affirm the existence of several truths without recognizing God as the source of those said truths; knowledge of Christ as the source of all truth does not preclude one's unknowing participation in "emanations" of the truth. Yet, to recognize the effects and emanations is insufficient for a relationship with Christ, the light source itself.

In light of this brief history of the *logos*, biblical and philosophical, one observes that when placing one's faith in Christ, who is the embodiment of the highest degree of reason, one must wonder where the space for an "only faith" attitude originates. That is, how would Christ be able to oppose that which is a part of his nature, that of which he is the highest degree?

Common Conspiracy Formulas

Having laid the groundwork for understanding how the *logos* requires seeing faith and reason harmoniously, we can now ask how and why Christians become vulnerable to believing conspiracy theories. First and foremost, what conspiracies often have in common is the observation that since one does not possess all knowledge of an event, there must be a malicious hidden agenda occurring behind the scenes. If the unknown components of an event remain

clopedia of Philosophy (1998), accessed September 11, 2021, doi:10.4324/9780415 249126-A090-.

8. Christian Tornau, "Saint Augustine," in *The Stanford Encyclopedia of Philosophy*, September 25, 2019, https://plato.stanford.edu/archives/sum2020/entries /augustine/.

undisclosed to others, the event is susceptible to conspiracy theories being created about it by those who feel like they are not in the know.

The larger the parties or the stakes involved, the more extravagant the belief. The result is to claim that a sinister and powerful individual or group of people collectively are responsible for secretly misleading the public regarding specific societal or global events, all to bring about their desired, often larger, goals of extending their power. Because a conspiracy theory can comprise one individual or many sinister individuals, be completely false or slightly true but mostly false, and have operations that are either secret or public, strict definition of a conspiracy theory is difficult.[9] Thus, this difficulty in providing a clean-cut definition makes it even more difficult for one to recognize when one is being led astray by a conspiracy theory.

However, on a more basic level, conspiracies are often born out of a group's more foundational beliefs about those they consider their adversaries. If X already did not trust Y, and if Y is in a position of power over X, then anything that Y does that is unknown to X is more likely to be conceived by X as something done out of malice. When enough of these unknowns accumulate in the eyes of X, then X finds himself or herself at the origination of a conspiracy theory. One who believes one is being denied one's equal due (truth, power, rights, or freedoms) by another in power or authority, when combined with an accumulation of unknown activities by that same person in power or authority, is ripe to fall victim to a conspiracy theory.

As difficult as it can be to identify a conspiracy theory, failing to check all beliefs is counter to the call from Christ for Christians to "be wise as serpents and innocent as doves" (Matt. 10:16 NRSV). This is also apparent in the book of Acts when the Berean Jews searched their scriptures, in what for us now is the Old Testament, to see if there was any truth to what the apostle Paul proclaimed about Jesus (Acts 17:10–12); that is, the knowledge of God's Word was sufficient to prevent the Bereans from being susceptible to false beliefs of their day. Furthermore, this supports the faith and reason thesis because reason can help to better interpret things of faith and thus commune more with the truths of the world, and ultimately with its maker.

Blind Faith: The Rejection of Faith and Reason

It is becoming more acceptable to envision a Christian faith that fails to interact with reason and science. A clear example of this is Christians in-

---

9. Marc Pauly, "Conspiracy Theories," in *Internet Encyclopedia of Philosophy*, accessed June 10, 2022, https://iep.utm.edu/conspira/#H8.

volved in the QAnon conspiracy. While this theory is not exactly Christian, it has been interpreted by its Christian adherents to be consistent with biblical eschatology.[10] Christians point to the biblical command to look out for the antichrist, a malevolent figure whose wide influence will lead several Christians astray from the faith (2 Thess. 2:3–12; 1 John 4:1–6). Furthermore, the antichrist's rise will occur before Christ's second coming and ultimate return to earth to gather Christ's faithful flock (1 John 2:18–27). However, a sector of Christians heavily put forth the interpretation that the antichrist will be a political leader (Rev. 13–17).

When one combines this eschatological interpretation with a context of America's growing de-religiosity, then the adherents of the QAnon conspiracy, both Christian and non-Christian, observe a common enemy—those who are more politically left leaning.[11] This is especially true when one compares current American de-religiosity to that of previous generations, with this trend being particularly the case within the Democratic Party.[12] Christians within the QAnon conspiracy conclude that it is the eschatological garden of the left from which the antichrist will blossom. Therefore, like a child anticipating the return of a military-deployed parent, one will, understandably, look to explain every occurrence in light of one's expectation and anticipation of one's beloved parent's return. This expectation occurs during the child's simultaneous recognition of the multiple groups of people who failed to expect the soldier's return and ridiculed the child for his or her expectation. A disjunctive relationship between faith and reason, where faith is preferred regardless of the discoveries of philosophical and scientific reason, shows itself in the following two ways: advocating biblical interpretations that ignore necessary literary elements, and diminishing any possibility that truth to the contrary of the conspiracy's claims can exist in other groups.

---

10. Dawn Araujo-Hawkins, "The Making of the QAnon Conspiracy Cult," *Christian Century*, November 30, 2020, 16.

11. Araujo-Hawkins, "The Making of the QAnon Conspiracy Cult," 16.

12. "In U.S., Decline of Christianity Continues at Rapid Pace," Pew Research Center, October 17, 2019, https://www.pewforum.org/2019/10/17/in-u-s-decline-of-christianity-continues-at-rapid-pace/; Daniel Cox and Robert P. Jones, "America's Changing Religious Identity," Public Religion Research Institute, September 6, 2017, https://www.prri.org/research/american-religious-landscape-christian-religiously-unaffiliated/.

Further Logical Consequences

Not only is the rejection of faith and reason within Christianity dangerous because it lends itself to affirming falsehoods within conspiracy theories, but it also distracts, if not prevents entirely, one from affirming other conclusions that have more evidence of being true. One of the largest proofs of this within American Christianity is the continual skepticism or outright rejection of claims of anti-Black racism, all despite a history rife with proof of the matter. Instead, the most common response is to advocate for a view of America that simply is not true, a view of America that says that such claims of negative racial treatments are all in the country's past and all that's left is the minimal residual cases that media outlets overblow.[13] Therefore, large-scale efforts to end racial animus are seen as unnecessary. Some even believe they are unpatriotic. However, racism has been and remains alive and well. From 1619, when the first black slaves arrived in America; to the 1830s, when blacks were considered three-fifths of a person; to the Emancipation Proclamation during the Civil War (which was fought over states' rights to own enslaved bodies) and Jim Crow's pushing back the gains of black Americans in the Reconstruction era; to the Great Migration, in which black Americans were escaping the terrors of lynching; to the civil rights era, where Blacks could finally register to vote in federal elections; to the drug war, which became nothing more than a war on Black men; to efforts to gut the Voting Rights Acts in the name of "voter security"—all this was done to Black families by white Christians in a nation where it was claimed that Christian values thrived and were to be protected at all costs.[14]

As already mentioned, Christians caught within the QAnon conspiracy, and even Christians who do not formally claim to affirm QAnon but reject the validity of this history regarding anti-black racism, must interpret these facts as lies and embellishments, or, even worse, try to justify these actions biblically. However, a more dire consequence of such a justification is the following: *one has to become more skeptical over the history of the last four hundred years, which has already been confirmed by several authorities on the matter, but still trust that biblical writers, who wrote close to two thousand years ago, told the truth on supernatural issues pertaining to Christ.* This places one

---

13. Jamar Tisby, *The Color of Compromise: The Truth about the American Church's Complicity in Racism* (Grand Rapids: Zondervan, 2019), 21.

14. Tisby, *The Color of Compromise*, 210.

in a position where one must blindly trust biblical writers with faith alone, regardless of one's historical proximity to facts that may suggest otherwise, and not faith *and reason,* which is able to affirm both the histories.[15]

One's Right to Believe What One Wants

Those viewing faith and reason harmoniously are not to deny that they choose what they believe. For not even God himself denied humanity a free will. However, that freedom did not mean that one could choose the consequences of said choice. As seen in the story of Genesis, God tells Adam and Eve they are free to eat anything they want in the garden except the fruit from the tree of knowledge of good and evil, for to do so means that they will surely die. Satan tempts Adam and Eve to disobey God on the basis that God is apparently holding out on them, stating that God is not concerned about their potential death, but rather God knows their eating from the tree will make Adam and Eve like him. There are consequences for such a choice, as with any decision.

15. This argument essentially says that those who adhere to the conspiracy of QAnon are more willing to rest the validity of their position on a position that is more recent and has less evidence than that which has an older history and yet more evidence on the matter. In 2021, we really should not be trying to convince people that racism is real and has long-lasting social effects for today. Often people will look at stories of Christ and say that they wish they had lived during biblical times so they could witness the events for themselves (equivalent to "Doubting Thomas" in John 20:24-29, whom Christ condemned for this type of strict skepticism); this seems to communicate a dissatisfaction with the evidence that exists in front of them. However, there is something pause-worthy about someone who is willing to faithfully believe the validity of the biblical events and yet deny the evidence of long-standing racism. This suggests that not only is one simply selective with that which one will believe, but that evidence to a conclusion does not matter on the level that it should. Hence, mass skepticism toward the effects of racism, especially from Christians, has the following effect: Why can we not get you to trust us when we say that racism is real and pervasive in America, but you do not express any doubt in the biblical events from two thousand years ago? The more reasonable position to take is that despite their differences (one concerns the history of miracles and one concerns a history of oppression), we are able to recognize that there is strong evidence for both cases in a way that does not cancel them both out; blind faith will exclude reason, while rational faith will use reason to better recognize the truths regarding other questions.

The consequences of Christians failing to check their beliefs in harmony with reason are (1) they become more vulnerable to believing that which is not true; (2) they stray from the faith, the very thing that they believe the conspiracy theories will prevent them from doing in the face of a changing society; and (3) they become less influential in the effort to show Christ to the nations. While the Genesis account is not traditionally considered a conspiracy theory (nor is this an argument I am making), there are some similarities to that which one finds in the Jim Jones cult, QAnon, and others: there was the truth of the matter (God told Adam and Eve to not eat from the tree) and the exploitation of unknown components by those claiming they were under an oppressive adversarial power (Eve did not know why they couldn't eat from the tree and therefore was convinced by the serpent that God was being cruel by forbidding them from eating from the tree), and thus, they (Satan) misled others (Adam and Eve) to believe the same. All had a free choice to act and choose their beliefs as they saw fit, but believing that one can believe whatever one wants without facing consequences for those beliefs proves the point at hand: reason does not show this to be a rational position in a communal world, but rather an irrational one.[16]

Athens and Jerusalem: Caving in to Worldly Thinking

Another response to Aquinas's position on the harmonization of faith and reason is to argue that one cannot expect a nonbeliever to understand the things of God. Therefore, this harmonization is just a way of caving in to worldly thinking. In other words, in the words of Tertullian, "What does Athens have to do with Jerusalem?"[17] The answer to this question exists in one of the closest things within the human experience: language. Consider the following: At the end of Malachi, the people of Israel were held

16. The point being made here is that having the right to believe what one wants does not remove the possibility of believing wrongly and irrationally. We do not get to choose an irrational belief and abdicate the consequences of that choice. Therefore, instead of this being a successful argument, this proves the point of my argument.

17. Tertullian, "Prescription against Heretics," trans. Peter Holmes, in *Ante-Nicene Fathers*, ed. Alexander Roberts and James Donaldson (Peabody, MA: Hendrickson, 1994), 3:249. Accessed in Jay Green, *An Invitation to Academic Studies* (Phillipsburg, NJ: P&R, 2014), 8.

in Babylonian captivity. Next in line to rule over Israel are the Persians, then the Greeks, and then the Romans. While the Israelites held on to their Hebrew language, they also spoke a type of Greek heavily influenced by the societies of people around them.

Language encapsulates not only different terms of the people who speak it, but also their cultures. The biblical writers are not an exception to this rule regarding their Greek usage, as seen previously with John's use of "*logos*" as a description for Christ. Therefore, to the Tertullian-like question, one can respond that "the language of Athens can help clarify the concepts within the given language and can be adopted by Jerusalem." This act of clarifying concepts within the language is not an example of God's Word caving in at the feet of the secular throne, but rather it is using worldly thinking to aid in one's ability to better understand God's Word, which is comprised of worldly elements. Hence, this further displays the miracle of God's Word of which He uses human conventions to show his glory to the world.

Conclusion

We began by unpacking Thomas Aquinas's thesis on the harmonization of faith and reason. In this explanation, Aquinas splits the difference between the two methods of understanding reality, that of faith and that of reason; they are different because they start with different principles, but they are the same in that they take the same method of moving from principle to conclusions. The principle of science explains the general understanding of the world, but principles of faith explain the specifics of God's interaction with the world. Because both are means of knowing God's truth and truth cannot contradict itself, their contradicting conclusions are only apparent and are resolved either through the course of time, reconsidering both positions, or in the heavenly life to come.

The next section explained how Christ is the *logos*, the embodiment of truth as the highest principle, emphasizing that one should always seek truth because understanding all truth brings us in closer communion with Him. The following section pivoted toward an explanation of the typical formulas that conspiracy theories take. It then highlighted how conspiracy adherents often advocate for a "faith only" approach rather than a faith-and-reason approach, particularly within the context of a more recent QAnon conspiracy theory. The next section analyzed some of the logical consequences of that theory's rejection of faith and reason. The last consideration featured responses to this analysis.

Christians should avoid believing in conspiracy theories for many reasons. However, foundational among them is that we ought to be committed to truth, including truth delivered by faith, truth delivered by reason, and truth delivered by harmonizing the two.

References

Araujo-Hawkins, Dawn. "The Making of the QAnon Conspiracy Cult." *Christian Century*, November 30, 2020.

Cox, Daniel, and Robert P. Jones. "America's Changing Religious Identity." Public Religion Research Institute, September 6, 2017. https://www.prri.org/research/american-religious-landscape-christian-religiously-unaffiliated/.

Emilsson, Eyjólfur Kjalar. "Plotinus (AD 204/5–70)." In *The Routledge Encyclopedia of Philosophy* (1998). Accessed September 11, 2021. doi:10.4324/9780415249126-A090-.

"In U.S., Decline of Christianity Continues at Rapid Pace." Pew Research Center, October 17, 2019. https://www.pewforum.org/2019/10/17/in-u-s-decline-of-christianity-continues-at-rapid-pace/.

Pauly, Marc. "Conspiracy Theories." In Internet Encyclopedia of Philosophy. Accessed June 10, 2022. https://iep.utm.edu/conspira/#H8.

Stead, Christopher. "Logos." In *The Routledge Encyclopedia of Philosophy* (1998). Accessed September 11, 2021. doi:10.4324/9780415249126-A065-1.

Tertullian. "Prescription against Heretics." Translated by Peter Holmes. In *Ante-Nicene Fathers*, edited by Alexander Roberts and James Donaldson. Peabody, MA: Hendrickson, 1994.

Thomas Aquinas. *Summa theologiae*. Translated by the Fathers of the English Dominican Province. 5 vols. Christian Classics. New York: Benziger Brothers, 1948.

Tisby, Jamar. *The Color of Compromise: The Truth about the American Church's Complicity in Racism*. Grand Rapids: Zondervan, 2019.

Tornau, Christian. "Saint Augustine." In *The Stanford Encyclopedia of Philosophy*. September 25, 2019. https://plato.stanford.edu/archives/sum2020/entries/augustine/.

14

THE GREATEST CONSPIRACY EVER

Susan Peppers-Bates

In the mid 1990s I heard a sermon that I will never forget.[1] In discussing the parable of the good Samaritan, and Christ's call to love our neighbor, the pastor paused and rhetorically asked, "What do you know of the Samaritans?" The Samaritans were not Jews (though they followed some parts of the Torah), and they were viewed disparagingly by the Jews. The fact that those viewed as upright in the story, the priest and the Levite, walked by the wounded and naked man in the ditch, fearing to sully their own ritual purity or inconvenience their day, was an important lesson not to neglect our obligations to others for selfish reasons. Even more importantly, the fact that the despised "other," the Samaritan, showed compassion and followed God's law that we love our neighbor as ourselves was the deeper message of the parable. The outcast is our neighbor, and may be a better neighbor to us than we are to him or her or to our community members. The priest paused and said, "Who is the Samaritan today? Is it the gay man that you shun? Is it the third-world immigrant crossing the US border? What lessons of God's love do you miss when you turn away from those different from you with fear and judgment?"

In this chapter I want to draw on the work of Miranda Fricker and feminist theologians such as Pamela Sue Anderson, Mary Daly, Cheryl Townsend Gilkes, Grace Jantzen, Judith Plaskow, and Rosemary Reuther

1. I do not recall the date, but the sermon was from Father Lou Temme, Trinity Memorial Church, Philadelphia. Given the passing of time, although I use quotation marks, this is more of a paraphrase.

to argue that the seemingly peculiar phenomenon of US evangelical Christians accepting baseless conspiracy theories is grounded in a prior, deeper tendency of Judeo-Christianity in general to reduce God to a white male idol, and in particular to silence or ignore the voices of women, people of color, LGBTQI, and other marginalized groups. When our symbols hold up only a subset of humanity as made in the image of God, it becomes easier to view those who differ as unworthy to lead or join the Christian community. Once some are viewed as second-class citizens in the body of Christ, their voices and witness fall on deaf ears. And once a group is demeaned, it becomes much easier to believe that they engage in pedophilia, drink blood, cause COVID, or any number of wild claims. Only when the Christian community struggles to expand our understanding of the divine, and to truly see and attend to all of our neighbors—regardless of their differences from us—will this tragic ethical and intellectual flaw be healed.

Making Unjust Meanings by Excluding Some Knowers

Human beings are social, rational animals. Philosophers in the West from Plato and Aristotle to today have argued that a fundamental component of our being is our capacity for wonder, curiosity, and innovation: we are thinkers. Unlike animals and physical objects, we transcended mere instinct and natural law to choose our actions freely and to create language. With language come systems of complex and abstract meaning and representation. Human beings have a sense of self, an ability to think and reflect on their own thoughts and beings, that animals apparently lack. Our shared social life gives rise to "the symbolic," the "broad conceptual patterns of civilization," including not only language but also music, art, ritual, and politics.[2] Judeo-Christian theologians further claim that our faculties or powers of knowing and willing mark us as made in the image of God. And as many feminist philosophers have critiqued, the foundation of the dominant Western understanding of the divine rests on God as Father, the font of abstract reason, power, and guarantor of meaning.

Across the centuries, religious symbols of God and the divine have shaped both individual senses of self and the structures of society itself. As Judith Plaskow describes this: "Religious symbols give resonance and authority to a community's self-understanding and serve to support and

2. Grace M. Jantzen, *Becoming Divine: Towards a Feminist Philosophy of Religion* (Bloomington: Indiana University Press, 1999), 10.

sustain its conception of the world. The male images Jews use in speaking to and about God emerge out of and maintain a religious system in which men are normative Jews and women are perceived as Other."[3]

The metaphor of God as father, lord, shepherd, king—traditionally masculine imagery—reinforces social expectations that men better approximate the divine, leading in synagogue, church, and the world. Indeed, in the Middle Ages, theologians even debated whether women were merely *less* in the image of God or *not at all* in the divine image, thus requiring salvation through marriage and childbirth.[4] As Mary Daly succinctly describes this patriarchization, "if God is male, then the male is God."[5]

Thus, we get the paradox that, on the one hand, God is incorporeal and ineffable, but on the other, language and symbolism insist on his maleness. What should have merely been one metaphor among others has shrunk down the human imagination and reduced the symbolized to the symbol—few things can as quickly produce vitriol and attack as using feminine symbols or language to describe God.[6] As such, God's masculinity has become an idol: "The metaphor is no longer simply a way of pointing to God but is identified with God, so that any change in the image seems to defame or disparage God 'himself.'"[7] In a similar fashion, Western art, church icons, and stained glass all too often display white, blond, and blue-eyed images of Christ, his disciples, and the Virgin Mary, despite the historical inaccuracy of such skin and hair tones.

Rosemary Radford Ruether explains the logic motivating the whitewashing of Christ as the logical conclusion of four centuries of conquest, enslavement, and theft of native lands: "It is in the context of this implied godly, moral and redeemed reality higher nature that 'whiteness' implies a connection to Christ, the epitome of goodness, godliness, and redeemed and redemptive being over against its opposites. That Christ must 'look'

---

3. Judith Plaskow, *Standing at Sinai: Judaism from a Feminist Perspective* (New York: HarperCollins, 1991), 170.

4. See Nancy Tuana, *The Less Noble Sex: Scientific, Religious, and Philosophical Conceptions of Woman's Nature* (Bloomington: Indiana University Press, 1993), chap. 3.

5. Mary Daly, *Beyond God the Father* (Boston: Beacon, 1974), 19.

6. For a fascinating historical examination of a time when feminine imagery of God was not so problematic for Christianity, see Caroline Walker Bynum, *Jesus as Mother: Studies in the Spirituality of the High Middle Ages* (Berkeley: University of California Press, 1982).

7. Plaskow, *Standing at Sinai*, 171-72.

and 'be' white in Christian thought and art, although perhaps beginning as an ethnic convention, takes on a theological meaning."[8]

The cultural symbolism that portrays God as male portrays Christ as white, and the message of natural hierarchy suffuses the culture. Indeed, the whiteness of Christ's family continues to be so normalized in the twenty-first century that Fisher-Price just released a little white holy family set for toddlers to play with.[9] Professor and theologian Anthea Butler captures how problematic this continued white imagery is with her succinct tweet, "Every time you see white Jesus you see white supremacy."[10]

What does it mean to female believers, to believers of color, when they do not see themselves in the dominant religious language, leadership, or symbols? Miranda Fricker has helpfully named this problem as one of being left out of creating a culture's shared understandings, to describe being socially subordinated and thus excluded from generating social meaning in religion, law, academia, politics, etc.[11] When you have experiences with no social concepts or metaphors to capture them, your capacity as a knower, and even your self-understanding, has been wrongfully stunted. Fricker clarifies with the following example: before society recognized sexual harassment as a wrong, women had no words to describe what they suffered at the hands of male colleagues and bosses; the law likewise could not recognize a problem with no name.[12]

In other words, with marginalized groups, their experiences in general will be excluded, and this reinforces prejudices against them, culminating in their absence from society's project of creating shared meanings: "the injustice of having some *significant area of one's social experience obscured from the collective understanding owing to a structural identity prejudice in the collective hermeneu-*

8. Rosemary Radford Ruether, "Is Christ White? Racism and Christology," in *Christology and Whiteness: What Would Jesus Do?*, ed. George Yancy (London: Routledge, 2012), 105.

9. Emily McFarlan Miller, "Christian Group Petitions Fisher-Price to Replace Nativity Playset Depicting Holy Family as White," Religion News Service, August 6, 2021, https://religionnews.com/2021/08/06/christian-group-petitions-toy -company-to-replace-nativity-playset-depicting-holy-family-as-white/.

10. Anthea Butler, Twitter post, June 24, 2020, https://twitter.com/rns/status /1330171613195702759.

11. Miranda Fricker, *Epistemic Injustice: Power and the Ethics of Knowing* (Oxford: Oxford University Press, 2010), 11–12. Her technical terms are "hermeneutical injustice" and "epistemic injustice."

12. Fricker, *Epistemic Injustice*, 150–52.

tical resource."[13] Once you are marked as not the right "kind" (here male) of person whose experiences matter, you also become the wrong kind of person to lead churches, synagogues, universities, companies, or countries.

Consider a similar example of being excluded as unworthy of inclusion in the religious meaning-making community focused on the experiences of people of color. During the age of Euro-American conquest and enslavement, theologians formulated unbiblical doctrines of "polygenesis" to argue that Africans and Native Americans were created by God in separate, secondary creations from white people.[14] Indeed, some argued that such "savages" were soulless, and thus despoiling them of lands and their very bodies was not a sin against one's neighbor: For how could the subhuman, distant, or fully separate from God be one's neighbor? American Christian slave owners banned the enslaved from learning to read and used the Bible to justify their sinful behavior, much as segregationists and racists refused and still refuse to worship with people of color and continue to treat them as though they were not also children of God. Debates over integrating the clergy and churches were ugly affairs, as debates about women clergy and LGBTQI clergy continue to fuel hate and not *agapē*.

Perhaps it should come as no surprise that despite the rise of academic books and articles focused on the concepts of intellectual (epistemic) injustice, little has been written about religion as a source of this cognitive vice. Indeed, the one recent article by Ian James Kidd that I found focused on the secular community's worldview silencing or marginalizing the viewpoint of people of faith: if your naturalistic framework itself excludes God, then your worldview denies credibility to religious experiences by definition. As Kidd describes this phenomenon: "Most cases of epistemic injustice involve deficiencies of epistemic goods—credibility and intelligibility—that stem from negative prejudice or lack of hermeneutical resources. I want to suggest that, in certain cases, the very possibility of credibility or intelligibility is removed, and that this can result from adoption by an epistemic agent of a certain worldview."[15]

Thus, while Kidd wants naturalism to count as a worldview that can discount the veracity of religious believers and rule them out as viable

---

13. Fricker, *Epistemic Injustice*, 155.

14. See discussion in Terence D. Keel, "Religion, Polygenism and the Early Science of Human Origins," *History of the Human Sciences* 26, no. 2 (2013): 3-32.

15. Ian James Kidd, "Epistemic Injustice and Religion," in *The Routledge Handbook of Epistemic Injustice*, ed. Ian James Kidd, Jose Medina, and Gaile Pohlhaus Jr. (New York: Routledge, 2017), 393.

contributors to shared social meaning, I am arguing that patriarchal white supremacy is a worldview that discounts whole classes of people as credible participants in the creation of religious meaning. Further, as I argue in the next section, by marginalizing knowers who are outside the white male dominant norm, this worldview leaves its holders vulnerable to intellectual vice and conspiratorial credulity.

Testimonial Injustice and Conspiracy Theories

Members of marginalized groups that have been excluded from making meaning, and from inclusion in religious symbolism, suffer a second injustice at the hands of large portions of the Christian community: their words are not heard, or if heard, they are not believed or given credence. As Fricker describes this general phenomenon, when prejudicial images in any community's social imagination lead a listener to deflate the credibility of a speaker, she has been "wronged specifically in her capacity as a knower."[16] Giving and exchanging testimony, being heard and believed, is part of what makes us human. Indeed, traditionally, possession of an intellect or reason is one of the characteristics that mark human beings as being made in the divine image. So, if a Black woman shares her religious experience of God as on the side of a suffering Black community facing police brutality, and white Christians accuse her of "playing the race card," they wrong her and also stunt their own growth as Christians.

In a recent op-ed, Peter Wehner contrasts the lack of Southern Baptist Convention (SBC) condemnations of the QAnon theory with six SBC seminary presidents' condemnations of critical race theory (CRT) as "incompatible with the Baptist Faith & Message."[17] To make this clearer: critical race theory argues that racism is not a matter of individual bad apples but rather a system of racial privilege and inequality written into America's founding documents and institutions. At its heart, CRT is a cry from the wilderness for white Americans to face up to and dismantle our founding sin of enslavement, theft of native lands, legalized discrimination, and continuing de facto discrimination.

In contrast, QAnon argues that Donald Trump is fighting a cabal of pedophiles and traffickers run by Democrats, Hollywood elites, and, in some

---

16. Fricker, *Epistemic Injustice*, 20.

17. As quoted in Peter Wehner, "Will Christian America Withstand the Pull of QAnon?" *New York Times*, June 18, 2021, https://www.nytimes.com/2021/06/18/opinion/southern-baptist-convention-christianity.html.

versions, aliens. Yet, no SBC seminary presidents have issued statements condemning QAnon as incompatible with the Baptist faith and mission. Indeed, a recent survey by the American Enterprise Institute (AEI) found that 31 percent of white evangelical Christian Republicans think this conspiracy is true.[18] Commenting on the survey, the director of the AEI Survey Center on American Life, David Cox, said, "As with a lot of questions in the survey, white evangelicals stand out in terms of their belief in conspiracy theories and the idea that violence can be necessary. They're far more likely to embrace all these different conspiracies."[19] In another recent article, sociology professor Samuel Perry commented, "I'm actually not surprised that evangelicals are more likely to believe those kinds of things. . . . Evangelicals are not socially isolated, but they are informationally isolated."[20]

I would argue that there is a direct line from the otherization and exclusion of women, people of color, and LGBTQI people historically from Christian religious meaning making and symbolism that continues and manifests through demonization, silencing, and failing to listen to members of those communities. Worse still, this prior interpretive and testimonial silencing make some Christians prone to believe conspiracies about members of marginalized groups—and perhaps make it easier to dehumanize and thus promote violence against them. Consider just two recent news stories:

> Pastor Rick Wiles has consistently spread conspiracy theories about COVID-19 on his show, and as senior pastor at Flowing Streams Church, blames Jewish people, Chinese people, gay men, and transgender kids for the disease, as divine punishment. When he and several of his news crew had a COVID outbreak, fill-in host Lauren Witzke blamed demonic spirits for attacking the show because they hosted proclaimed ex-gay Milo Yiannopoulos.[21] These responses follow a long tradition of hate

18. Wehner, "Will Christian America Withstand the Pull of QAnon?"

19. As quoted in "A 'Scary' Survey Finding: 4 in 10 Republicans Say Political Violence May Be Necessary," NPR, February 11, 2021, https://www.npr .org/2021/02/11/966498544/a-scary-survey-finding-4-in-10-republicans-say -political-violence-may-be-necessa.

20. Kaleigh Rogers, "Why QAnon Has Attracted So Many White Evangelicals," FiveThirtyEight, March 4, 2021, https://fivethirtyeight.com/features/why-qanon -has-attracted-so-many-white-evangelicals/.

21. Alex Bollinger, "Televangelists Say Satan Gave Them COVID-19 Because

that paints Jewish people, people of color, and gay people as sources of disease rather than children of God.

The headline blared: "Dozens Arrested in Los Angeles as Anti-Trans Protest Outside Spa Turns Violent." Following reporting by Tucker Carlson of Fox News criticizing the spa's trans-inclusive policies, protesters chanted the popular QAnon slogan of "save our children" as they harassed patrons of the spa. One woman described being thrown to the ground by protesters, who also threw water on her and yelled about Jesus.[22]

Sadly, I could list many more recent news stories of Christians who embrace hate-mongering conspiracy theories that do not demonstrate love or charity or compassion for one's neighbor. Governors push bills to allow professionals and businesses to deny services to LGBTQI individuals. Laws continue to be proposed in multiple states to ban trans youth from playing sports. Bills to block LGBTQI individuals from fostering or adopting children proliferate. Certainly, such behavior has led to millennials leaving the church.[23]

How is such vitriol given a pass by those who profess to follow Jesus? I believe that the background failure, rooted in misogyny, racism, and other forms of marginalization, first silenced and dehumanized marginalized groups. This first collective myopic idol worship of God as only white, male, straight, and able-bodied prepared the second individual vice of failing to see or hear any neighbors who fell outside the dominant group, taken as the only ones made fully in the divine image. The stories that have haunted me in particular are those of bills being promulgated in Texas and Arkansas, to deny professional services—including medical care—to people thought or perceived to be LGBTQI on grounds of religious freedom. In other words, to be Christian means you can walk by bleeding persons on the side of the road if they look gay to you. Who is the Samaritan today? How could white evangelicals who embrace QAnon conspiracy theories and clamor to ban critical

Milo Went Ex-Gay," *LGBTQ Nation*, June 8, 2021, https://www.lgbtqnation.com /2021/06/televangelists-say-satan-gave-covid-19-milo-went-ex-gay/.

22. Lois Beckett and Sam Levin, "Dozens Arrested in Los Angeles as Anti-Trans Protest Outside Spa Turns Violent," *Guardian*, July 17, 2021, https://www.theguard ian.com/society/2021/jul/18/dozens-arrested-in-los-angeles-as-anti-trans-protest -outside-spa-turns-violent.

23. Adam Gabbatt, "'Allergic Reaction to US Religious Right' Fueling Decline of Religion, Experts Say," *Guardian*, April 5, 2021, https://www.theguardian.com /world/2021/apr/05/americans-religion-rightwing-politics-decline.

race theory learn from the Samaritan if she were gay or black or Muslim or disabled? What if Christ asks us for food or shelter or medical attention, and we fail to heed the call because we cannot see or hear the Samaritan?

Christ has called us to follow the Samaritan's example: note that this means one viewed as a heretic by the religious leaders of the day showed God's way, and acted to love his neighbor as himself. Christians caught up in conspiracies that promote throwing stones, rejecting children with gay parents from school,[24] and demonizing and slandering "others" must take a hard look at themselves. Miranda Fricker would argue that such people are failing intellectually and ethically at justice. Surely, they also are failing to heed the call of Christ to "love because he first loved us" (1 John 4:19). Describing his attempt at "restorative conversations" with church members espousing QAnon and similar conspiracy theories, the Reverend Mark Fuggit of Round Grove Baptist Church (Miller, Missouri) likewise suggested "emphasizing (religious) virtues like loving your neighbor."[25]

Although I converted to Christianity as a college student and spent many years attending Roman Catholic and Episcopalian services, I do not recall more than that one sermon I discussed above focusing on the status of Samaritans as outsiders, and on what that meant as an analogue for today's oppressed groups. I recently discovered, through the work of Cheryl Townsend Gilkes, that the African American preaching and musical tradition frequently turned to Jesus's travels and ministry in Samaria, viewing "Jesus' presence in Samaria as indicative of his determination to stand with the poor and the oppressed."[26] In addition to the story of the good Samaritan, Jesus healed a group of ten lepers: and only the Samaritan stayed to praise and give him thanks, much as the religious elite walked by the injured man and the Samaritan helped him. Both the Good Samaritan and the leprous Samaritan had the eyes to see people in their need or in

24. Tyler Butler, "Child Expelled from School over Same-Sex Parents," KTUL/WKRC, August 7, 2021, https://local12.com/news/nation-world/child-expelled-from-school-over-same-sex-parents.

25. Mya Jaradat, "Why Would Christians Embrace Conspiracy Theories?" *Deseret News*, March 28, 2021, https://www.deseret.com/indepth/2021/3/28/22334183/what-group-of-christians-most-likely-believe-conspiracy-theories-white-evangelicals-qanon-faith.

26. Cheryl Townsend Gilkes, "Jesus Must Needs Go through Samaria: Disestablishing the Mountains of Race and the Hegemony of Whiteness," in Yancey, *Christology and Whiteness*, 59.

their generosity and to act accordingly. Drawing on Fricker's language, we might say that their standpoint from the margins of society gave them a more expansive view of reality, whereas the myopic view of the privileged insiders gave them cognitive blinders.

When Jesus spoke to the Samaritan woman at the well, Gilkes argues, and asked her for water, he broke across boundaries not simply of gender but also of in-group Judeans versus outcast Samaritans.[27] He saw her in her humanity, taught her, and John's Gospel describes her as going forth and making disciples for Christ. This is the power of being seen and loved, the radical power of God's universal mission. Christ excludes no one. The tragedy of contemporary Christians who cleave to wild conspiracy theories that demonize the "different" is not only their intellectual vice of failing to hear the voices of testimony of the oppressed, but also their failing to see and to offer compassion and love to those whom God has commanded them to love.[28]

References

Beckett, Lois, and Sam Levin. "Dozens Arrested in Los Angeles as Anti-Trans Protest Outside Spa Turns Violent." *Guardian*, July 17, 2021. https://www.theguardian.com/society/2021/jul/18/dozens-arrested-in-los-angeles-as-anti-trans-protest-outside-spa-turns-violent.

Bollinger, Alex. "Televangelists Say Satan Gave Them COVID-19 Because Milo Went Ex-Gay." *LGBTQ Nation*, June 8, 2021. https://www.lgbtqnation.com/2021/06/televangelists-say-satan-gave-covid-19-milo-went-ex-gay/.

Butler, Tyler. "Child Expelled from School over Same-Sex Parents." KTUL/WKRC, August 7, 2021. https://local12.com/news/nation-world/child-expelled-from-school-over-same-sex-parents.

Bynum, Caroline Walker. *Jesus as Mother: Studies in the Spirituality of the High Middle Ages*. Berkeley: University of California Press, 1982.

Daly, Mary. *Beyond God the Father*. Boston: Beacon, 1974.

Fricker, Miranda. *Epistemic Injustice: Power and the Ethics of Knowing*. Oxford: Oxford University Press, 2010.

Gabbatt, Adam. "'Allergic Reaction to US Religious Right' Fueling Decline of Religion, Experts Say." *Guardian*, April 5, 2021. https://www.theguard

27. Gilkes, "Jesus Must Needs Go through Samaria," 65–66.

28. My thanks to Mike Austin, Christopher Bell, Stephen Davis, Kadhapriya Lindo, Todd Peppers, Joshua Rust, and Rebecca Selover for helpful feedback on drafts of this chapter.

ian.com/world/2021/apr/05/americans-religion-rightwing-politics -decline.

Jantzen, Grace M. *Becoming Divine: Towards a Feminist Philosophy of Religion.* Bloomington: Indiana University Press, 1999.

Jaradat, Mya. "Why Would Christians Embrace Conspiracy Theories?" *Deseret News*, March 28, 2021. https://www.deseret.com/indepth /2021/3/28/22334183/what-group-of-christians-most-likely-believe-co nspiracy-theories-white-evangelicals-qanon-faith.

Keel, Terence D. "Religion, Polygenism and the Early Science of Human Origins." *History of the Human Sciences* 26, no. 2 (2013): 3–32.

Kidd, Ian James. "Epistemic Injustice and Religion." In *The Routledge Handbook of Epistemic Injustice*, edited by Ian James Kidd, Jose Medina, and Gaile Pohlhaus Jr. New York: Routledge, 2017.

Miller, Emily McFarlan. "Christian Group Petitions Fisher-Price to Replace Nativity Playset Depicting Holy Family as White." Religion News Service, August 6, 2021. https://religionnews.com/2021/08/06/christian-group -petitions-toy-company-to-replace-nativity-playset-depicting-holy-fa mily-as-white/.

Plaskow, Judith. *Standing at Sinai: Judaism from a Feminist Perspective.* New York: HarperCollins, 1991.

Rogers, Kaleigh. "Why QAnon Has Attracted So Many White Evangelicals." FiveThirtyEight, March 4, 2021. https://fivethirtyeight.com/features /why-qanon-has-attracted-so-many-white-evangelicals/.

Ruether, Rosemary Radford. "Is Christ White? Racism and Christology." In *Christology and Whiteness: What Would Jesus Do?*, edited by George Yancy. London: Routledge, 2012.

"A 'Scary' Survey Finding: 4 in 10 Republicans Say Political Violence May Be Necessary." NPR, February 11, 2021. https://www.npr .org/2021/02/11/966498544/a-scary-survey-finding-4-in-10-republi cans-say-political-violence-may-be-necessa.

Tuana, Nancy. *The Less Noble Sex: Scientific, Religious, and Philosophical Conceptions of Woman's Nature.* Bloomington: Indiana University Press, 1993.

Wehner, Peter. "Will Christian America Withstand the Pull of QAnon?" *New York Times*, June 18, 2021. https://www.nytimes.com/2021/06/18/opin ion/southern-baptist-convention-christianity.html.

15

TESTING TEACHINGS
AND TORCHING TEACHERS

Rick Langer

Many years ago, I had a conversation with a couple of friends who were experiencing a very divisive church conflict. Things had gotten truly ugly. After recounting some of the ugliness, one friend pointed out that the combatants probably just felt like they were trying to be faithful to Paul's command to test every teaching (1 Thess. 5:21). My other friend sighed and said, "Yes, I suppose so. But we are supposed to test the teaching, not torch the teacher."

"Test the teaching, don't torch the teacher." It is a good line. It would make a great bumper sticker. It is pithy, but it includes some deep wisdom. It warns against two pitfalls. First, "test the teaching" warns against a sin of negligence—that we might swallow everything that is taught us without giving careful consideration to its truth. Second, "don't torch the teacher" warns against a sin of excess—that we go overboard as we test teachings and end up attacking or vilifying teachers instead.

One might suppose there is enough distance between these two pitfalls to leave room for a pretty broad playing field—just like there seems to be plenty of room between lighting your stove and burning down your house. You can pretty easily do one and avoid the other. But unfortunately, when it comes to our current communication climate, the challenge is greater than it first appears.

Here's a good example of the problem. A friend of mine is a seminary professor who recently wrote a blog post encouraging Christians to get the COVID vaccine. He argued that even people who aren't worried about

COVID themselves should get the vaccine simply as an act of neighbor love. He pointed out that getting the vaccine benefits not just yourself but also others. It diminishes the risk of spreading the virus to others; it makes things safer for people who cannot get the vaccine for medical reasons; it makes it easier for people who are worried about COVID to come to church or join in other group activities; and finally, high levels of vaccination allow for a quicker return to normal relative to the social restrictions that are fraying the nerves of so many. The blog seemed relatively uncontroversial to me. It was a nice, short packaging of an argument that I have heard many others make. It raised a point worth raising: when it comes to the vaccine, we should think of others, not just ourselves. It was barely over seven hundred words—short and sweet.

Or perhaps not . . .

When a link to the blog was posted to his university's Facebook page, it went viral. Here's a quick sample drawn from the hundreds of comments that were posted online (all direct quotes):

- What's next? "Love thy neighbor, get the abortion"? that has about the same level of logic as this argument.
- This is awesome insight on scripture! Every time in the New Testament we read the word "love" we should translate it into "get the shot."
- Vacuous virtue signaling . . . un-factual, un-informed, logical fallacies . . . bad hermeneutics . . .
- Who would've thunk that seminary profs would turn liberal Pharisee?
- Boo . . . why would you take a stance on this? You know it's all political right? And you know the shot doesn't work . . .
- You're on some ridiculous high horse to twist the words of Jesus in such a disgusting way.
- This is about the worst article and UNBIBLICAL POST I've seen! Jesus would NOT take the vax . . . he'd heal people . . .

Other posts accused my friend of being stupid, "woke," liberal, ignorant, and arrogant. I won't take the time to identify logical fallacies or rebut particular claims in these comments. What I would like to point out is simply this. The original blog made a fairly straightforward claim—that one could love one's neighbor by getting the COVID vaccine. This was a teaching— and, as with any teaching, it needed to be tested. Unfortunately, instead of testing the teaching, the commenters torched the teacher. Where was that bumper sticker when we needed it?

The goal of this chapter, then, is to help readers avoid torching teachers while still testing teachings. These skills might better be thought of as (1) *habits of heart* that help avoid torching teachers and thereby failing to love our neighbors, and (2) *habits of mind* that help us test teachings and thereby reject what is false and hold fast to what is true. Cultivating these habits will equip us not just to be civil but to be faithful to the truth and loving to our neighbors—goals to which I would hope every Christian would aspire.

Habits of the Heart

I will start with the heart because of a tendency, seen in the online comments above, that once one decides one does not *like* a teaching, one skips over the tedious process of testing the teaching and goes straight to torching the teacher. Torching becomes a *replacement* for testing. If our hearts are prone to torch, or even just willing to torch, testing is preempted. So, our first need is to convince ourselves that torching really isn't an option.

Hearts that are prone to torch are more dangerous, widespread, and insidious than one might think. I read a quote not long ago that expressed this concern well:

> We spend our strength in arguing, bickering, contending, quarrelling, troubling, and opposing one another rather than magnifying, blessing, and praising the name of God for the mercy we enjoy. We are a divided people whose hearts, heads, and hands are all divided. Peace and unity seem to have flown from us, and a spirit of contention and division has come upon us.
>
> The church is divided. The state is divided. The city is divided. The country is divided. Towns are divided. Families are divided. Godly people are divided. Ministers almost everywhere are divided. Yes, and what heart is there at this time that is not divided within itself?[1]

This quote certainly isn't saying anything surprising—countless others have made similar observations. What is surprising is that these words were written by Jeremiah Burroughs *almost four hundred years ago*. Apparently, heart disease is nothing new.

---

1. Jeremiah Burroughs, *Peace and Healing: Restore Harmony*, Be United in Christ Outreach Ministry, accessed June 14, 2022, https://www.beunitedinchrist.com/all-categories/product-announcement/peace-and-healing-now-available/, 15.

In Burroughs's day, they couldn't fight over Donald Trump or critical race theory, but fight they did. This book was written after a century of the Wars of Religion on the Continent, and at the outset of the English Civil War. These religious wars were not culture wars—they were real, not metaphorical. Today when we talk about political leaders losing their heads, we are referring to out-of-control rhetoric in a presidential debate. Not so for Burroughs. Shortly after his book was completed, King Charles I was literally beheaded.

Burroughs offers some profound insights into both the causes of divisions and possible cures. He begins with the causes, asking what makes us so prone to fight and divide. He argues that we mistakenly blame external circumstances for what might better be blamed on our own hearts. As he puts is, "The main source of our strife is internal, not external. Hearts divided from God always divide from others."[2] Our outward strife is just the visible manifestation of an illness of the heart deep inside. Or, as Jesus puts it, "Out of the abundance of the heart [the] mouth speaks" (Luke 6:45 ESV). Burroughs goes on to identify some "dividing principles"—principles that, if practiced, inevitably lead to division. Here are a few principles drawn from his longer list, with a few added comments of my own in parentheses:

1. Everyone must believe like me. (I'm right, and it is important that you share in my rightness. It is not enough to agree to disagree; you need to agree with me.)
2. People can believe anything. (An approach to conflict that hopes to solve disagreements by refusing to care or believe that there is anything important to care about. This leads to division simply because there actually are things we care about, and most of us know it.)
3. Always share what you believe. (The tendency to speak when silence might serve better. In modern terms, the tendency to tweet [or retweet] things that will stoke your side's righteous indignation but do nothing to edify or make peace.)
4. Misjudge motives. (Assume that people on the other side of the issue are not ill-informed but ill-motivated.)
5. Overreact to differences. (No wrong on the part of the other side can be overlooked because so much is at stake. The country, the church, the cause of Christ all hang in the balance, and downplaying differences just allows them to fester and become more dangerous.)[3]

2. Burroughs, *Peace and Healing*, 13.
3. Burroughs, *Peace and Healing*, 24.

Burroughs does not merely diagnosis our disease, he also suggests a cure, which includes some ways of approaching other people that make it easier to avoid division.

1. We should give the **best interpretation possible to other people's actions.** (Practice a hermeneutic of charity with others by overlooking minor faults in reasoning. Also, this might include affirming the good parts of a position that we nonetheless reject.)

2. We should **focus on ourselves, not others,** because we know the evils of our heart. Practice a hermeneutic of suspicion toward oneself. Be self-critical, knowing our confirmation bias will welcome a truth claim even if it has weak support. By the way, it is easy to invert these two hermeneutics—we often exercise a hermeneutic of suspicion toward those with whom we disagree and a hermeneutic of charity to those who are on our side.)

3. If we feel certain our view is correct, **we should thank God for revealing this truth to us rather than condemn those he has not yet revealed it to.** (We need to be nonjudgmental and not assume others are lacking in intelligence or character simply because they have a different view. We should see our own wisdom as a gift, so we will be grateful to God, not resentful of others.)

4. We should keep in mind that **our own convictions have changed at times,** so we should be gracious with those whose convictions currently differ. (Others may have different views because they have thought *more* about the issue, not less.)

5. We want others to assume the best of us, therefore we should do the same for them (Matt. 7:12). (**The Golden Rule**—this is just one specific expression of Jesus's most famous moral teaching, which also applies to every other item in this list.)[4]

Let's also look at the *Westminster Larger Catechism*, a document written about the same time as Jeremiah Burroughs's book. This wonderfully rich work of practical theology includes some helpful instruction about how we speak to one another. Question 144 (yes, it is a *large* catechism) concerns the duties entailed by the ninth commandment (which forbids bearing false witness). Here are a few excerpts:

What are the duties required in the ninth commandment?

4. Burroughs, *Peace and Healing*, 44.

- the preserving and promoting of truth . . . and the good name of our neighbor
- speaking the truth, and only the truth, in matters of judgment and justice
- a charitable esteem of our neighbors; loving, desiring, and rejoicing in their good name; [and] sorrowing for, and covering of their infirmities
- freely acknowledging of their gifts and graces, defending their innocency [*sic*]
- a ready receiving of a good report, and unwillingness to admit of an evil report, concerning them
- . . . discouraging talebearers, flatterers, and slanderers[5]

Take a moment to savor these phrases: "a charitable esteem of our neighbors," "preserving and promoting . . . the good name of our neighbor," "rejoicing in [our neighbors'] good name," "covering [our neighbors'] infirmities," "freely acknowledging of [our neighbors'] gifts and graces." Does this even remotely resemble language of the online posts we recorded above? These posts were directed not toward just any neighbor, but toward a brother in Christ. Is there a special Facebook exemption from having to honor the ninth commandment? It would be a wonderful spiritual discipline to read this description of the ninth commandment before beginning any session on social media.

Since these teachings are almost five centuries old, it should be clear that a heart prone to torch is not just a passing phase brought on by social media. Torching is a besetting sin that permeates the pages of our newspapers as well as church history and the New Testament. Contentious quarreling is a cancer that has stalked the church through the centuries and saps its strength from within. We dare not take it lightly.

But what about severe cases, when people are *really* wrong and have been deceived by the devil and captured to do his will? Fortunately, God has not left us without guidance. Paul writes to Timothy: "Have nothing to do with foolish, ignorant controversies; you know that they breed quarrels. And the Lord's servant must not be quarrelsome but kind to everyone, able to teach, patiently enduring evil, correcting his opponents with gentleness. God may perhaps grant them repentance leading to a knowledge of the truth, and they may come to their senses and escape from the snare of the devil, after being captured by him to do his will" (2 Tim. 2:23–26 ESV). What

5. "Larger Catechism: The Orthodox Presbyterian Church," The Orthodox Presbyterian Church, accessed June 14, 2022, https://opc.org/lc.html.

should we do if someone has been snared by the devil to do his will? We should correct the person with gentleness, patience, and kindness. There is really no way to avoid it. There is no Facebook exemption; there is no captured-by-the-devil exemption. We are simply obliged, as followers of Christ, to discard habits of wrath, anger and divisiveness, and cultivate habits of gentleness, peacemaking, and kindness.

Habits of the Mind

Thus far I have considered torching the teacher; I must now turn my attention to testing the teaching. It is natural to think of testing teachings in philosophical terms like sound reasoning, good logic, and a discerning eye for evidence. Testing a teaching doesn't require a PhD in philosophy, but perhaps a course in critical thinking would be in order. Surely, if people are failing at a philosophical task, the solution is some sort of philosophical training.

Strangely enough, I disagree.

Though I do think testing a teaching is a philosophical task, I don't think our current problems are primarily philosophical. Let me offer an analogy by way of explanation. I live near a park that is thick with dogs running around without a leash. Our city actually has a leash law, so how should we solve this problem? Buy more leashes? A quick walk through the park will reveal that all the owners actually have leashes for their dogs, and they almost always have the leashes with them. My local park doesn't have a leash problem; it doesn't even have a dog problem. It has a people problem—people who refuse to use the leashes they already have. Likewise, with testing teachings. Most of us actually have enough philosophical chops to test a teaching. Doubtless, we could improve our abilities, but our biggest need is to use the philosophy we've already got. What keeps us from using our philosophical leashes? To keep it brief, I will just consider two reasons: convenient truths and inconvenient teachers.

Convenient Truths

A "convenient" truth is one that fits nicely with our preexisting beliefs. It is immediately welcomed into our thinking and quickly repeated to our friends and neighbors—both digitally and in person. Its convenience exempts it from testing. And it is important to realize that this definition of convenient statements includes not only positive things about one's own group but also negative things about the other group. A terrible truth claim—that the country is being run by a cabal of cannibal pedophiles, for example—is actually *convenient* if it reinforces your identity narrative. It is not welcome, you are not glad it is true, but it is convenient.

But of course, convenience is not actually a good truth test. There is such a thing as an inconvenient truth. We all have enough philosophy to know that. But we don't use the philosophy we have. Instead, we adopt the double standard that is common to dog parks: if your dog is mean, keep him on the leash; if your dog is nice, let him run free. If a truth claim is *inconvenient*, we are sure to test it. If the truth is *convenient*, we want to let it run free. In fact, we take the leash off and shout, "Run, Forrest, run!"

Why are we so prone to let convenience serve as an exemption to truth testing? A convenient truth supports, enhances, or advances a narrative to which one is committed. It may be a *micro-narrative*—perhaps you are a vegan and you see an article that claims vegans live longer. It may be a *meta-narrative*—perhaps you are a Christian and see an article that says people who go to church are happier and more successful than people who don't. And, most importantly for our current concerns, a truth may confirm your *group narrative*—the midlevel narrative that reflects the identity, values, and core commitments of your closest circle of friends. You and your friends might identify with a conservative (or progressive) political narrative. You might see an article that says people in blue states (or red states) have fewer friends, have shorter marriages, and are less generous than those in red states (or blue states). This statement is convenient relative to your group narrative, and you will be prone to believe this statement without testing. It doesn't matter what the group narrative is, as long it is *important to the people who are important to you.*

It is this last phrase that is particularly noteworthy because it is at this point that testing a teaching has moved from being a *philosophical* matter to being a *sociological* matter. Philosophical reasoning is preempted by a sociological cost-benefit analysis. Here's how it works. We quietly ask ourselves, "What would happen if I raised a question about this teaching?" Of course, one thing that might happen is that I might discover if the teaching is true or false. But I'm not sure this is what first comes to mind for many of us. Instead, we think, "If I tested this teaching, my friends would be upset." In fact, it is possible that my friends would look askance at me even if the truth claim was confirmed by my testing. The mere act of testing can seem like a betrayal. It makes other people wonder if you are really "one of us." If I simply pass this teaching along as if it were true, I maintain membership in good standing among the committed. I preserve intact my core relationships and my most nourishing friendships. I avoid the cost of losing these friendships altogether. For the vast majority of human beings, our relationships are far more important than an incremental increase in the overall ratio of true truth claims to false truth claims that you believe.[6]

Inconvenient Teachers

The counterpoint to the convenient truth is the inconvenient teacher. It is natural to think of an inconvenient teacher as someone teaching inconvenient truth claims. For example, a teacher, or a website, or a political figure who offers up truth claims that are inconvenient to my favored narrative. This is a reasonable enough, but it is not what I mean in this case.

The reason we cannot define an inconvenient teacher merely as someone offering opposing truth claims is that in reality such people are often quite convenient! To keep our group identity together, we actually need the other side. Who would Bugs Bunny be without Elmer Fudd? Nancy Pelosi is very convenient for a broad swath of conservative Americans, just as Donald Trump is convenient for a broad swath of progressives. It is so easy to say, "Did you hear the latest thing Pelosi [or Trump] said?!!" One can so easily pass along an outrageous quote, the truth of which you didn't really have to check because you know that your audience won't check it either. There are lots of celebrity figures on the other side who are convenient (even necessary) for keeping the discourse going within one's own group.

For me, the real inconvenient teachers are the ones whose names I probably don't even know. These are the thoughtful, sober-minded, reasonable defenders of a truth claim that I don't like. These are people who do not naturally penetrate my information bubbles. The algorithm (whether Facebook's or Google's) does not push their names into my browser window. Why? Well, if I bump into one of their articles online, I am prone to stop reading before I'm done—I don't scroll down. I'm unlikely to retweet, post, or quote the article. Simply put, when I read the blog of a truly inconvenient teacher, it doesn't generate clicks. In contrast, pieces written by the

---

6. Several books and articles have addressed the problem of groupthink and the sociological problems associated with knowledge, including: Irving L. Janis, *Groupthink: Psychological Studies of Policy Decisions and Fiascoes*, 2nd ed. (Boston: Cengage Learning, 1982); Jonathan Haidt, *The Righteous Mind: Why Good People Are Divided by Politics and Religion* (New York: Pantheon, 2013).

"pseudo-inconvenient teacher" might very well generate clicks, tweets, and posts. They would all begin with the phrase, "Did you see the latest thing Pelosi/Trump/Fudd said . . . ?" So, the information bubble that I occupy almost guarantees that no one within my circle of friends, no podcast to which I subscribe, no news program that I watch is likely to introduce me to the best thought of these inconvenient teachers.

If I want to hear from inconvenient teachers, I will have to seek them out. Why would I seek out inconvenient teachers who offer thoughtful, sober-minded, well-reasoned arguments for a viewpoint that I don't share? Simply because these people will help me think better. They will refine my convictions and improve my reasoning. They will help me see the other side more clearly. They might even help me love a friend or family member who sees things differently than I do, but who isn't particularly good at giving an account of his or her beliefs. In short, I might want to seek out inconvenient teachers not because I want to test their teaching, but because I want to let their teaching test me.

The inconvenient teacher is, in effect, a particular sort of friend. One who says things that can make me aware of my own sins and shortcomings, who can help me understand people I don't like but am commanded to love, and who can help me think more clearly about issues that are truly important. We should like inconvenient teachers, not hate them. And if the algorithm doesn't find them for us, we should seek them out ourselves.

Conclusion

I will conclude with a few practical tips for improving our communication patterns:

1. Before posting, tweeting, or raging with a friend about a controversial issue, ask yourself if your comment is preserving and promoting truth and the good name and charitable esteem of your neighbor.
2. Intentionally offer comments, posts, or tweets that acknowledge the gifts and graces of people on the "other side." When occasion allows, defend them from unfair statements and mischaracterizations.
3. Reflect on the reward mechanism for what you are about to say, tweet, or post. Consider whether it will edify others, or if it will simply stir the pot of outrage by repeating an error or excess of which your hearers are already aware. Ask yourself what you are hoping to gain.
4. If you are active online, read back through your last year's tweets

and posts. Test them against the Westminster Catechism's list of duties of the ninth commandment or Burroughs's list of principles for avoiding division.

5. Seek out inconvenient teachers who challenge your beliefs and help refine your thinking. Make reading beyond your comfort zone a spiritual discipline.

6. Curate your news sources. Intentionally read news sources that span the political spectrum. It is easier than you think. Check out AllSides.com—a newsfeed that aggregates news sources from across the spectrum on a single website.

7. Make a new friend. Befriend someone with whom you disagree. There is nothing like personalizing a viewpoint that you normally view only in abstract.

References

Burroughs, Jeremiah. *Peace and Healing: Restore Harmony*. Be United in Christ Outreach Ministry, accessed June 14, 2022. https://www.beunitedin christ.com/all-categories/product-announcement/peace-and-healing -now-available/.

Haidt, Jonathan. *The Righteous Mind: Why Good People Are Divided by Politics and Religion*. New York: Pantheon, 2013.

Janis, Irving L. *Groupthink: Psychological Studies of Policy Decisions and Fiascoes*. 2nd ed. Boston: Cengage Learning, 1982.

"Larger Catechism: The Orthodox Presbyterian Church." The Orthodox Presbyterian Church, accessed June 14, 2022. https://opc.org/lc.html.

16

WORD SPOKEN
AT THE PROPER TIME

Tim Muehlhoff

"Please reschedule!"

Before heading out to get my annual flu shot, I stopped by my campus office to quickly collect my mail. I mentioned to our administrator that I didn't want to be late for my shot. With tears in her eyes, Kate asked me to reconsider.

"Tim, don't put that into your body. Even if it means missing your appointment, please let me share my concerns and research." Over the past year Kate and I had become friends through discussing not only work but our common faith. I didn't know, until that moment, that she was deeply committed to a perspective that viewed most vaccinations as a type of poison. Her request to reschedule put me in an awkward place. To be honest, I found her perspective naïve and wanted to politely dismiss it. But her concern for me was moving. For the sake of our relationship, I rescheduled my appointment for the following week. Better to consider her perspective than hurt feelings and possibly put a strain on our friendship. After all, regardless of our differing views, we still had to work together.

Can you relate?

Do you have a spouse, relative, fellow church member, or coworker that holds a view you find wildly untenable? If it was held by an acquaintance or stranger on social media, you'd most likely summarily dismiss it, or dismantle it with *real* research. But, what to do if this is your son home from college, a person in your church small group, or a spouse? And, what if in each of these scenarios the disagreement is between followers of Jesus?

Is it possible to address the conspiracy without harming or even severing the relationship? "Like apples of gold in settings of silver," assert the ancient writers of the book of Proverbs, "is a word spoken at the proper time" (25:11 NASB).[1] What work needs to be done to ensure that it's the proper time to address a perspective you view as misinformed, wrong, or even dangerous?

In addition to being a communication professor, I'm the codirector of the Winsome Conviction Project, which seeks to reintroduce compassion, perspective taking, and civility into our disagreements. We have found the topic of conspiracy theories to be deeply divisive among Christ followers. Those who hold to views that others find naïve or misinformed feel not only dismissed but disrespected. Once this happens, relational walls go up that are difficult to dismantle. Thus, an offended brother is compared to a fortified city (Prov. 18:19). Our experience has shown that disagreements can be broken down into three segments: our emotional and intellectual state heading into the conversation, the actual conversation, and the aftermath, where we process the interaction. Each step is vital to attempting to construct a productive and civil conversation where truth is not only spoken but the relationship is also preserved.

Before the Conversation Starts

If we are to successfully engage others, much work needs to be done before the first word is uttered. Not only should we address our attitude toward the other person but we should also address our view of communication itself.

Adopt a ritual view of communication. Why do we want to have this conversation in the first place? If we are honest, many of us simply want to set a person straight in his or her thinking. Bad or naïve ideas need to be corrected by information or authorities we deem credible. While not an official debate, this is a time to challenge erroneous thoughts. This attitude is what scholars call the *transmission view of communication*, where the primary focus is on imparting, sending, or giving information to others.[2] This dominant view of communication, while useful in many ways, may cause

---

1. Unless otherwise noted, all Scripture quotations in this chapter are taken from the New International Version.

2. James Carey, "A Cultural Approach to Communication," in *Communication as Culture: Essays on Media and Society*, 2nd ed. (New York: Routledge, 2008), 57.

unexpected problems when engaging a person holding a theory you think is deeply flawed. When Kate and I did talk about her view of vaccinations, we adopted a transmission view and sent each other emails with links to our favorite sources of information. However, the trading of information simply amplified our disagreement by showing how we each trusted "experts" who wildly disagreed with each other. As soon as she produced a study, I countered it with a different—and in my estimation—superior one. While we were transmitting much information, we made little progress.

The transmission view can easily veer off into volatile tangents. For example, President Biden is being severely critiqued for his administration's attempt to flag and have removed from social media information about COVID vaccines that he determines is spreading misinformation.[3] "You see," say some friends, "there would be more studies and information showing the dangers of vaccines if it were a level playing field. My view is being systematically censored at the highest levels." Such a suspicious view fits neatly under what social critic Michel Foucault calls discarded discourse, where dissenting information is suppressed by those in power. The battle over information, or misinformation, "is by no means anything new at all," states Mathew Baum, Kalb Professor of Global Communication at the Kennedy School.[4] If all we do is stay within the confines of a transmission view of communication, then the information battle will surely continue and we'll be caught in a downward spiral of challenging each other's sources and experts as tensions mount.

Is there a view of communication that doesn't altogether discard a transmission view but shifts the focus? A *ritual view of communication* focuses on coparticipation, fellowship, and sharing of thoughts *and* emotions. A key part of this view is what Gregory Shepherd calls *sympathetic awareness*: when we "experience another in communication, we come to be in sympathy or in common feeling, with that other."[5] While information separated Kate and me, what brought us together was attempting to see the

3. Editorial, "Biden Has No Business Being Judge of 'Truth,'" *Detroit News*, July 31, 2021, https://www.detroitnews.com/story/opinion/editorials/2021/08/01 /editorial-biden-has-no-business-being-judge-truth/5428168001/.

4. Jacob Sweet, "Can Disinformation Be Stopped? Scholar's Perspectives on a Pervasive New Threat," *Harvard Magazine*, July–August 2021, 31.

5. Gregory Shepherd, "Communication as Transcendence," in *Communication as . . . Perspectives on Theory*, ed. Gregory Shepherd, Jeffery St. John, and Ted Striphas (Thousand Oaks, CA: Sage, 2006), 24.

world through the eyes of the other and sympathize. *How would I feel if those I care about were putting poison into their bodies? A poison that could hurt or even kill? And what if the information that could help is being censored?* Living within Kate's worldview—what communication scholars call perspective taking—made me appreciate her concern for me and to respect the courage it must have taken to share her views with me.

In his seminal study of communication climates, Jack Gibb noted that a key way to foster a defensive climate is to approach another person's point of view with *detached neutrality*. How do we react to the information or stories others share with us? Do we treat it merely as data to be debunked, or as insight into what drives their convictions and emotions? If we treat the stories of others in a detached manner, then we should not be surprised when they become defensive and stop sharing altogether.[6]

Sympathetic awareness mirrors the author of Hebrews' command to not only remember those in prison but to do so as if "you were together with them in prison, and those who are mistreated as *if you yourselves were suffering*" (13:3). Adopting Kate's perspective not only made me appreciate the time and attention she'd given to this issue, but it opened me up to the strong emotions associated with her view. Instead of debating, I sought to adopt her view as if it were my own and understand it from the inside out.

Beware of emotional contagion. Before the conversation starts, we also need to become cognizant of our disposition toward the person we'll be engaging. What is our attitude toward him or her? What range of emotions are you feeling? Are you disappointed that this person has adopted a view you think is obviously fallacious? Over time, has disappointment morphed into anger? It's at this point that we make a crucial mistake that can sabotage the conversation even before it starts. We assume that our self-talk about a person—if not verbalized—is harmless. In other words, while we'd never articulate how disappointed we are with a person, or how angry we are that the person has bought into a conspiracy, we allow ourselves to articulate those emotions to ourselves. "I can't believe Karen would be so stupid to buy into this crap!" "Ted prides himself on his discernment, and yet he's consulting websites that are ludicrous." "How long can my father ignore the facts?" Mounting research shows that these thoughts bleed out into the conversation even if not verbalized.

---

6. Jack Gibb, "Defensive Communication," *Journal of Communication* 11, no. 3 (1961): 141–48.

Understanding your emotional state before entering a conversation is key because your emotions will be passed on to the other person, and vice versa. This transfer of emotions is called *emotional contagion.* "We catch feelings from one another as though they were some kind of virus," notes behavioral scientist Daniel Goleman.[7] In one study, participants took a survey assessing their emotional mood and level of emotional expressiveness. Researchers specifically paired a self-identified low-expressive individual with a high-expressive individual. After the survey, the pair spent two minutes alone in a room waiting for the study to enter into another phase. Participants were not allowed to speak to each other. At the end of the two minutes, a researcher came in and asked them to take the same survey again. In each case, the less emotionally expressive person took on, in some degree, the emotions of the more expressive person just by being in the same room with the other.[8]

Behavioral experts like Goleman explain that our complex brains have a low and high road when taking in information such as emotions. The high road is the part of our brain that is keenly aware of facts and analyzes them accordingly. The low road is "circuitry that operates beneath our awareness, automatically and effortlessly, with immense speed." While the high road allows us to think about the data we are receiving, the low road lets us feel before we are even aware of it. When we "sense the sarcasm in a remark, we have the low road to thank."[9] We cannot avoid emotional contagion and the transfer of our emotions because our low road is always subconsciously taking in information, as evidenced by two participants merely sitting in the same room. This makes assessing and controlling our emotions and self-talk before a difficult conversation crucial!

Paul commands young believers at Ephesus to put away bitterness, anger, rage, slander, and malice (Eph. 4:31). Paul understands how these emotions and communication styles can fracture a church. In today's argument culture, we've all seen the devastating effects of venting our anger. Many of us attempt to keep negative emotions in check when talking to another

---

7. Daniel Goleman, *Social Intelligence: The New Science of Human Relationships* (New York: Random House, 2006), 115.

8. Ellen S. Sullins, "Emotional Contagion Revisited: Effects of Social Comparison and Expressive Style on Mood Convergence," *Personality and Social Psychology Bulletin* 17 (1991): 166–74.

9. Goleman, *Social Intelligence*, 16.

person. If what researchers like Goleman are uncovering is true, then we need to pay equal attention to our self-talk. When we find our internal dialogue deteriorating into slander, or anger, we need to replace it with compassion (Eph. 4:32) or, as already suggested, sympathetic awareness. For many of us, reeling in our self-talk or taking thoughts captive (2 Cor. 10:5) will be a struggle, since we often give them free rein. Yet, the realization that our emotions may sabotage a conversation before it starts should serve as strong motivation to replace internal rage with compassion.[10]

Starting a Conversation

Many conversations begin due to mounting frustration. You've been upset about the family finances for months but have held your tongue. When the frustration reaches a certain level, you just have to voice your opinion! The problem is that your anger or frustration fosters an equally exasperated response. "A harsh word," asserts wisdom writers, "stirs up anger" (Prov. 15:1). The result is a negative communication spiral where communicators not only mirror but also intensify negative emotions where shouting begets more shouting. In interacting with a person you care about, your goal isn't just to debate the issue but to construct a positive experience where the relationship is maintained or strengthened even if issues remain unresolved.

Over the past few years, the Winsome Conviction Project has sought to facilitate conversations centering on potentially explosive topics such as critical race theory, a divisive 2020 presidential election, mask wearing, and assorted conspiracy theories. People are often surprised to learn that these conversations—while often passionate—can be constructive and civil. Through much trial and error, we've discovered that adopting a simple outline of how the conversation is to proceed is crucial. While individuals are free to say whatever they want, their response must follow this four-step process. Participants say the steps seem awkward at first, but their value surfaces when the conversation gets heated. "I was frustrated with the steps, but later realized it's helpful to have speed bumps when things get going," noted one participant. While space doesn't permit me to go into detail, here is the outline we ask people to work through when engaging each other.

10. The conversation about emotional contagion was adapted from my book, *I Beg to Differ: Navigating Difficult Conversations in Truth and Love* (Downers Grove, IL: InterVarsity Press, 2014).

- Here's what I heard you say.
- Here's what resonated with me at a heart level.
- Here's where I agree with you.
- If I could, here is one thing I'd like to add to the conversation.

While nothing revolutionary, we've found this format helps in several ways.

Here's what I heard you say. Paraphrasing back to a person what you heard the person say can be a powerful way of validating the person's perspective. Communication theorists assert that acknowledgment is central to fostering a positive communication climate. In a terse proverb, the wisdom writers state that it is folly and shame to speak before listening (Prov. 18:13). Notice that this first step adopts a transmission view of communication and allows a person to express thoughts unchallenged.

Here's what resonated with me at a heart level. Letting a person know how the person's fears, arguments, or story has emotionally resonated with you mirrors a ritual view of communication and places an emphasis on sympathy—*I can't imagine having my view constantly made fun of in social media, or so easily dismissed. It must be infuriating.* While moderating a conversation between gay people and conservative Christians, a gay participant noted, "I know we still disagree with each other, but thank you for feeling my hurt." Letting a person know his or her story or perspective moved you is not synonymous with condoning that view. It shows that the person's narrative matters and you are eschewing the impulse to merely treat this as a sterile debate. Weeping with those who weep (Rom. 12:15) establishes emotional connection even in the midst of disagreement.

Here's where I agree with you. Uncovering areas of agreement during a difficult conversation is becoming a lost skill in today's argument culture. Many today see agreement as a sign of weakness, or the condoning of a differing perspective that is deemed dangerous. As our communities, churches, or families become fractured, cultivating common ground when there appears none will be an invaluable skill and mind-set.

Organizational psychologist and researcher Adam Grant asserts that what separates average negotiators from skilled negotiators is an expectation of finding common ground. One study asked negotiators to describe their preparation prior to the actual negotiation. The majority "went in armed for battle, hardly taking note of any anticipated areas of agreement." In contrast, negotiators who were the highest rated "mapped out a series of dance steps they might be able to take with the other side, devoting more

than a third of their planning comments to finding common ground."[11]
Fostering areas of agreement is a sign of intellectual humility in which
I resist the urge to demonize views as all bad. Common ground allows us to
establish points of agreement as we slowly move toward disagreement.

One of the key benefits of cultivating common ground is that it evokes
what communication scholars call the *rule of reciprocation*. This rule states,
"We should try to repay, in kind, what another person has provided for
us."[12] Not only has this rule been noticed by anthropologists,[13] but it also
finds scriptural support. In writing to the churches at Galatia, the apostle
Paul shares his own version of the rule of reciprocation. He exhorts believers to not grow weary in doing "good to all people" (Gal. 6:10). Weariness is
minimized knowing that in due time "a man reaps what he sows" (6:7).[14] If
we regularly do good to others, we can expect that goodness to eventually
be reciprocated.

To illustrate his point, Paul utilizes a practice familiar to his rural
readers—harvesting. A farmer can only expect to harvest that which he
has planted. You can't expect to harvest apples when you plant oranges.
This same principle is true of human relationships. You cannot keep being sarcastic to your spouse and expect sympathy; you cannot neglect a
relationship with a neighbor and expect it to thrive. What Paul is saying
has great consequence to us as we attempt to engage those who are dear
to us. We can expect to be treated in the same manner in which we treat
people holding views we reject. We cannot be harsh toward others and
expect compassion in return. We cannot dominate the conversation and
then expect people to be silent when we are speaking. We cannot ignore
areas of agreement and then be disappointed when others do not agree
with our views.

11. Adam Grant, *Think Again: The Power of Knowing What You Don't Know* (New
York: Viking, 2021), 105.

12. Robert Cialdini, *Influence: The Psychology of Persuasion* (New York: Morrow,
1984), 17.

13. To read more about the rule of reciprocation from an anthropological standpoint, see Richard Leakey and Roger Lewin, *People of the Lake: Mankind and Its
Beginnings* (New York: Anchor, 1978).

14. The principle of reaping and sowing is not limited to the book of Gala-
tians. The theme can be traced throughout Scripture: Job 4:8; 31:8; Ps. 126:5; Prov.
11:21; 22:8; Jer. 12:13; Mic. 6:15; Matt. 6:26; 25:24, 26; Luke 19:21; John 4:36–37; Rev.
14:15–16.

If I could, here is one thing I'd like to add to the conversation. When we get to this part of the outline, people assume it's time to launch a rebuttal. *Yes, there are some areas of agreement, but I strongly disagree with your central premise! And most of your facts are just plain wrong.* When I teach a course on engaging perspectives, I explain that this last part of the outline should be guided by this simple formula: *With this person, at this time, under these circumstances, what is the one thing I should say?* Let's say you are conversing with a family member who not only holds beliefs you deem untenable but every time you've tried to tackle this topic it ends in anger or raised voices. However, this time voices were not raised and you surprisingly found areas of agreement. The one thing you might want to say is, "I'm so pleased we could talk about this without either of us getting angry."

When deciding how to respond, we need to remember that communication exists on two levels, not one. The *content level* consists of our convictions, arguments, and messaging, while the *relational level* includes the amount of perceived respect between individuals, compassion, and acknowledgment. Communication theory is predicated on the assertion that if the relational level is lacking, then people will not listen to our content—no matter how sound our arguments. Thus, before we give our content, we need to assess the relational level: Does this person feel disrespected by me? Am I compassionate to his or her perspective or story? While not necessarily agreeing with the arguments, do I acknowledge the time and research put into this issue? If the answer is no to one or more of these questions, then, from a communication standpoint, your content will likely be dismissed. Better to temporarily shelve your content and work on shoring up the relational level.

"The heart of the righteous weighs its answers" (Prov. 15:28). The word "weighs" literally can be translated *meditates* or *studies*. What should we meditate on or study before we offer our opinion to those around us? We should meditate on or study not just our arguments (content level), but also the quality of our communication climate (relational level).

After the Conversation

Once the conversation is over, many people report being flooded with thoughts: *Why didn't I push back against bogus facts even more strongly? I spent too much time listening—they walked all over me! Next time, I won't be so nice!* Have you ever wondered why we often beat ourselves up after a conversation? How easily anger seems to take root when reviewing a conversation?

What makes communication so difficult with fellow believers is that the Scriptures clearly state that we have a spiritual adversary who wants—at all costs—to disrupt unity. This attempt at disunity often comes in the form of negative thoughts or extreme second-guessing. Where might these thoughts come from?

While Scripture gives no indication that demons can read our mind, there is evidence that they can plant thoughts, as seen in the incident where King David is incited by Satan to shift his confidence from the Lord to troop strength (1 Chron. 21:1), when the idea of betrayal is put into Judas (John 13:2), when Ananias is given the thought to lie about the amount of an offering (Acts 5:3), and even when Jesus is given a mental panoramic view of all earthly kingdoms—past and present—by Satan (Matt. 4:1–11).[15] This leads New Testament scholar Keith Ferdinando to conclude that "a critical theatre of the believer's spiritual warfare is the battle for the mind."[16]

While Christian communicators must be alerted to spiritual opposition at every stage of engaging a fellow believer, we must be particularly aware of how our spiritual adversary will want to negatively color our perception of the conversation once it's over. We must guard against discounting areas of agreement and the strengthening of the relationship by giving in to a sudden flood of negative thoughts. Surely, the spiritual armor Paul vividly describes to the early church must be adorned by modern believers attempting to resist today's argument culture (Eph. 6).

Conclusion

With all the rancor and vitriol surrounding the COVID-19 vaccine, it was nice to read a conversation in a national paper where civility was maintained. While the two participants strongly disagreed on the trustworthiness of the vaccine and the responsibilities of citizenship, they were cordial as they went the extra mile to understand each other. What made the difference? The two participants were, in fact, brothers.[17] Like many families fac-

---

15. To read more about the strengths and limitations of spiritual adversaries, see Clinton E. Arnold, *3 Crucial Questions about Spiritual Warfare* (Grand Rapids: Baker Academic, 1997); and Clinton E. Arnold, *Powers of Darkness: Principalities and Powers in Paul's Letters* (Downers Grove, IL: IVP Academic, 1992).

16. Keith Ferdinando, *The Message of Spiritual Warfare* (Downers Grove, IL: InterVarsity Press, 2016), 194.

17. Nicole Carroll, "The Backstory: My Brother Is One of Millions Who Won't

ing COVID, siblings found themselves on opposite sides. While COVID has unfortunately torn families apart, these two brothers maintained their relationship. Certainly, this is a good reminder for fellow Christ followers as we disagree about competing theories. While Kate and I have yet to agree on the efficacy of vaccines and our conversations can leave both of us frustrated, we have maintained our friendship as brother and sister in the faith.

In the end, we must fiercely cling to the idea that our current disagreements are not between combatants but rather among family members intent on seeking Jesus's kingdom. With all humility and patience, asserts the apostle Paul, bear with one another "in love" (Eph. 4:2). These qualities will be manifest—to those inside and outside the church—as we do the hard work to speak words in their proper time.

References

Arnold, Clinton E. *Powers of Darkness: Principalities and Powers in Paul's Letters.* Downers Grove, IL: IVP Academic, 1992.

———. *3 Crucial Questions about Spiritual Warfare.* Grand Rapids: Baker Academic, 1997.

Carey, James. "A Cultural Approach to Communication." In *Communication as Culture: Essays on Media and Society.* 2nd ed. New York: Routledge, 2008.

Carroll, Nicole. "The Backstory: My Brother Is One of Millions Who Won't Get the COVID-19 Vaccine. I Asked Why. Here Are His Reasons, My Responses." *USA Today*, August 6, 2021. https://www.usatoday.com/story/opinion/2021/08/06/covid-vaccine-why-do-people-refuse-the-vaccine-here-are-reasons-and-responses/5491922001/.

Cialdini, Robert. *Influence: The Psychology of Persuasion.* New York: Morrow, 1984.

Gibb, Jack. "Defensive Communication." *Journal of Communication* 11, no. 3 (1961): 141–48.

Goleman, Daniel. *Social Intelligence: The New Science of Human Relationships.* New York: Random House, 2006.

Grant, Adam. *Think Again: The Power of Knowing What You Don't Know.* New York: Viking, 2021.

Get the COVID-19 Vaccine. I Asked Why. Here Are His Reasons, My Responses," *USA Today*, August 6, 2021, https://www.usatoday.com/story/opinion/2021/08/06/covid-vaccine-why-do-people-refuse-the-vaccine-here-are-reasons-and-responses/5491922001/.

Leakey, Richard, and Roger Lewin. *People of the Lake: Mankind and Its Beginnings*. New York: Anchor, 1978.

Muehlhoff, Tim. *I Beg to Differ: Navigating Difficult Conversations in Truth and Love*. Downers Grove, IL: InterVarsity Press, 2014.

Shepherd, Gregory. "Communication as Transcendence." In *Communication as . . . Perspectives on Theory*, edited by Gregory Shepherd, Jeffery St. John, and Ted Striphas. Thousand Oaks, CA: Sage, 2006.

Sullins, Ellen S. "Emotional Contagion Revisited: Effects of Social Comparison and Expressive Style on Mood Convergence." *Personality and Social Psychology Bulletin* 17 (1991): 166–74.

Sweet, Jacob. "Can Disinformation Be Stopped? Scholar's Perspectives on a Pervasive New Threat." *Harvard Magazine*, July–August 2021.

17

FOLLOWING CHRIST INTO CONTROVERSY

Jason Cook

We have built a society that in many ways thrives on controversy.[1] Intense, public disagreements over injustices, both real and imagined, preoccupy our news outlets. They shape the conflicts dramatized in our favorite TV shows. They influence the advertising agendas of businesses across a variety of industries. They form a pervasive network of focal points for the social media landscape. The ubiquity of smart phones and digital social media means that public debate is often mediated to us through venues that hinder productive dialogue and by algorithms that tend to confirm our biases and amplify our differences.[2] Sometimes it seems that the particulars of a specific controversy are secondary to our culture's obsession with indignation as its own end. Our technology-shaped culture encourages self-indulgent outrage over everything from demonstrably false conspiracies to complex policy debates. Because of the ways people and institutions participate in controversy, our society grows increasingly vulnerable to conspiratorial thinking, misguided activism, and social fragmentation.[3]

---

1. Gregory L. Bock has been a wonderful conversation partner as I worked through the ideas in this chapter. I gratefully acknowledge his friendship, feedback, and suggested revisions on preliminary drafts.

2. Jonathan Haidt, "Why the Past Ten Years of American Life Have Been Uniquely Stupid," *Atlantic*, April 11, 2022, https://www.theatlantic.com/magazine/archive/2022/05/social-media-democracy-trust-babel/629369/.

3. Haidt, "Why the Past Ten Years of American Life Have Been Uniquely Stupid."

Bearing Witness to Christ in Controversy

As Christians, we aim to live faithfully according to the moral and ethical standards inherent in the gospel. When controversies revolve around issues of freedom and justice, we may feel morally obligated to participate. Because so much is at stake, we may feel morally justified in our outrage. But responding to public controversy about potential moral failures is not merely a social duty. It is one of the critical ways we bear witness to Christ. Since those with opposing views often assume a non-Christian or even secular worldview, our involvement in public debates bears all the weight of a cosmic battle between good and evil. Yet for Christians, and particularly for leaders in the church, the inclination to indulge our righteous indignation is counterbalanced by New Testament exhortations to be meek, long-suffering reconcilers who seek to live peaceably with all (Matt. 5:5, 9; Rom. 12:12–18; 2 Cor. 5:18). This is all the more important because of the cultural and technological forces that tempt us to participate in controversy in ways that arouse unrighteous impulses.

But even as we acknowledge our own vulnerability to sin, we still face the challenge of navigating the controversies and conspiracies of our day. In a society with more controversies than we can attend to, how do we choose which ones to get involved in? How do we decide which venues of participation to use? How do we lead fellow church members who bring conspiracy theories and activist inclinations into our congregations? How do we keep our flesh in check when opponents provoke us? In short, how can we follow Christ faithfully as we encounter and participate in controversy?

Christ and Controversy

In this chapter, I attempt only the beginning of a response to the questions above. I write as a Christian and fellow sojourner, groping my way through the peculiar mix of controversies that has caused so much disruption in recent years and trusting in the testimony of Scripture as a reliable guide. In particular, I reflect on the accounts of Jesus's life and ministry, especially in Matthew's Gospel. The Gospels show us that the first coming of Christ was filled with controversy, conspiracy, and the self-righteous indignation of his contemporaries. He was the intended victim of several conspiracies against his life (Matt. 2:7–18; 12:14). He was repeatedly accused of making outrageous claims that threatened the religious sensibilities and political influence of the Pharisees (Matt. 9:1–8). They also made outrageous claims against him (Matt. 12:22–28). Christ's closest disciples misunderstood the nature of his political ambitions (Matt. 16:21–23; Luke 9:51–56). Finally, his resurrection occasioned even more conspiracies (Matt. 28:11–15).

Jesus's responses to the controversies and conspiracies surrounding him varied throughout his ministry. Sometimes he withdrew (Matt. 12:14–16). Sometimes he waited to be engaged by his opponents (Matt. 12:9–13; 26:36–55). Sometimes he deliberately provoked his opponents (Luke 4:23–30). When his hearers failed to understand him, sometimes he corrected them (Matt. 22:29). Sometimes he left their misunderstanding intact (Matt. 13:10–11). The range of Jesus's responses to controversy gives us an opportunity to consider his example and attempt to discern the wisdom he modeled for us. In what follows, I consider three episodes from the life of Jesus and how they might inform our participation in controversy. For each episode, I pose one overarching question for reflection that can help us discern how to faithfully follow Christ's example as we consider whether, and how, to involve ourselves in the controversies of our own time and place.

Private Preparation for Public Controversy

Have you fasted lately? Perhaps the connection between fasting and how we deal with controversy seems counterintuitive. But before Jesus entered into any public debates with antagonistic scribes and Pharisees, he spent forty days and forty nights fasting in the wilderness (Matt. 4:1–2). Prior to that, John the Baptist had condemned the Pharisees and Sadducees who came for his baptism as a "brood of vipers" who only feigned repentance (Matt. 3:7). So, public controversy was in the air, and Jesus had opportunities to engage with it. However, his priorities first led him away from society and into the wilderness.

Jesus's forty-day retreat from the typical entanglements of society should lead us to recall the forty days and nights that the prophet Moses spent on Mount Sinai when he received the Ten Commandments from the Lord (Exod. 34:27–28). It should also remind us of the forty days and nights Elijah went without food on his journey from the wilderness to Mount Horeb, where he too encountered the presence of the Lord (1 Kings 19:8). In all three cases, this period of fasting, solitude, and divine encounter served as a time of preparation for the demands of the contentious prophetic ministry that would soon follow.

In the case of Jesus, we know that he was led by the Spirit into the wilderness specifically to be tempted by the devil (Matt. 4:1). This beginning of temptations, this first of adversaries, reveals the spiritual undercurrent beneath all his future conflicts with hostile religious leaders and sometimes his own misguided disciples. Before he dealt with demonic temptations working indirectly through others in public controversy, he confronted the weakness of his flesh and the wickedness of demonic temptation directly. If Jesus had any vulnerability to sinful inclinations, his confrontation with the devil would have exposed it.

In his response to the devil's first two temptations, we witness the absence of insecurity about his identity. The devil enticed him to demonstrate his divine Sonship (Matt. 4:3-6). But Jesus felt no obligation to prove himself on the devil's terms. The devil then invited him to gain worldly power and glory. But again, Jesus did not lust after worldly power on the devil's terms. Instead, he was preoccupied with honoring, trusting, and worshiping God. These three temptations became a pattern for the controversy Jesus faced throughout the rest of his ministry. Antagonistic religious leaders repeatedly challenged and undermined his divine identity (Matt. 9:1-7; 21:23; Mark 2:7). Similarly, the suffering and insults he endured led to a recurring temptation to avoid persecution by exercising his power in self-aggrandizing ways (Matt. 26:52-53). Instead, he modeled meekness and tolerated suffering with steady fortitude (Matt. 26:57-68).

Question 1: What Is at Stake for Me?

Jesus's example in the wilderness is important for us as we contemplate our own potential involvement in the political and social controversies of our generation because it reminds us of the spiritual nature of these conflicts that often goes unacknowledged. The information and misinformation that fuel our debates about masks, vaccines, elections, protests, immigration, military conflict, and corrupt politicians are only part of the story. Christians often acknowledge and react strongly to the moral and ethical concerns involved in all these issues. Yet the spiritual character of how these controversies play out entails an ongoing cosmic struggle between the angelic and human servants of God and the powers of darkness that oppose him (Eph. 6:10-12). If we are only concerned with influencing public policy or winning an argument, we can easily overlook the reality that demonic spirits are at work. Being thus distracted, we will tend to rely on political rather than spiritual means to deal with a problem that is fundamentally spiritual. Such a failure leaves us vulnerable to the schemes of the devil. Just as he attempted with Jesus, the devil also seeks to exploit our personal insecurities, our preoccupation with comfort, and our desire for power.

Whether our engagement in controversy is through political activism, social media posts, or informal debates, we should prepare ourselves for the attendant spiritual conflict by asking ourselves this question. "What is at stake for me?" You may be factually correct about a conspiracy theory and still fall prey to temptation because of personal insecurity. You may be on the morally right side of a debate and still fall into sin because of lust for worldly power. So, it is wise to prepare yourself for the temptations that will surely come in the midst of emotionally charged controversy by acknowledging what is personally at stake for you.

It could range from the mild embarrassment of losing a private argument to public humiliation. It could be a matter of preserving social status, a job, a clear conscience, family harmony, or a cherished friendship. Your potential involvement in a controversy could have significant consequences on your mental and physical health, and your moral integrity. At times, your participation in controversy may threaten your acceptance in the community you belong to or the coherence of your most deeply held convictions. Therefore, it is wise to count the cost before you throw yourself into the arena of controversy, especially when the personal stakes are high.

Regardless of the topic of controversy, give yourself time to evaluate what is truly at stake for you. It is spiritually risky to enter into a raging controversy as an idealistic champion for justice, only to discover you are actually fighting for the approval of someone you idolize. In a scenario like this, your involvement can easily become self-indulgent and self-protective. Instead of bearing witness to Christ, we may find ourselves resembling hypocritical Pharisees. When the stakes are high, the self-protective impulse entices us to make moral and ethical compromises.[4] It takes spiritual discipline to resist the passions of the flesh when something we love is threatened. Thus, Jesus began his ministry with an extended fast.

Demonic Exploitation and Spiritual Discernment

Even if you are supporting a defensibly Christian perspective, a self-centered manner of engaging in controversy exposes you to demonic ex-

---

4. People's vulnerability to self-serving bias has been well documented. This pattern of bias can affect our moral judgments even when we recognize the susceptibility of others to it. Konrad Bocian and Bogdan Wojciszke, "Self-Interest Bias in Moral Judgments of Others' Actions," *Personality and Social Psychology Bulletin* 40, no. 7 (April 2014): 4–5, https://www.researchgate.net/publication/261757400_Self -Interest_Bias_in_Moral_Judgments_of_Others'_Actions.

ploitation. I recognize that the notion of demonic exploitation may evoke incredulity among some readers, as though I'm suggesting that careless involvement in controversy puts you at risk of demonic possession. Actually, what I have in mind is more along the lines of Peter rebuking Jesus when Jesus foretold his impending suffering and death (Matt. 16:21-22). On the surface, Peter seemed to be expressing his allegiance to the man he recognized as "the Christ, the Son of the living God" (16:15-16).[5] But Jesus responded to Peter by saying, "Get behind me, Satan! You are a hindrance to me. For you are not setting your mind on the things of God, but on the things of man" (16:23). The kind of demonic exploitation that Peter yielded to is more subtle and mundane than demonic possession. Yet it undermines our efforts to faithfully represent Christ to our generation.

Discerning what's at stake is not always easy. Discernment of this sort is not simply an intellectual task, but rather a spiritual one. In this lies the wisdom of fasting. Fasting, along with prayer, allows us to acknowledge our vulnerability to temptation and fortify our capacity to discern and resist the subtle ways in which demonic influence attempts to exploit our weaknesses. Through the spiritual disciplines of prayer and fasting, we take seriously the spiritual undercurrent of any controversy we consider entering. We acknowledge this spiritual undercurrent by preparing ourselves for the spiritual risks that our participation may entail for ourselves and others.

Question 2: What Is at Stake for Them?

One of the most exasperating experiences in conflict is to express a compelling case for your own convictions based on established facts and clear logic only to be rebuffed on the basis of some irrational objection. We live in a society enamored with information. Consequently, we sometimes fall into the delusion that if we could just present a sufficient amount of relevant information, our opponents would have to acknowledge our rightness and their wrongness. But this assumes that the fundamental difference between us and those with whom we disagree is a lack of valid information. Certainly, the fragmentation of our news sources and the difficulty of verifying facts complicate our conflicts. But humans are not computers. We don't rely exclusively on rationality to navigate the controversies we care most about. The reason controversies become so intensely debated is precisely that they arouse deeply felt emotions. And they do that because the parties involved believe the stakes are high. Just as it's important to

5. Scripture quotations in this chapter are from the English Standard Version.

recognize what's at stake for yourself, it is wise to consider this second question. What is at stake for the other party?

Felt Needs and Underlying Issues

Despite the way our society tends to prioritize reason over emotion, our emotions serve the important function of manifesting our desires. What people desire is a fundamental consideration in our engagement with controversy. Our emotions sometimes expose our threatened loves even before we are cognitively aware of the perceived threat. In short, emotions provide a window into felt needs. We ought to pay attention to the emotions and felt needs of others, whether in public controversy or private debate, for two significant reasons. First, the felt needs of our opponents may be needs we can sympathize with, needs that become a point of contact that allows us to build bridges (Matt. 15:21–28). They can remind us of our common fears and frustrations. They can awaken our compassion when we feel tempted to focus only on protecting our own interests.

For example, those who are strongly against vaccinations and espouse vaccine conspiracy theories might have had some negative experiences in the past, such as a real (or perceived) vaccine injury. Their child may be the victim of a real (but rare) vaccine side effect, or they may think their child's autism was caused by a vaccine, even though the scientific evidence doesn't support this causal connection. Regardless of whether their belief is supported by good evidence or not, taking the time to understand where it comes from and what's at stake for them can help us intuitively regard them as fellow humans in need of sympathy, and not just enemies to be defeated. Practicing compassion and selflessness is among the most compelling ways Christians have historically demonstrated the character of the gospel in the midst of controversies with the unbelieving world.

Second, the felt needs of potential opponents will sometimes make it unprofitable to pursue certain kinds of engagement with controversy. For years I have been fascinated by Jesus's confrontation with the chief priests and elders concerning John's ministry of baptism.

> And when he entered the temple, the chief priests and the elders of the people came up to him as he was teaching, and said, "By what authority are you doing these things, and who gave you this authority?" Jesus answered them, "I also will ask you one question, and if you tell me the answer, then I also will tell you by what authority I do these things. The baptism of John, from where did it come? From heaven or from man?" And

they discussed it among themselves, saying, "If we say, 'From heaven,' he will say to us, 'Why then did you not believe him?' But if we say, 'From man,' we are afraid of the crowd, for they all hold that John was a prophet." So they answered Jesus, "We do not know." And he said to them, "Neither will I tell you by what authority I do these things." (Matt. 21:23-27)

Jesus recognized that the Jewish leaders' opposition to him did not stem from an absence of information. So, he refused to answer their request for information. But he did so in a way that exposed their apathy toward the truth. Jesus correctly discerned that the basis of his authority was irrelevant to them. They were concerned with preserving their own authority and regarded Jesus's popularity and ministry as a subversive threat. In this case, both parties were correct. They could and did argue about other things, but Jesus's recognition of the fundamental motivation of these leaders clarified the wastefulness of participating in the controversy about his authority on the terms they presented. Instead, he spoke to them in parables, one of which invited them to indirectly announce their own guilt for rejecting him (Matt. 21:28-32).

One of the practical implications of identifying what is at stake for potential opponents in controversy is that we must learn to recognize the role of symbols in public debate. Public debates become more complicated when people deploy symbols because the same object, phrase, and actions mean different things to different people. For example, what is the significance of a red MAGA hat after the election of 2020? What does it mean to have a formal initiative for "diversity, equity, and inclusion" in your organization? What does it mean to kneel during the national anthem at a football game? Symbols such as these often lead to peripheral debates about what a particular symbol means and who has legitimate authority to interpret its meaning. These debates can then become vague and counterproductive proxies that fail to address the actual underlying issues at stake. Jesus's example models the recognition that sometimes we need to reframe controversy before we engage in it, instead of accepting it as presented to us. Taking the time to discern what is at stake for our opponents and to understand how their symbols reflect their felt needs can help us avoid distraction by secondary issues and participate in controversies more wisely.

Question 3: Am I Willing to Lose?

If we can take seriously the presence of spiritual undercurrents in contemporary controversies, and if we acknowledge the habit of deceit among wicked spirits, we can anticipate that the aims of individuals and institutions that Christians oppose may be distinct from the aims of our spiritual adversaries.

Consider this scenario. A husband and his unbelieving wife may engage in a tense, ongoing debate about whether the coronavirus is spread through 5G technology and whether COVID-19 vaccines contain tracking devices. The wife spends inordinate amounts of time searching the Internet for information that confirms her conviction and participating in online chats with fellow "believers." She stops getting adequate sleep, her performance at work declines, and she becomes less emotionally available to their young children. The exasperated husband in turn becomes obsessed with proving the absurdity of these theories. He too spends excessive time on the Internet searching for information. He too neglects sleep, work, and their children. The strain gradually erodes the stability of their marriage and the mental health of their children. The husband never realizes that the devil's aim is to instigate a divorce that will result in the mother gaining custody of their children and raising them away from the influence of a Christian community.

This hypothetical scenario reflects the reality that when we participate in controversy, we often find ourselves simultaneously fighting on two fronts, one in the social sphere, and one in the spiritual sphere. This creates the ironic possibility of winning on one front while losing on the other. Because of this possibility, we ought to reflect on this third question. Am I willing to lose?

Sometimes, what appears to be and feels like defeat may actually be a necessary step toward victory. The preeminent example of victory through apparent defeat is Jesus's crucifixion. By yielding to the betrayal of a friend, an unjust sham of a trial, and a humiliating crucifixion, Christ overthrew the reign of sin, death, and the devil. Christ consistently taught his followers to expect persecution and suffering for the sake of his kingdom (Matt. 5:11-12; 10:16-25; 16:24). Furthermore, he modeled patient endurance under persecution throughout his ministry.

We live in a society obsessed with winning. We want to win games, awards, arguments, trials, and elections because our society rewards winners. Winning is not inherently wrong. Indeed, the basis of Christian hope is Jesus's ultimate victory over all the destructive forces of evil. However, the overwhelming desire to win can distract us from which contests are most worth winning. Sometimes earning trust, reconciling a relationship, demonstrating compassion, or modeling moral integrity is the primary victory we ought to pursue when we participate in a controversy. At times, accomplishing such victories includes defeat in your pursuit of a secondary goal.

Distinguishing Primary and Secondary Goals

To follow the example of Jesus in this regard, we need to do two things. First, we must distinguish between primary and secondary goals. Second, we must be willing to endure the consequences of losing secondary battles for the sake of winning our primary battles. In the scenario above, the wife's conspiracy theories create real problems for the family. But the husband must decide which of his goals should be primary: changing his wife's mind or keeping his family intact. If he chooses the latter, he will have to endure some losses. He will also need to model the humility, compassion, and self-discipline of Christ. These are precisely the characteristics Christ aims to form in his followers. Of course, these are also the characteristics the devil aims to undermine in the followers of Christ. The cosmic battle between good and evil that rages all around us also rages within. When we consider our participation in controversy, we must determine which battles we are willing to lose in order to win the battles that are most necessary to win.

Faithful Participation in Controversy

As we contemplate how to follow Christ faithfully in the way we participate in controversy, the questions proposed above—What is at stake for me? What is at stake for the other party? Am I willing to lose?—don't guarantee safe passage through the highly charged, and overwhelmingly complex, debates that have caused so much disruption in our public discourse and personal relationships. In fact, they presume that our involvement in controversy is risky. We should expect to suffer some loss. However, these questions remind us to take seriously the spiritual risks that we sometimes overlook. First, acknowledging our own susceptibility to sinful inclinations to pursue comfort, self-validation, and power at the expense of others can help us enter into controversy with greater self-awareness and soberness. Doing so allows us to recognize when it may be wiser to remain uninvolved. Second, making the effort to understand the felt needs of others gives us the opportunity to extend dignity and compassion to others, even when we disagree with them. Furthermore, taking time to discern how others express their values and concerns through literal and symbolic means can help us engage more wisely in our conflicts with them. Third, part of our preparation for getting involved in controversy is clarifying which victories are most important and committing ourselves to them, even when that involves losing on a secondary front.

To answer the third question well, we actually need to return to the first question. What is at stake for me? Clearly understanding what is at stake for us prepares us to determine which victories are spiritually most significant. It shows us what we might lose along the way. Greater self-awareness of our own weaknesses can also awaken greater forbearance for the weaknesses of others. All three questions are interrelated. Reflecting on them ought to help us cultivate wisdom, compassion, and humility. The world often rewards the proud and overbearing. Yet the Christ who leads us into controversy by his own example is the one who conquered sin through sacrificial love and death. His life should be our pattern because his reward is greater.

References

Bocian, Konrad, and Bogdan Wojciszke. "Self-Interest Bias in Moral Judgments of Others' Actions." *Personality and Social Psychology Bulletin* 40, no. 7 (April 2014): 4–5. https://www.researchgate.net/publication/261757400_Self-Interest_Bias_in_Moral_Judgments_of_Others'_Actions.

Haidt, Jonathan. "Why the Past Ten Years of American Life Have Been Uniquely Stupid." *Atlantic*, April 11, 2022. https://www.theatlantic.com/magazine/archive/2022/05/social-media-democracy-trust-babel/629369/.

18

THE RELIGIOUS RHETORIC OF QANON

Chase Andre

In the afternoon of January 6, 2021, less than two minutes after the vice president of the United States is ushered out of the Senate chamber, over which he is presiding, a ragtag group of would-be insurrectionists breach the chamber doors.[1] A few men are dressed in tactical gear, some in plain clothes, others are draped in various patriotic or pro-Trump flags. One, bare-chested, wears William-Wallace-meets-American-Patriot face paint and Nordic horns on his head. This man, Jacob Anthony Angeli Chansley—the conspiritualist known to the world as the QAnon Shaman[2]—chants and pounds the flagpole flying Old Glory with fervor. Then, he raises a bullhorn to rally everyone in the Senate chamber to prayer.

"Conspirituality," a term popularized in 2011 by researchers Charlotte Ward and David Voas, describes Chansley well. Noticing a melding of "conspiracy theory and alternative spirituality" occurring online, Ward and Voas advance this term to capture a "politico-spiritual philosophy" that weaves together conspiracy theorists' claim that a shadowy league pulls unseen levers of political and social control with the guiding belief

---

1. Lauren Leatherby et al., "How a Presidential Rally Turned into a Capitol Rampage," *New York Times*, January 12, 2021, https://www.nytimes.com/interactive/2021/01/12/us/capitol-mob-timeline.html.

2. After writing, but prior to publication, Chansley entered a plea deal with prosecutors about his role during the January 6, 2021, insurrection and requested to no longer be known by the moniker QAnon Shaman.

of New Age spirituality seekers, that humanity must be awakened to a new paradigm.[3]

Chansley is a made-for-Instagram model of these colliding worldviews. He claims to have been on a "shamanic path for over a decade," and his torso is adorned in tattoos depicting the hammer of Thor and other icons of "Norse paganism."[4] The young, white conspiracy theorist from the American West takes up shaman spirituality to declare himself the apostle-like mouthpiece of an otherwise anonymous, fringe Internet movement and becomes an unlikely chaplain during an insurrection.

Standing behind Vice President Pence's desk, one of the group raises an arm, shouting, "Jesus Christ, we invoke your name! Amen!" And a chorus of amens resound. Seizing the moment as resident clergy, Chansley speaks up: "Let's all say a prayer in this sacred space," then continues:

> Thank you Heavenly Father for gracing us with this opportunity to stand up for our God-given unalienable rights.... To allow us to exercise our rights, to allow us to send a message to all the tyrants, the communists, and the globalists that this is our nation not theirs, that we will not allow the America—the American way, of the United States of America—to go down....
>
> Thank you divine, omniscient, omnipotent, and omnipresent creator God for blessing each and every one of us here and now.... Thank you for allowing the United States of America to be reborn. Thank you for allowing us to get rid of the communists, the globalists, and the traitors within our government. We love you and we thank you, in Christ's holy name we pray![5]

And all the insurrectionists said, "Amen."

Is QAnon a Christian movement? In the January 2021 American Perspectives Survey, the Survey Center on American Life found that Repub-

---

3. Charlotte Ward and David Voas, "The Emergence of Conspirituality," *Journal of Contemporary Religion* 26, no. 1 (2011): 103-4, doi:10.1080/13537903.2011.539846.

4. Jack Jenkins, "The Insurrectionists' Senate Floor Prayer Highlights a Curious Trumpian Ecumenism," Religion News Service, February 25, 2021, https://religionnews.com/2021/02/25/the-insurrectionists-senate-floor-prayer-highlights-a-curious-trumpian-ecumenism/.

5. "A Reporter's Video from Inside the Capitol Siege," *New Yorker*, January 17, 2021, https://www.newyorker.com/news/video-dept/a-reporters-footage-from-inside-the-capitol-siege.

licans who are evangelical are "much more receptive to conspiracies than non-evangelical Republicans."[6] The Public Religion Research Institute (PRRI) found a similar connection between Christians who are conservative Republicans and QAnon beliefs.[7] This harmonizes with what pastors are reporting across the country. Lifeway Research reports that "49% of U.S. Protestant pastors say they frequently hear members of their congregation repeating conspiracy theories they have heard about why something is happening in our country."[8] When it comes to Q, some pastors feel pushed out of the pulpit. "It's not easy watching people that you've invested time in becoming radicalized so quickly right in front of you," one confesses.[9] Whether we recognize it or not, the movement known as QAnon is reshaping the topography of many churches.

If we are watching conspiracism create fissures where churches once stood on common ground, what are the tectonic plates shifting beneath the surface? What is the thread that connects QAnon to a prayer invoked in Christ's name during a violent insurrection? And for that matter, who is Q, and why did this once-fringe movement, spawned from the bowels of the Internet, take root in churches across the United States? To attempt to discover this, I analyze each of the "Q drops," or messages from Q, posted during 2020—when Q's notoriety surged—to look for the language that would resonate with a Christian audience in the United States. Amidst the memes and coded conspiracies, I discover five categories of religious rhetoric employed by Q to speak to the religious inclinations of the movement's target audience. For the sake of Christian discipleship, pastors and Christian leaders must understand why and how the language of Q became seen as acceptable within churches across the country, and congruent with what the church is about.

6. Daniel A. Cox, "Rise of Conspiracies Reveals an Evangelical Divide in the GOP," AEI, February 12, 2021, https://www.aei.org/articles/rise-of-conspiracies-re veals-an-evangelical-divide-in-the-gop/.

7. PRRI Staff, "Understanding QAnon's Connection to American Politics, Religion, and Media Consumption," Public Religion Research Institute, May 27, 2021, https://www.prri.org/research/qanon-conspiracy-american-politics-report/.

8. Aaron Earls, "Half of U.S. Protestant Pastors Hear Conspiracy Theories in Their Churches," Lifeway Research, January 26, 2021, https://lifewayresearch .com/2021/01/26/half-of-u-s-protestant-pastors-hear-conspiracy-theories-in-th eir-churches/.

9. Sophia Ankel, "Pastors Are Leaving Their Congregations after Losing Their Churchgoers to QAnon," *Business Insider*, March 14, 2021, https://www.businessin sider.com/pastors-quit-after-qanon-radicalize-congregation-2021-3.

Who Is Q?

In October 2017, a user known only as Q posted on the anonymous message board 4chan about the imminent arrest of Hillary Clinton. That was not the only Q prophecy that failed to come to pass. And yet, over the next three years, Q would publish nearly five thousand posts across anonymous message boards—first 4chan, then 8chan, which then rebranded as 8kun. These three sites exist in the space of the Internet that ostensibly champions free speech. In practice, however, they are hollows of vitriol, racism, sexism, anti-Semitism, and a tacit competition to post the most bombastic, shock-inducing meme of the day. Users on these sites are anonymous (the "Anons" in QAnon), but subsequent posts by particular users can be identified through a verified code—a kind of digital signature. This is how whoever posts as Q, an alleged Washington, DC, insider with Q-level security clearance, can remain anonymous yet be identified as Q by the denizens of the sites.[10]

Even amidst the anonymity, many have attempted to unmask the persona known as Q. Documentaries have been dedicated to that end. After an in-depth analysis of the text of the 4,950 Q drops, researchers posited that two separate individuals are behind the Q persona.[11] Citizen journalists, through the examination of metadata encoded in pictures posted by Q, propose two time zones from which Q operated.[12] While understanding who Q is may help uncover motivations behind the persona, it's a moot point. Q's anonymity is part of the cult appeal.

Technically anonymous, Q would not have the reach that the movement amassed if the posts remained on these sites. Once these Q drops began

---

10. Q-level security clearance is the equivalent to top-secret security clearance granted by the Department of Energy. It's worth noting, though departmentally equivalent, it is not synonymous with the US Department of Defense's top-secret clearance. In practice, there's little reason to think someone with Q-level clearance, specifically, would have intimate working knowledge of the president's day-to-day affairs.

11. "Style Analysis by Machine Learning Reveals That Two Authors Likely Shared the Writing of QAnon's Messages at Two Different Periods in Time," Orph-Analytics, December 21, 2020, https://www.orphanalytics.com/en/news/whitepa per202012/OrphAnalyticsQAnon2020.pdf.

12. Abigail W. Xavier and Robert Amour, "Where in the World Is Q? Clues from Image Metadata," *Bellingcat*, May 10, 2021, https://www.bellingcat.com/news/rest -of-world/2021/05/10/where-in-the-world-is-q-clues-from-image-metadata/.

to garner acclaim on 4chan, syndicates published their contents to Reddit and a variety of Q-devoted sites. Since the crackdown on Q-content post-January 6, Reddit and other sites have removed much Q-affiliated media. I used the site QAnon.pub as the repository for my research.

Q drops are intentionally cryptic. It takes the work of dedicated interpreters who crawl the Internet to make meaning of each post. In this way, Q invites the audience of "anons" into the cocreation of these coded briefs—a seductive invitation that gives participants a sense of agency and community as they decode, assemble, and amplify the message together.

Central to that message is Donald Trump: hero and true patriot who's fighting a thinly veiled battle against a powerful cabal of Satan-worshiping, child-trafficking elites composed of Democrats and Hollywood royalty. In their research, PRRI adds two more core tenets to define QAnon believers: first, "There is a storm coming that will sweep away the elites and restore the rightful leaders," and second, "American patriots may have to resort to violence in order to save our country."[13] But QAnon has been dubbed a "big-tent" conspiracy, incorporating theories surrounding 9/11 and Kennedy family deaths, as well as fueling doubts about COVID-19 and the 2020 election. Because of both the disparate nature of the conspiracies under the roof of Q and the participatory nature of the interpretation and amplification of Q drops beyond their source site, some are taken by conspiracies within QAnon's domain, even while rejecting the more severe iterations of its core beliefs.

While the task of untangling Q's grip on evangelicalism in the United States will undoubtedly benefit from the gifts of theology, psychology, history, and philosophy, examining how these conspiracies spread communicatively will strengthen our ability to recognize future patterns of rhetoric and address them before new conspiracies take root in Christian communities. Are evangelicals prone to conspiracy theories, or is there something specific about how QAnon has won their appeal? This question is rhetorical in nature, not in the sense that it doesn't warrant an answer, but in the sense that only a close examination of Q's rhetoric—the way, the why, and the how of Q's communication—will illuminate a response. In Q's drops, five categories of religious rhetoric significantly help shed a light on Q's sway over evangelicals.

13. PRRI Staff, "Understanding QAnon's Connection to American Politics, Religion, and Media Consumption."

Category One: Civil Religion

The first rhetorically significant category is best described as "civil religion." These are references to a vaguely Judeo-Christian deity, common throughout American public life. Civil religion pays homage to a Creator from whom we receive inalienable freedoms, but its theology does not become much more granular than that. It is the religious vernacular of American leaders who speak to a nation of many creeds. For example, I can't name a president, whether Republican or Democrat, that failed to conclude some speech with "God bless America"—a palatable religious reference that's far from distinctly Christian. Beyond this prosaic refrain, the clearest examples of civil religious rhetoric came in phrases like "Will we be a free nation under God?"—another familiar, albeit imprecise idiom.[14] Indistinct religious references are a present, innocuous part of American political discourse, and present in the Q drops. As a product of American political culture, there's little relevance to them, outside how they operate as part of the larger structure of religious rhetoric in the United States.

Category Two: Spiritual Language

The second category is best described as "spiritual language." This is the linguistic home of the New Age vein of conspirituality. These messages may feel familiar to Christian spirituality, but they often contradict common colloquialisms in Christian culture.

One frequent refrain within this category is the call to "Have faith in humanity."[15] It strikes me as dissonant against the more explicitly Christian "insider" language Q proffers. "Have faith in yourself" or soft New Ageisms such as "Let light guide you" or "Unity is Peace" were only once paired with "Have faith in God"—a much more familiar admonition in Christian circles.[16]

The ubiquity of spiritual language in Q's rhetoric demonstrates affiliation to the New Age element of conspirituality. However, even if conspiratorial thinking has laid claim inside Christian communities, these communities typically do not interface with humanist and New Age culture. So,

14. Q Drop #4545, June 29, 2020, https://qanon.pub/#4545.

15. Q Drop #4427, June 5, 2020, https://qanon.pub/#4427.

16. Q Drop #4550, June 30, 2020, https://qanon.pub/#4550; Q Drop #4429, June 6, 2020, https://qanon.pub/#4429.

QAnon represents a bridge between conspirituality and Christianity; the rhetor behind Q may speak from within the conspirituality community to a Christian audience. Rather than presenting as a Christian cultural insider, for Q, Christian rhetoric is utilitarian; it serves to speak to, and create an identity with, a particular public. This becomes more evident when the remaining three categories are considered.

Category Three: Spiritual Warfare

Third, a distinct category of spiritual warfare rhetoric is present throughout the Q drops. This category reveals the other side of the conspirituality coin. Where "spiritual language" is a New Age appropriation of religio-spiritual rhetoric, "spiritual warfare" contains the more militant expressions of Q's conspiratorial worldview. Statements in this category serve as an invitation for soldiers in the conspiracy to enlist as soldiers in an ongoing war of cosmic significance—one where the soul of the nation is at stake. As Q puts it, "If America falls darkness will soon follow."[17] While often borrowing from a Christian understanding of spiritual warfare, this war is always bracketed within the scope of Q's conspiracy mythos: a battle for the United States; a constant threat of powerful unseen, yet human, enemies; and a self-aggrandizing of this national struggle to the heights of global or universal significance.

This war framing is necessary to galvanize would-be combatants. It motivates conspiracism and invites opportunity to see oneself caught up in that cosmic cause. Reflecting on the rhetoric of spiritual warfare in conspiracism, Michael Mertes writes: "In the modern era, superhuman forces shaping humankind's destiny—above all, Satan—have been replaced by real or imaginary secret societies of various kinds: the Illuminati; the Freemasons; the Jesuits; the Elders of Zion; Opus Dei; the Bilderberg Group; the liberal American East Coast press; Wall Street; the military-industrial complex; international corporations; the 'deep state'; the Bill & Melinda Gates Foundation; George Soros's Open Society Foundations—the list goes on."[18] Q sets sights on a number from this list; the deep state has become a new Satan.

While the language of spiritual warfare might appeal to a Christian audience, the focus is no longer "against the rulers, against the authorities,

---

17. Q Drop # 4545, June 29, 2020. https://qanon.pub/#4545.

18. Michael Mertes, "Contemporary Conspiracism: The Return of Satan," *Israel Journal of Foreign Affairs* 14, no. 3 (2020): 421, doi:10.1080/23739770.2020.1840811.

against the powers of this dark world and against the spiritual forces of evil in the heavenly realms" (Eph. 6:12 NIV). Q describes the enemies of the patriots as a swamp aligned with Satan; Q says that "these people are pure evil"[19] and that the coming storm will be "Children of light vs children of darkness. United against the Invisible Enemy of all humanity."[20] In this way, spiritual warfare rhetoric serves two purposes: first, it strips the humanity from the people in the groups Q sets out against; second, the spiritual warfare rhetoric grants Q a baptized spiritual authority and a sense for followers of the eternal significance of their quest.

Careful students of both history and communication may recognize this othering rhetoric as the precursor to violence. It's easier for humans to justify killing when the object of our violence are not bearers of the *imago Dei* but cockroaches, rats, a cancer, or as Q puts it, "Demons" who "serve the devil."[21] Dehumanizing rhetoric is elemental to the world's worst atrocities. So typical an ingredient, dehumanization via hate propaganda is listed as the fourth of Gregory H. Stanton's ten stages of genocide.[22] When those with authority or attention direct their followers to see the opposition as less-than-human, calls for violence may be close.

For many who follow Q, the appropriation of the Christian articulation of spiritual warfare provides a powerful sense of cosmic struggle against evil, bolstering the significance of their participation in Q's war. Anons respond to these spiritually tinged battle cries with real-world violence. On June 29, 2020, a Q drop included the lines: "Like past battles fought, we now face our greatest battle at present, a battle to save our Republic, our way of life, and what we decide (each of us) now will decide our future." While Q often frames the battle as cosmic, spiritual, and ultimate, Q forms a direct connection here to "past battles" fought "to save our Republic"— the implication being that this battle demands more than prayer. And QAnon's devotees seem to perceive exactly what this battle will take.

Over time, the violent, real-world actions associated with QAnon continue to climb. In October 2020, the *Guardian* released a report of twelve incidents related to QAnon, from reckless driving while live-streaming conspiracy rants to allegedly murdering a mob boss.[23] No Q drops posted

19. Q Drop #3967, April 15, 2020, https://qanon.pub/#3967.

20. Q Drop #4545, June 29, 2020, https://qanon.pub/#4545.

21. Q Drop #4402, June 29, 2020, https://qanon.pub/#4402.

22. Visit the Genocide Education Project for more. https://www.genocideeducation.org/wp-content/uploads/2016/03/ten_stages_of_genocide.pdf.

23. Lois Beckett, "QAnon: A Timeline of Violence Linked to the Conspiracy The-

from December 8, 2020, about a month prior to the insurrection at the Capitol in Washington, DC, until June 24, 2022.[24] And yet, eight months into that silence, Q made headlines when a father killed his two toddlers with a spearfishing gun. According to the FBI affidavit, the Santa Barbara, California, resident told authorities he had been "enlightened [by] QAnon and Illuminati conspiracy theories" and was convinced that he was saving the world from the monsters his children were going to grow up into, because of his wife's serpent DNA.[25] In his mind, his kids and his wife were something other than fully human. Ethereal conspiracies and dehumanizing hate speech descend into real-world tragedies. And a misapplication of spiritual warfare theology may have offered a push.

Category Four: Explicitly Christian Content

Fourth, there were statements that could not be categorized as anything other than explicitly Christian. These took the shape of distinctly Christian prayers or passages of Scripture. Notably, Q gravitates toward passages and prayers that reemphasize the theme of spiritual warfare. One passage, dealing with the armor of God in Ephesians 6:10–18, was cited in full or in part in over 10 percent of the examined set of Q drops with religious rhetoric. These verses underscore the spiritual warfare element of Q's rhetoric while reaffirming the purported Christian grounds for its cause. Notably, other than the New Age humanist mantras found in category two, no rhetoric from any other religion or perspective filtered through in Q's writings. Again, an appeal to a Christian audience seems intentional.

The Bible is not peripheral in the minds of Q's audience—and Q seems to leverage this to reemphasize the significance of Q's cause. Explicitly Christian content functions as a reaffirmation of identity for Q's audience, and to underscore Q's cause. For example, Q posted a prayer written by

---

ory," *Guardian*, October 16, 2020, https://www.theguardian.com/us-news/2020 /oct/15/qanon-violence-crimes-timeline.

24. Jack Brewster, "'Q' Hasn't Posted in Six Months—but Some QAnon Followers Still Keep the Faith," *Forbes*, June 8, 2021, https://www.forbes.com/sites /jackbrewster/2021/06/08/q-hasnt-posted-in-6-months-but-some-qanon-follow ers-still-keep-the-faith/?sh=2269c39b6071.

25. "Santa Barbara Surf Instructor Accused of Killing His Two Young Children," *Ventura County (CA) Star*, August 17, 2021, https://www.vcstar.com/story/news/lo cal/communities/county/2021/08/11/owner-santa-barbara-surf-school-accused -killing-his-children-ventura-county/8099844002/.

author Rebecca Barlow Jordan in 2015 but failed to cite the source, so that it appeared as though the prayer originated from Q.[26] The effect? Q broadcasts an image of devotion with a rich, bold, and public prayer life. The truth? I found no proof of a prayer crafted by Q. Once again, Q's Christianity seems performative for an intended public, rather than born from within the church community or from a space of personal piety.

The topic of Jordan's prayer only proves the point. Several iterations of Jordan's prayer can be found by searching the Web for "spiritual warfare prayers"—which may suggest the depth of Q's content research. Q is selective, only sharing what can be bent toward Q's cause, citing, "Make me brave, so I can stand and fight the spiritual battles in my life and in our world. . . . Together, Lord, we'll win"—but leaving out a line from the original that petitions "Lord Jesus" to "Guard us from those who scheme against righteousness [and] twist truth into lies to accomplish their evil intents."[27] Even when it comes to explicitly Christian content, Q exploits Christian identity for the service of another cause.

Q imagines an audience of anons who think of themselves as Christians and are familiar with the language of Christian culture. For Q's target audience, religious markers are as fundamental to their self-concept as their unwavering patriotism. And this bipartite identity structures the basis for the final category.

Category Five: Christian Nationalism

When woven together, these threads of civil religion, spiritual and warfare language, and explicitly Christian rhetoric form another, stronger cord: Christian nationalism. In *Taking America Back for God: Christian Nationalism in the United States*, Andrew L. Whitehead and Samuel L. Perry note that Christian nationalism isn't synonymous with Christianity but is a cultural architecture "undergirded by a combination of conservative political ideology, belief in the Bible, apocalyptic visions of societal decline, and divine militarism" encapsulated by the phrase "You stand at the flag and

---

26. Q Drop #4739, September 20, 2020, https://qanon.pub/#4739. Cf. Rebecca Barlow Jordan, "Spiritual Warfare Prayers for Supernatural Help in the Battle," IBelieve.com, September 21, 2015, https://www.ibelieve.com/faith/a-prayer-for -spiritual-warfare.html.

27. Q Drop #4739; Jordan, "Spiritual Warfare Prayers for Supernatural Help in the Battle."

you kneel at the cross."[28] Christian nationalism offers a salient identity for those within its cultural bounds. A conflation of God and country, Christian nationalism is built on an assumption that God is on the side of America, rather than following the wisdom of Israel's prophets who implored the country to be right with God. Christian nationalism weaves the symbols of the American mythos with the symbols of the Christian faith, until blood shed by soldiers is sanctifying blood, and Jesus died for America.

Christian nationalism leverages the language of Christianity, but it is not synonymous with it. Whitehead and Perry continue, "Christian nationalism is significant because calls to 'take America back for God' are not primarily about mobilizing the faithful toward religious ends. . . . They are instead seeking to retain or gain power in the public sphere."[29] Like Q's serpentine use of civil religion, spiritual warfare framing, and explicitly Christian content for ulterior motives, Christian nationalism leverages the language of faithfulness for the purpose of power. And it demands faithful allegiance from its adherents. As historian Kristin Kobes Du Mez summarizes, "If you believe that America is God's chosen nation, you need to fight for it and against others."[30] Much wrong can be justified when people think God is on their side.

Throughout the history of the United States, Christian nationalist apologia has rendered, implicitly or not, America as a new Israel and enforced through its rhetoric a form of ethnic purity, drawing the line marking who is—and isn't—a *true* American. For example, Samuel Davies Baldwin, in the mid-1800s, wrote that the immigrants arriving on America's shores were fulfillment of the end-times prophecy that Israel would gather the nations, and he believed Ezekiel 38 pointed to a war between the United States and "a Russian-led European alliance."[31] More recently, Anthea Butler points out that, post-9/11, some evangelical leaders began to frame conflict with Muslims in spiritual warfare terms.[32] This blurs the lines between the War

28. Andrew L. Whitehead and Samuel L. Perry, *Taking America Back for God: Christian Nationalism in the United States* (New York: Oxford University Press, 2020), 13, 80.

29. Whitehead and Perry, *Taking America Back*, 153.

30. Kristin Kobes Du Mez, *Jesus and John Wayne: How White Evangelicals Corrupted a Faith and Fractured a Nation* (New York: Liveright, 2021), 303.

31. Paul S. Boyer, *When Time Shall Be No More: Prophecy Belief in Modern American Culture*, Studies in Cultural History (Cambridge, MA: Belknap Press of Harvard University Press, 1992).

32. Anthea Butler, *White Evangelical Racism: The Politics of Morality in America* (Chapel Hill: University of North Carolina Press, 2021), 104.

on Terror abroad and neighbors of differing creeds at home—it also blurs the line between the blood shed on the battlefield and the blood of the cross. As in Chansley's Senate chamber oration, God saves patriots from "all the tyrants, the communists, and the globalists" because "this is our nation not theirs."[33] To the Christian nationalist, the blessing of America is a duty that God performs.

Q draws this antagonistic us-versus-them demarcation even tighter than the circle of national or ethnic lines. On August 26, 2020, Q posted an image that ties the logo for the Democratic National Committee with a satanic symbol, and writes: "One party discusses God. One party discusses Darkness. One party promotes God. One party eliminates God. Symbolism will be their downfall. The Great Deceiver(s). When was the last time you witnessed a [D] party leader being Patriotic [exhibiting National Pride (love of Country)]?"[34] The only evidence suggested as proof of promoting God is national pride; for the Christian nationalist, eliminating love of country eliminates God. Q intentionally pits faithful patriots against fellow American citizens, turning neighbors into enemies and aligning Democrats with the devil in the hive-mind of the Q community.

Christian nationalism relies on explicitly Christian rhetoric, even when that rhetoric is misapplied, such as Q's use of Christian spiritual warfare. Christian nationalism is not mere civil religion; it is not synonymous with conservative politics, and it extends far beyond healthy expressions of patriotism. While nominally Christian, it bears little resemblance to the cross of Christ. Instead, Christian nationalism is an ideology centered on acquiring or maintaining power over others; "God wins" is a ubiquitous QAnon refrain.[35] But, when God serves to bless this group's country, president, and political exploits, it's clear that the anthem "God wins" is not a statement about God, but rather, about the one who speaks it.

Christian Nationalism and the Community of Q

Christian nationalism's centrality to the culture of Q is apparent not only in the rhetoric of the Q drops but also in how the community communicates. On March 21, 2020, Q posted a link to a YouTube video of instrumental music entitled "Future World Music—Victory of Life"; one of the more

33. "A Reporter's Video from Inside the Capitol Siege."
34. Q Drop #4627, August 26, 2020, https://qanon.pub/#4627.
35. E.g., Q Drop #4396, June 3, 2020, https://qanon.pub/#4396.

than ten thousand comments, all seemingly Q-affiliated, states, "I'm new to Q but look at everyone! Praising God! Even now I can see that Q has brought us closer to God and to each other. God bless our President Trump, and God bless America!"[36] Notice the tight connection between God, Q, and Trump: Q elicits praise to God, who then serves to bless the president and country.

Another reads: "FOR GOD AND COUNTRY. NO FEAR HERE AS PATRIOTS ARE IN CONTROL.... WE HEAR YOU AND WILL STAND BEHIND YOU ALWAYS Q+."[37] Here, patriots—not Christians, nor even Americans, but true American patriots—are the ones with the upper hand. The Christian nationalist refrain, for God and country, rings like a mantra. It's worth noting, too, that allegiance here isn't paid to God, nor to country, but to Q.

In the Q drop from April 15, 2020, Q amplifies an anon's post that states "Just like Q & Q+ put on that Armor of God Patriots! Keep Praying! In the end, God Wins!"[38] Evoking Q's favorite Bible passage, the writer makes clear the armor is not for Christians, but for patriots. To these praying patriots, their team is bound to win. "God" is worn like a jersey, a sign that they're on the winning side.

The rhetoric of Christian nationalism is the key that unlocked the evangelical community for Q. It enunciates identity. For the Christian bent toward Christian nationalism, there seems little dissonance between the good news of the kingdom of God and the gospel of Q. While extending beyond the aim of this brief chapter, this claim could be further verified by investigating the religious rhetoric of the platforms that expanded Q's reach. Were the audiences and followers of conspiracist Alex Jones, Fox News host Sean Hannity, activist Charlie Kirk, or any other early amplifiers of QAnon feeding on a steady diet of Christian nationalism from these platforms? Or did Christian nationalism arise in Freedom Sunday church services, and other overt entangling of God and country from behind pulpits across the country? Q's religious rhetoric fashions a message for a receptive audience of Christian nationalists. But that receptivity predates Q's arrival.[39]

36. XDarkLegacyx2, "Future World Music—Victory of Life (Volume 11 Preview-Early 2011)," YouTube, January 5, 2011, https://www.youtube.com/watch?v=_MK0 j765k04&lc=Ugw1xGFar3UcOqcqGf94AaABAg.

37. "Future World Music."

38. Q Drop #3967, April 15, 2020, https://qanon.pub/#3967.

39. For an in depth, yet brief, survey of the relationship between Christian na-

Beware of the Leaven of Nationalism: A Church without Q

Returning to the image of the Senate chamber prayer, I can't help but think of the missiologists with whom I've studied. If I told them about a shaman spiritualist, in ritualistic garb and covered in tattoos symbolizing pagan gods, who prayed to Jesus after incantational chanting while keeping time with a pagan totem, many would readily describe the scene as "syncretism"—the melding of two distinct religions to create a new set of beliefs and practices. What might it take for American Christians to see this particular amalgamation of God and country as equivalently syncretistic?

The rise of Q-affiliation in churches may be less a feature of Protestantism, or conservatism, and more due to pervasive God-and-country Christian nationalism that co-opts Christian language and culture. How do we know when familiar Christian language is being twisted for another purpose? Consider discerning with these questions:

First, does the spiritual language we encounter promote a love for God, for neighbor—and I'd add, for enemy—or does some other object, person, or ideal take the center? This isn't just the case of placing Q at the center. Even a love of good objects and ideals, like country, flag and freedom, esteemed too highly, might raise these goods to the pedestal of worship in the priorities of our hearts.

Next, consider what is communicated about the other. Are those (presumed) not in the room spoken about with honor and given the benefit of the doubt regarding their motives, or used as scapegoats bearing blame or enemies to be vanquished? It is the language of mere nations to demonize an enemy; it's the language of God's kingdom to love an enemy.

Finally, when "we" is employed in Christian settings, pause to consider who it includes: Can Christians outside the United States find themselves in that "we"? Or Christians across the political aisle? What implications hold for drawing boundary lines too tightly?

Q weaves a persona with the fabric of Christian nationalism, and the audience of anons dons the familiar garb. For Q, God is not a socially palatable reference to a Creator, or specific to the crucified Jesus, but shorthand for the winning team. To explain why Christians in the United States are

---

tionalism and the events at the Capitol on January 6, see the report released by the Baptist Joint Committee for Religious Liberty, Freedom from Religion Foundation, and Christians against Christian Nationalism, available online at https://www.christiansagainstchristiannationalism.org/jan6report.

taken by Q's big tent of conspiracism, scholars, theologians, pastors, and platformed Christian celebrities must examine how the syncretistic tangle of God and country has fashioned a Christian identity for a national culture war and promised that *God wins*.

References

Ankel, Sophia. "Pastors Are Leaving Their Congregations after Losing Their Churchgoers to QAnon." *Business Insider*, March 14, 2021. https://www .businessinsider.com/pastors-quit-after-qanon-radicalize-congrega tion-2021-3.

Boyer, Paul S. *When Time Shall Be No More: Prophecy Belief in Modern American Culture*. Studies in Cultural History. Cambridge, MA: Belknap Press of Harvard University Press, 1992.

Brewster, Jack. "'Q' Hasn't Posted in Six Months—but Some QAnon Followers Still Keep the Faith." *Forbes*, June 8, 2021. https://www.forbes.com/sites /jackbrewster/2021/06/08/q-hasnt-posted-in-6-months-but-some-qan on-followers-still-keep-the-faith/?sh=2269c39b6071.

Butler, Anthea. *White Evangelical Racism: The Politics of Morality in America*. Chapel Hill: University of North Carolina Press, 2021.

Cox, Daniel A. "Rise of Conspiracies Reveals an Evangelical Divide in the GOP." American Enterprise Institute, February 12, 2021. https://www .aei.org/articles/rise-of-conspiracies-reveals-an-evangelical-divide-in -the-gop/.

Du Mez, Kristin Kobes. *Jesus and John Wayne: How White Evangelicals Corrupted a Faith and Fractured a Nation*. New York: Liveright, 2021.

Earls, Aaron. "Half of U.S. Protestant Pastors Hear Conspiracy Theories in Their Churches." Lifeway Research, January 26, 2021. https://lifewayre search.com/2021/01/26/half-of-u-s-protestant-pastors-hear-conspiracy -theories-in-their-churches/.

Greenwood, Sue. 2020. "How British Grannies Are Spreading QAnon Conspir acy Theory Memes on Facebook." *Conversation*, September 25, 2020. https://ray.yorksj.ac.uk/id/eprint/4781/1/how-british-grannies-are -spreading-qanon-conspiracy-theory-memes-on-facebook-145820.

Jenkins, Jack. "The Insurrectionists' Senate Floor Prayer Highlights a Curi ous Trumpian Ecumenism." Religion News Service, February 25, 2021. https://religionnews.com/2021/02/25/the-insurrectionists-senate-floor -prayer-highlights-a-curious-trumpian-ecumenism/.

Jordan, Rebecca Barlow. "Spiritual Warfare Prayers for Supernatural Help in

the Battle." IBelieve.com, September 21, 2015. https://www.ibelieve.com
/faith/a-prayer-for-spiritual-warfare.html.

Leatherby, Lauren, Arielle Ray, Anjali Singhvi, Christiaan Triebert, Derek Wat-
kins, and Haley Willis. "How a Presidential Rally Turned into a Capitol
Rampage." *New York Times*, January 12, 2021. https://www.nytimes.com
/interactive/2021/01/12/us/capitol-mob-timeline.html.

Mertes, Michael. "Contemporary Conspiracism: The Return of Satan." *Israel
Journal of Foreign Affairs* 14, no. 3 (2020): 421. doi:10.1080/23739770.2
020.1840811.

PRRI Staff. "Understanding QAnon's Connection to American Politics, Religion, and Media Consumption." Public Religion Research Institute,
May 27, 2021. https://www.prri.org/research/qanon-conspiracy-american
-politics-report/.

"A Reporter's Video from Inside the Capitol Siege." *New Yorker*, January 17,
2021. https://www.newyorker.com/news/video-dept/a-reporters-foot
age-from-inside-the-capitol-siege.

"Santa Barbara Surf Instructor Accused of Killing His Two Young Children."
Ventura County (CA) Star, August 17, 2021. https://www.vcstar.com/story
/news/local/communities/county/2021/08/11/owner-santa-barbara-surf
-school-accused-killing-his-children-ventura-county/8099844002/.

"Style Analysis by Machine Learning Reveals That Two Authors Likely Shared
the Writing of QAnon's Messages at Two Different Periods in Time."
OrphAnalytics, December 21, 2020. https://www.orphanalytics.com/en
/news/whitepaper202012/OrphAnalyticsQAnon2020.pdf.

Whitehead, Andrew L., and Samuel L. Perry. *Taking America Back for God:
Christian Nationalism in the United States*. New York: Oxford University
Press, 2020.

Xavier, Abigail W., and Robert Amour. "Where in the World Is Q? Clues from
Image Metadata." *Bellingcat*, May 10, 2021. https://www.bellingcat.com
/news/rest-of-world/2021/05/10/where-in-the-world-is-q-clues-from
-image-metadata/.

19

LOVING OUR ONLINE COMMUNITIES

Rachel I. Wightman

Think back over the past twenty-four hours: How many times did you use a computer or smart phone? Did you read the news? Watch a show? Text a friend? Buy something from Amazon? Scroll through a social media feed? If you're like many people in the United States (and elsewhere), you probably looked at a device more than once. Most likely more than once each hour. "According to a survey conducted in February 2021, nearly half of the respondents stated that on average they spent five to six hours on their phone on a daily basis, not including work-related smartphone use. A further 22 percent of respondents said that they spent three to four hours on average on their phone daily."[1] Over and over we reach for our devices, and in the past twenty-five to thirty years (at least) we have seen a huge shift in our culture as our use of these devices and the Internet has grown. From shopping to learning about current events to attending school to communicating with our friends and family, we use the Internet in many aspects of our lives, and in many ways our community has shifted into online spaces.

Prior to the Internet, we went to a store, called a friend, or read a physical newspaper or book. In the past, our physical community was a large

---

1. SellCell.com, "How Much Time on Average Do You Spend on Your Phone on a Daily Basis?" Statista, June 14, 2022, https://www.statista.com/statistics/1224510/time-spent-per-day-on-smartphone-us/.

source of information. These older media formats created a mediated information landscape, one where people got much of their information through modes that required someone else to curate or compile it: journalists, authors, librarians, etc. However, that's not to say biased or inaccurate news and information didn't exist. Its form was just different. How people learned about the world around them was different than how we learn about the world today.

The effects of the changes in technology and the Internet on the economy, our education systems, and our communication methods are not hard to see. We see changes not only in our culture but also in how we gather information. From news to school assignments to Googling our latest medical symptom, we use the Internet to meet many of our information needs. We can open an Internet browser and search for an answer to all kinds of questions. We do so much searching online that the name Google has become synonymous with searching. In casual conversation, we hear "just Google it" to mean "I'll look it up quickly and find the answer." In his 2017 TED talk, Michael Patrick Lynch used the term "Google-knowing" to refer to the quick looking up of information, and this is a reminder that just because we look something up doesn't mean we deeply understand or are an expert at what we find.[2]

Every day we look for and engage with information through these different forms of technology. From reading or watching the news to looking up the menu of our favorite restaurant to watching videos on YouTube or Tik Tok, we engage with information in hundreds of ways. We don't necessarily think about our online habits in terms of "information," but that's what we're doing: finding and using information. The Merriam-Webster dictionary defines "information" as "knowledge obtained from investigation, study, or instruction."[3] In our online spaces, we're often obtaining knowledge, even if that knowledge is simply finding the hours of the local grocery store.

As all these changes have taken place in our culture and we have turned to the Internet for our information needs, there is also a shift in mistrust

2. Michael Patrick Lynch, "How to See Past Your Own Perspective and Find Truth," TED video, 2017, https://www.ted.com/talks/michael_patrick_lynch_how_to_see_past_your_own_perspective_and_find_truth?language=en.

3. Merriam-Webster.com, last updated June 7, 2022, https://www.merriam-webster.com/dictionary/information, s.v. "information."

of online spaces, especially social media.[4] People read or hear news from different sources that seem to contradict each other. Or they find "news" stories that are really opinion pieces or advertisements parading as news, which makes their time online more confusing. We have so many choices on where to get our news and information. We are bombarded with it when we open a browser or scroll through social media. We get decision fatigue trying to decide where to go for information, or trying to figure out if something is trustworthy, or trying to decide whether engaging with a friend online will help or hurt our relationship. And it's getting harder to distinguish between credible information and unreliable information since it all looks the same on a screen.

At the same time that we get overwhelmed by everything we see online and on social media, we're also seeing more and more division in our culture and our relationships. We see it in our families as we struggle to talk through issues with the ones we love the most. Our churches, too, see the division as we sort out the issues we're seeing in our world. It's evident by the comments we see on social media and in our everyday conversations. It doesn't take us long to see how much division there is in our culture, churches, homes, workplaces, and cities. During the COVID-19 pandemic, people posted and shared opinions and information on everything from wearing masks to getting vaccines to remote school options. During the unrest following the killing of George Floyd in Minneapolis in 2020, we saw all kinds of comments about policing, racism, and more. For many people, the division is exacerbated when different groups follow different "experts" and can't seem to agree on who is actually "right" on the issue.

The information landscape is complex and confusing. It has provided us with lots of conveniences—online shopping, video calls to connect with loved ones, and easy access to current events—but it has also created spaces that are overwhelming, not just for people of faith but for everyone. As Christians, we have an opportunity to engage differently in these online spaces. If we want to be light in dark places, we'll need to examine our online spaces and reflect on our own behaviors and habits to see how our faith shows up in these places. But before we ask *how* our faith shows up, we need to ask ourselves, *does* our faith show up?

4. Sora Park et al., "Global Mistrust in News: The Impact of Social Media on Trust," *JMM: The International Journal on Media Management* 22, no. 2 (2020): 83–96, doi:10.1080/14241277.2020.1799794.

Defining Some Terms

Before we go too far, it would be helpful to define some terms. First, for the purposes of this chapter, online spaces are any place you show up and use the Internet (note that there is overlap in many of these):

- email
- social media, for example, Instagram, Facebook, Twitter, Tik Tok, SnapChat
- YouTube
- news coverage—reading or watching
- general websites and blogs

Frequently we find these spaces are on our smart phones, although many of us started exploring these spaces on our computers in the past. Some of us can remember the days of dial-up Internet, when online spaces felt new and exciting. But regardless of where or how we access the Internet, in all these spaces we have a choice: we can passively scroll, watch, or consume, or we can pay attention, invite the Spirit, and use these spaces in our kingdom work.

Other terms that are often used and left undefined are "misinformation" and "disinformation." Both can be found in all those online spaces. Both are problematic. But it's important to know the difference. Misinformation is information that is out of context or incorrect. It's easy to share and can circulate easily in online spaces. Disinformation is also false information but intentionally so. It can also circulate easily online and shows up in online spaces. These two terms, while they may be used interchangeably, are actually quite different, as the intention behind them is not the same. And, in addition to misinformation and disinformation, the term "fake news" is often used in casual conversation but can mean anything from misreporting, to biased news, to blatantly false information.[5] Additionally, deep fakes are videos that have been intentionally altered to spread misinformation. To make matters more confusing, all these terms are often used interchangeably, creating a heightened sense of false information in our media.

Additionally, it is very easy for anyone with the right technology—a smart phone, a computer, the Internet—to create, post, or share information on-

---

5. Maria D. Molina et al., "'Fake News' Is Not Simply False Information: A Concept Explication and Taxonomy of Online Content," *American Behavioral Scientist* 65, no. 2 (February 2021): 180–212, https://doi.org/10.1177/0002764219878224.

line. This is not necessarily a bad thing. We see many instances where people have live-streamed events, which has allowed the world to see what happened in real time. Certainly, during the COVID-19 pandemic we saw musicians and artists use streaming platforms in creative ways for performances. Or, in 2020, when George Floyd was pinned to the ground by police officer Derek Chauvin, many people saw what happened because of bystander video. (While bystander video during police encounters is controversial, having access to videos like that does allow those not in the vicinity to see the event as opposed to reading about the event in the news.)

However, the ability for people to create and share information so easily also creates spaces for conspiracy theories and misinformation or fake news to thrive. Most reputable news outlets have some sort of code of conduct or code of ethics, such as the *New York Times'* "Ethical Journalism: A Handbook of Values and Practices for the News and Editorial Departments."[6] These codes provide guidelines within which journalists work and create information that has been vetted and edited. However, in other spaces, without these codes, there is little regulation, and almost anyone can post anything on Twitter, YouTube, Tik Tok, or a myriad of other platforms. Some of these platforms have codes of conduct or are taking steps to remove misinformation, but it remains relatively easy for people to post content online. It is not difficult for people to create and post misinformation and conspiracy theories on their online accounts on many platforms. This content can then be easily shared and commented on, regardless of its accuracy. And as more people comment, like, or share the content, it becomes more "popular," which moves the content higher in our news and social media feeds, creating the viral moments we've become accustomed to seeing in the last decade.

These environments also create spaces where highly emotional content and reactions thrive. For example, when people see headlines or information that prompts an emotional response, they may respond out of emotion and not always logic. This might also lead to the increase in division and false information we see in our social media feeds. When emotions are high, people may be less likely to pause and fact-check what they see or hear.

In 2020 we saw many examples of both the emotional content and the ease with which people could create and post information. People from

6. "Ethical Journalism: A Handbook of Values and Practices for the News and Editorial Departments," *New York Times*, accessed June 15, 2022, https://www.ny times.com/editorial-standards/ethical-journalism.html.

all types of professions posted and created content about the COVID-19 pandemic, some of it fact and some of it opinion. Other information was completely false, but because it was easy to create and share content, it was hard to stop its spread. There was so much misinformation and disinformation about COVID-19, the World Health Organization used the phrase "Infodemic" to describe the current situation.[7] The world was dealing not only with a global health crisis but also with an information crisis, as people shared and believed false information and conspiracy theories.

Finally, it is especially important to understand filter bubbles and algorithms and the roles they play in our online experiences. Search engines and social media rely heavily on personalization. This means that your search results, your social media feeds, and what you see online are all highly tailored to you. This personalization is built into the constantly running algorithms that determine what you'll see next in your feed or at the top of your search results. This personalization comes from many different factors, such as your geolocation, your browsing history, your browser, your device, your previous search history, etc. These platforms take into account all these factors and predict what you would like to see next. It's highly complicated, and it's happening in your social media feeds and online searches.

On the one hand, many of us love receiving personalized Target coupons or having Amazon ask if we'd like to reorder a specific product. On the other hand, the personalization of our online spaces can also mean we miss a great deal of content. If our feeds and results are tailored to ourselves, we can end up in "filter bubbles"—a term coined by Eli Pariser in 2011.[8] These filter bubbles are essentially hyperfocused echo chambers created by the personalization of our online searches and social media feeds. We see the same things—the same views, biases, etc.—over and over in our online spaces.

Why does it matter? Personalization is great for companies that advertise to us, and it may lead us to discover new products or people that align with our values or interests. On the other hand, we may miss out on content from different perspectives or different parts of the world. For Christians, it means we may also end up in self-created bubbles, surrounding ourselves

7. World Health Organization, "Infodemic," accessed June 15, 2022, https://www.who.int/health-topics/infodemic/.

8. Eli Pariser, *The Filter Bubble: How the New Personalized Web Is Changing What We Read and How We Think* (New York: Penguin Press, 2012).

only with other Christian points of view. While it can be tempting to think that only consuming Christian views is the best, it can also result in a narrowing of our perspective. We may miss out on the opportunity to learn from others if we stay in our filter bubbles. In order to love our neighbors, we need to listen to them and understand their points of view. If we live in a bubble (online or not), we may miss out on opportunities to connect with people who are different from ourselves and the opportunity to see the breadth and beauty of all God's created humanity.

A Christian Response

What is the role of Christians in this environment? As we see the emotional intensity with which people post and share information, it is imperative for Christians to understand the information landscape and how it works. In order to have an impact on our culture, our communities, and those around us, we need to understand how our online spaces work and the role they play in our lives. So much of our lives now takes place in online spaces—from shopping to getting news to video phone calls to education. Almost all aspects of our lives and those of our families, neighbors, and friends are touched or impacted by the Internet and technology. We have an opportunity to love our neighbors in new ways as we interact with them not only next door but also online.

Generally, Christians want to be truth-tellers. Like Jesus, we want to seek truth and share it with others. He loved the marginalized and cared about justice. He taught us to love our neighbors and to be a good Samaritan. As we engage on social media, we too have an opportunity to speak the truth to others. Sharing misinformation (whether intentionally or unintentionally) is not a part of Jesus's truth-telling kingdom. But to speak truth well, we need to understand the information landscape in which we find ourselves. Knowing how filter bubbles and search engines work (even just generally) can make us more effective searchers and wise news consumers and sharers.

We have an opportunity to pay attention to what the Holy Spirit might be teaching us and where we are being led in our online spaces. Are we paying attention to the Spirit's promptings when we're using our social media apps, or are we getting sucked into the shiny technology as we passively consume content? What is the posture of our hearts in these spaces? Do we approach our online spaces with an intent to prove others right or to learn from others? Do we simply passively consume content without engaging?

Our actions on social media and online also give us an opportunity to love our neighbors better. We talk about loving our neighbors in church all the time: making a meal for a neighbor that just had a baby, running an errand for a friend that had surgery, donating to the local homeless shelter. All of these are good things. But what does it look like to love your neighbors in your online spaces? Another way to think about this is, what would the Holy Spirit think about your online interactions and engagement? Are you speaking truth into your online spaces, and are you respecting others and loving the marginalized as Jesus did? (Yes, it's possible to do these things online.) Our online culture is full of "sound bites"—quick comments, likes, tweets, and shares. It can be easy to lose sight of the people behind the posts. When simply looking at words on a screen, we forget that the person that posted them has a story and is made in the image of God.

This does not mean we radically change our beliefs, although being a better consumer of information could result in learning new things! What does it look like to practice a posture of humility as we engage with information online? As we hold some truths in our faith (i.e., Jesus's role as Savior), is it also possible for us to read or engage with information and change our minds on some issues or topics? Ultimately, do we pause to ask ourselves, what is the posture of our hearts as we step into an online environment? Are we actively choosing to approach our online spaces with kindness? Do we recognize that the individual who posted was created in God's image just as we were? Do we approach sharing online the same as if the person or people we are communicating with were across the table from us?

Some Practical Steps and Tools

In addition to these big picture questions and understanding of the information landscape, there are also a number of practical tools we can use to help us engage wisely online. These practices and tools give us a place to start and allow us to respond in kind and wise ways.

Notice your emotions.

First, notice your emotions when you are online. This doesn't mean we shouldn't have emotions when we read or watch the news or other online content. But a lot of online content is designed to get at our emotions, which can lead to quick responses and sharing before we actually know what is true. The emotional response can lead us to spread the misinformation before we even know it's misinformation. Noticing our emotions is not a habit many of us have, but it can be valuable in online spaces. We can be wise in online spaces by pausing and noticing our emotions and how they manifest themselves when we engage with news or other online content.

Pause before responding on social media.

Second, take time and pause before sharing, liking, retweeting, etc. Because it is so easy to comment and share content online, we often do so without thinking. We click "like" or "share" before we've really digested the information. Or we share a news article with someone simply based on its headline, to get a point across. Consider pausing before you share, like, retweet, etc. Give yourself time to process what you've read or watched before you pass it along. Ask the Holy Spirit how he might have you respond. Fact-check the information to make sure you're not passing along misinformation.

Learn a few fact-checking skills.

This may seem complicated, but it doesn't have to be! We don't need to fact-check everything we read, see, or hear. But having a few skills that help us evaluate online information can be invaluable when we try to engage wisely online. There are many resources to help you learn fact-checking skills, but here are a few things to consider:

- Look up the author or creator when you come across new information. Is the person an expert on the topic? Can you find out anything about the hosting organization?
- Reverse-search an image. You can right click on an image online and search for it to see whether it might have been taken out of context.
- Use fact-checking websites, such as Politifact or Snopes. These websites employ fact-checkers to dig deeper into claims, and the best fact-checking sites will cite their sources.
- Dig deeper to find the original source. So much of news and information online is rereporting of the same content. See if you can find the original source, the original study, or the original news story.

Engage with news sources outside your normal ones.

One of the best ways to get outside our comfort zones and our filter bubbles is to read something new and practice a posture of humility and curiosity toward it. What does this look like? Instead of always reading the same news sources, consider looking at different ones to see how they're presenting current events. Allsides.com is a great resource if you're not sure where to start. They present many current events side by side from different news sources, helping you see the differences in how news outlets report on the same event. Practicing this step can give you a broader understanding of the world and what is happening. This shouldn't be an exercise in seeking out another perspective, to say, "I knew I was right!" but rather a way to understand the thinking of those who think differently than you do. As Christians, we can choose to love our neighbors by seeking out their perspectives and humbly trying to learn from them.

Conclusion

Ultimately, Christians have an opportunity to be salt and light in our online spaces. But simply adding our opinion to our online spaces might not always be helpful. We have an opportunity to slow down, be mindful, and love our neighbors well. But we also need to understand the platforms and landscape in which we experience these things. When we understand the bigger picture of how the information landscape is structured and how it works, we are better prepared to love our neighbors in our online spaces.

References

"Ethical Journalism: A Handbook of Values and Practices for the News and Editorial Departments." *New York Times*. Accessed June 15, 2022. https://www.nytimes.com/editorial-standards/ethical-journalism.html.

Lynch, Michael Patrick. "How to See Past Your Own Perspective and Find Truth." TED video, April 2017. https://www.ted.com/talks/michael_patrick_lynch_how_to_see_past_your_own_perspective_and_find_truth?language=en.

Molina, Maria D., S. Shyam Sundar, Thai Le, and Dongwon Lee. "'Fake News' Is Not Simply False Information: A Concept Explication and Taxonomy of Online Content." *American Behavioral Scientist* 65, no. 2 (February 2021): 180–212. https://doi.org/10.1177/0002764219878224.

Pariser, Eli. *The Filter Bubble: How the New Personalized Web Is Changing What We Read and How We Think.* New York: Penguin Press, 2012.

Park, Sora, Caroline Fisher, Terry Flew, and Uwe Dulleck. "Global Mistrust in News: The Impact of Social Media on Trust." *JMM: The International Journal on Media Management* 22, no. 2 (2020): 83–96. doi:10.1080/142 41277.2020.1799794.

SellCell.com. "How Much Time on Average Do You Spend on Your Phone on a Daily Basis?" Statista, June 14, 2022. https://www.statista.com/statis tics/1224510/time-spent-per-day-on-smartphone-us/.

World Health Organization. "Infodemic." Accessed June 15, 2022. https://www .who.int/health-topics/infodemic/.

20

CONSPIRACY THEORIES, POLITICAL TRUST, AND CHRISTIAN WITNESS

Daniel Bennett

At the intersection of Connecticut and Nebraska Avenues in Washington, DC, sits a pizza parlor. Since 2006 customers have visited the restaurant for pizza and chicken wings in a trendy atmosphere. It has been well received by local and national critics; celebrity restaurateur Guy Fieri even featured the venue on a 2010 episode of his program *Diners, Drive-Ins, and Dives*. Patrons also visit the restaurant to grab a beer, support local musicians, and play the occasional game of Ping-Pong.

But in 2016, Comet Ping Pong drew a whole new kind of attention. During that year's presidential election, leaked emails from top Democratic Party officials caught the eye of Internet conspiracy theorists, who believed these officials' seemingly banal messages belied something far more sinister. In what came to be known as "Pizzagate," these amateur detectives—many later affiliated with the larger QAnon community[1]—believed certain people's email references to pizza were coded messages for child sex trafficking, with the basement at Comet Ping Pong playing a central role.

Among those convinced by this conspiracy theory was Maddison Welch. A father of two from North Carolina, Welch gradually became convinced of the Pizzagate conspiracy theory, disgusted by what he read about a cabal of political elites trafficking and abusing children. Eventually, he'd had enough. About a month after the election, on December 4, Welch drove

1. Kevin Roose, "What Is QAnon, the Viral Pro-Trump Conspiracy Theory?" *New York Times*, September 3, 2021, https://www.nytimes.com/article/what-is-qanon.html.

several hours to Washington, DC, to investigate the restaurant for himself. Armed with a semiautomatic rifle, Welch entered Comet Ping Pong and fired several shots. No one was hurt, and after police surrounded the restaurant, Welch surrendered without incident.

In an interview with the *New York Times* following his arrest, Welch said that though he encountered no trafficked children in the restaurant's basement—indeed, the restaurant has no basement—he refused to dismiss Pizzagate altogether.[2] He said he had intended to "shine some light" on the supposed conspiracy, adding that he felt his "heart breaking over the thought of innocent people suffering." Welch also said he had recently discovered Christianity, saying he especially appreciated John Eldridge's book *Wild at Heart* and also referencing a tattoo of Bible verses—Isaiah 40:30-31—on his back.

Welch is not representative of American Christians in their attraction to conspiracy theories, but he is not exactly an outlier, either. Writing for the *New Yorker*, Zoe Heller says, "Perhaps one way to attack our intellectual hubris on this matter is to remind ourselves that we all hold some beliefs for which there is no compelling evidence."[3] No, most Christians will never bring a gun to a restaurant in order to shine light on a supposed sex-trafficking ring. But when beliefs motivate actions, it is important to consider the implications of these beliefs for the church in general, as well as her public witness.

As a Christian, I am troubled about the potential appeal of conspiracy theories and misinformation among my brothers and sisters in the kingdom, which can only hinder our witness to a world in desperate need of the gospel. And as a political scientist, I am concerned about the proliferation of these things and their effects on the American political experiment. Our constitutional order depends not on people agreeing with one another but on people drawing from the same basic reality in making political and civic judgments. Drawing on outlandish and feverish conspiracy theories obscures this shared reality, making it difficult for our system to operate as designed.

In this chapter I highlight research from my discipline about political trust, and how it has been weakened in recent years as a result not only of

2. Adam Goldman, "The Comet Ping Pong Gunman Answers Our Reporter's Questions," *New York Times*, December 7, 2016, https://www.nytimes.com/2016/12/07/us/edgar-welch-comet-pizza-fake-news.html.

3. Zoe Heller, "What Makes a Cult a Cult?" *New Yorker*, July 1, 2021, https://www.newyorker.com/magazine/2021/07/12/what-makes-a-cult-a-cult.

political polarization but also of misinformation and conspiracy theories. Scholars of political behavior have found that people today are less trusting of their political opponents than ever before, largely because of an increasingly polarized and sorted political environment. Seeking and relying on extreme sources of information, often with roots in misinformed and conspiratorial worldviews, do little to ameliorate this divide.

Next, I dive into just how prevalent conspiracy thinking and misinformation is among Christians. Naturally, this answer depends a great deal on what you consider to be misinformation and conspiracy theories. But even a sympathetic understanding of these ideas yields ample evidence that Christians are just as susceptible to this way of thinking as the average American, if not more so. Given scriptural admonitions to seek and embrace truth, this should be worrying for all those concerned with the long-term health of the church.

All of this leads me to this chapter's main argument: Christians should be at the forefront of rejecting conspiracy theories, and wise enough to be able to dismiss misinformation. We must be discerning enough to separate good information from bad and conspiracy from reality, but also confident and strong enough to do so even when it means having to face fears and challenges head-on. Not all Christians who get caught up in conspiracy thinking will end up like Maddison Welch, but our identity and hope in Christ must set a higher bar. God's people should be relentless in seeking truth, not the convenience conspiracy theories so often provide.

Polarization and Trust

Even casual political observers will notice that Americans are a polarized people. Over the past several decades our political institutions have become more divided than at any time since the Civil War. But political polarization is just the tip of the iceberg. Virtually everything about American society has been touched by polarization, from sports and entertainment to restaurants and shopping centers. Nothing is off limits; everything is political.

According to Lilliana Mason, the political scientist and author of *Uncivil Agreement*, this development was predictable.[4] Believe it or not, there was a time when Republicans and Democrats looked so much like one

4. Lilliana Mason, *Uncivil Agreement: How Politics Became Our Identity* (Chicago: University of Chicago Press, 2018).

another that the American Political Science Association published a letter urging the parties to oppose one another more concretely.[5] Over the span of several decades, these two major parties gradually became more distinct from one another, in response to incentives from voters and real differences in policy. Furthermore, as Republicans and Democrats increasingly embraced ideological—like conservative and liberal—labels, many Americans began to attach to these parties in the same sense that a sports fan attaches to a team. They came to see politics as less about a debate over policy and more as a simple contest, a matter of winning and losing. In this sense, the *result* of politics matters little; beating the other team is what counts.

Mason's research explains how political polarization eventually transformed into affective polarization, raising the stakes from policy disagreements to mutual disdain for nonpartisans. Early in her book she references the famous "Robbers Cave" experiment from 1954, where two groups of boys from nearly identical backgrounds were brought to neighboring summer camps. Over the course of a few weeks, the boys grew to despise one another solely because they were in opposite groups, resulting in physical violence and denying reality. Affective polarization is not a result of social media or the twenty-four-hour news cycle; it is rooted in our fallen human nature.

One consequence of affective polarization is increasing numbers of politically active people who should probably not be politically active. Consider this, from Mason: "Activism may have increased over the last few decades, but this is not necessarily a responsible, outcome-based participation. As Republican congressman Devin Nunes told *New Yorker* reporter Ryan Lizza in 2015, the types of people who reach out to him (a form of participation) are increasingly ignorant of the actual policies they wish to see enacted. They are participating, but they are doing so on the basis of misinformation and ill-formed ideas."[6] Political participation ought to be a boon for representative democracy. However, when people engage absent accurate information or even a basic understanding of government power and policy making, this participation ends up harming the political system. As people grow further and further apart and trust each other

5. "Toward a More Responsible Two-Party System: A Report of the Committee on Political Parties, American Political Science Association," *American Political Science Review* 44, no. 3 (1950).

6. Mason, *Uncivil Agreement*, 125.

less and less, the consequences for the American political experiment are serious indeed.

Other research bolsters Mason's concerning conclusions. Consider a 2007 study from political scientist Joel Turner.[7] Turner wanted to know how people's partisan identity shapes the way they consume media. To figure this out, he conducted a clever experiment. First, Turner presented a random sample of the population with news articles—one from CNN, one from Fox News—and, after having the sample read them, asked them to rate the articles based on trustworthiness. He also measured people's political viewpoints and leanings. Not surprisingly, people who reported more conservative viewpoints rated the Fox News article more trustworthy than the CNN article, while liberals rated the CNN article more trustworthy than the Fox News article.

But here's where Turner's experiment gets interesting. Using another segment of this random sample, he presented the same articles but reversed the authors, so that people thought the Fox News article was written by CNN, and vice versa. What Turner found speaks to the importance of polarization in our perceptions: conservatives rated the "Fox News" article (really from CNN) as more trustworthy, just as liberals did for the "CNN" article (really from Fox News). Nothing else in the articles was changed, but people's perceptions of who wrote them were enough to alter their evaluations.

More recently, another study highlighted the relationship between trust, partisanship, and something as simple as the decision to receive the COVID-19 vaccination.[8] A team of social scientists identified Republicans from a random sample of the population and then presented them with one of three messages: one from former president Trump encouraging people to get vaccinated, one from President Biden encouraging people to get vaccinated, and one from a neutral messenger not making a recommendation.

The results were discouraging, though not particularly surprising: "Unvaccinated Republicans who were exposed to the [Trump] endorsement reported 7.0% higher vaccination intentions than those who viewed the [Biden] endorsement and 5.7% higher than those in the neutral control condition."

7. Joel Turner, "The Messenger Overwhelming the Message: Ideological Cues and Perceptions of Bias in Television News," *Political Behavior* 29, no. 2 (2007): 441–64.

8. Sophia L. Pink et al., "Elite Party Cues Increase Vaccination Intentions among Republicans," *Proceedings of the National Academy of Sciences* 118, no. 32 (2021).

Moreover, Republicans who saw the Biden endorsement were significantly less likely to recommend the vaccine to others *and* reported far lower trust in the effectiveness and necessity of the vaccine. To summarize, you are more likely to believe a message coming from someone you trust than one coming from someone you don't, even when these messages are the same.

What does all this mean for the state of trust in American politics and society? The short answer is, it means that we are in a tough spot. Polarization is not relegated to politics; it has affected most everything in our society. As a result, we are less prone to trust those with whom we have disagreements, big or small. Moreover, we tend to trust people and voices who share our perspectives and goals, regardless of what the truth may be. This breeds reliance on familiar and comfortable voices, creating echo chambers that lead to even less trust for those with whom we disagree. And the cycle, unfortunately, continues to spiral.

Christians and Conspiracism

Conspiracism—the tendency to entertain and embrace conspiracy theories and related thinking—is not a new phenomenon. The idea that there must be another explanation to the natural order of things, just beyond our reach, is in some sense ingrained in our fallen nature. People tend to doubt official explanations, especially when our expectations or prior assumptions lead us to this doubt. Consider the belief that aliens crash-landed in Roswell, New Mexico, in 1947, or that President Kennedy's assassination was much more complicated than the official "lone gunman" theory. The best evidence and consensus of experts supporting official explanations are not enough; people just *know* something else is going on.

Conspiracism can be innocuous. The belief that the National Basketball Association is biased toward larger media markets does not threaten the stability of the social order (and as a fan of the Portland Trail Blazers, I've admittedly taken to this way of thinking to explain my team's relative lack of success). Or consider the belief in the existence of Bigfoot: while people may believe that entities are hiding the truth about a mysterious biped roaming the forests of the Pacific Northwest, few are taking up arms in response. Conspiracism can even be satirical, such as the Internet-driven "birds aren't real" movement.[9] Conspiracism need not lead down dark paths.

9. Anagha Srikanth, "'The Birds Aren't Real' Movement Says Federal Government Replaced All Birds with Surveillance Drones," *Hill*, June 28, 2021, https://thehill

But as the beginning of this chapter showed, entertaining conspiracy theories can also be quite harmful. In August 2021, a QAnon-obsessed father murdered his two young children after coming to believe they had inherited serpent DNA from their mother; killing them, he told the FBI, was the only way he could "sav[e] the world from monsters."[10] Conspiracism can also lead to mental and emotional harm, not just for the person who becomes enraptured in fringe theories about the world but also for the victims of these delusions. Take, for example, a confrontation between two conspiracy theorists and the pastor of First Baptist Church of Sutherland Springs, Texas, the site of a mass shooting that took the lives of twenty-six people, including the pastor's daughter. Yelling and cursing at the pastor, the two claimed that the victims were part of a "false flag" operation designed by the government. On more than one occasion, one of the pair is heard demanding to see the pastor's daughter's death certificate, suggesting she never existed in the first place.[11]

Just as Christians are called to worship God in spirit *and* truth,[12] we must be on guard against such a damaging and corrosive way of thinking. But just how pervasive is conspiracism and support for conspiracy theories in American society, and among Christians in particular? Consider the January 6, 2021, attack on the US Capitol. Prior to and during the violence, several Christian symbols were seen alongside symbols for QAnon, leading some to draw connections between Christians and the online group.[13] Andrew Walker, a professor at Southern Baptist Theological Seminary, is skeptical of this relationship, though. He recalled a conversation he had with a pastor of a large church in the Bible Belt, in which the pastor said he

.com/changing-america/sustainability/environment/560583-the-birds-arent-real-movement-says-federal.

10. Jonathan Edwards, "A QAnon-Obsessed Father Thought His Kids Would Destroy the World, So He Killed Them with a Spear Gun, FBI Says," *Washington Post*, August 12, 2021, https://www.washingtonpost.com/nation/2021/08/12/california-father-killed-children-qanon-illuminati/.

11. Meagan Flynn, "Conspiracy Theorists Harass Sutherland Springs Churchgoers, Pastor Whose Daughter Was Killed," *Washington Post*, March 8, 2018, https://www.washingtonpost.com/news/morning-mix/wp/2018/03/08/conspiracy-theorists-harass-sutherland-springs-churchgoers-pastor-whose-daughter-was-killed/.

12. John 4:24.

13. Michelle Boorstein, "A Horn-Wearing 'Shaman.' A Cowboy Evangelist. For Some, the Capitol Attack Was a Kind of Christian Revolt," *Washington Post*, July 6, 2021, https://www.washingtonpost.com/religion/2021/07/06/capitol-insurrection-trump-christian-nationalism-shaman/.

knew of one person in his congregation who entertained ideas related to QAnon. "But please," Walker wrote, "continue with The Narrative™."[14]

An article from Lifeway Research tells a different story.[15] Citing a study of American pastors, author Aaron Earls said that nearly half of those surveyed reported they regularly hear church members repeating conspiracy theories. Earls claims that conspiracism is not new among Christians, ranging from the belief that medieval Jews were drinking the blood of Christian children to the notion that the advent of the Internet foreshadowed the rise of the antichrist. And as for QAnon, Earls writes, "Many people in church pews have probably never heard of QAnon, but they've likely seen material on their social media feeds that originated with the group."

Recent surveys show that some Christians have not just seen this material but have been convinced by it. The Public Religion Research Institute surveyed more than five thousand Americans, and the results were discouraging: while 14 percent of Americans were identified as "QAnon believers"—expressing agreement with three statements prevalent in the QAnon community—the number for white evangelical Christians was 22 percent, the highest of any religious tradition measured.[16] These "QAnon believers" were more likely than other segments of the sample to express support for other conspiracy theories, including the idea that the 2020 presidential election was stolen from Donald Trump and the belief that the COVID-19 vaccine amounts to the "mark of the beast."

A survey from the American Enterprise Institute (AEI) yielded similar results. AEI found that white evangelical Christians were more likely to entertain conspiracy theories than other groups.[17] Specifically, white evangelicals identifying as Republicans were far more likely to believe that there

14. Andrew T. Walker, "A Pastor to Me through Text Message Just Now: 'I Pastor a Church of 1,500 in the Bible Belt and I Know One Guy Who Even Remotely Entertains the Idea of Q.' But Please, Continue with The Narrative.TM I Know Articles Need Written and Reputations Maintained," Twitter, June 25, 2021, https://twitter .com/andrewtwalk/status/1408422181835530244.

15. Aaron Earls, "Christians, Conspiracy Theories, and Credibility: Why Our Words Today Matter for Eternity," Lifeway Research, February 1, 2021, https:// lifewayresearch.com/2021/02/01/christians-conspiracy-theories-and-credibility -why-our-words-today-matter-for-eternity/.

16. "The Relationship between Libertarians, the Tea Party and the Christian Right," Public Religion Research Institute, October 29, 2013, http://publicreli gion.org/2013/10/the-relationship-between-libertarians-the-tea-party-and-the -christian-right/.

17. Daniel Cox, "Rise of Conspiracies Reveals an Evangelical Divide in the

was widespread voter fraud in the 2020 election than other Republicans (74 percent to 54 percent). And while 19 percent of all Republicans support at least one basic tenet of QAnon, that number jumped to 29 percent of white evangelical Republicans. So, while it is certainly not fair to accuse *all* Christians of getting caught up with conspiracism and conspiracy thinking, it is also not fair to claim that these beliefs are largely absent from our communities.

Christian Witness in the Misinformation Age

My family got our first computer in the late 1990s. It was a hefty machine, costing the same amount as a small used car though far less advanced than the simplest of today's smart phones. And while we relied on our landline telephone for access, we were nevertheless able to explore the Internet. I remember my mom, who was born in 1948, remarking that this technology was unlike anything she had imagined, allowing for instantaneous communication with people all over the world. This, she said, shined new light on Scripture detailing Jesus's inevitable return to earth, as depicted in Revelation. "How was it possible," she wondered, "that every eye would see Jesus descending from heaven?" The Internet, she suggested, made sense of that.

People living in the twenty-first century find it easier to access information and reach one another than at any point in human history. Social media gives every connected voice a platform. Emails transmit data and messages across the world in an instant. People can share Bible verses and encouragement with believers around the globe, including those living under the threat of social and legal persecution. In many respects, this could not be a better context for Christians seeking to fulfill the Great Commission, to make disciples of all nations.[18]

In practice, though, the information age has its downsides. While people do have more information at their fingertips than ever before, how does one sift through the noise to reach the truth? And while people can connect with others in ways unfathomable to previous generations, this does not guarantee that people will foster connections with others in a constructive and beneficial way. Instead of ushering in utopia in the areas of knowl-

---

GOP," American Enterprise Institute, February 12, 2021, https://www.aei.org/arti cles/rise-of-conspiracies-reveals-an-evangelical-divide-in-the-gop/.

18. Matt. 28:19.

edge and interpersonal connections, the information age has (among other things) exacerbated tendencies toward tribalism.

As Christians, we are called to present a hopeful witness to a skeptical and disinterested world.[19] But when we succumb to the tendency toward conspiracism and comforting explanations for uncomfortable realities, we are doing serious damage to our witness. As I wrote for *Christianity Today* in the aftermath of the attack on the US Capitol, "If Christians are broadcasting conspiracy theories . . . what credibility do we have when telling the world of the Good News of a resurrected Savior?"[20] As Christians, how we carry ourselves in the world matters a great deal.

Now, this does not mean we should sanitize our beliefs for the sake of a secular audience. We are called to proclaim what is true, and to stand on the foundation of the gospel. Nor should Christians naïvely bury our heads in the sand for fear of learning difficult or troubling information about the world around us. But conspiracism is not the sort of thinking that is needed for Christians in this moment. We are called to be wise and discerning, not to seek information that exclusively confirms our biases or beliefs.[21] We can question authority without falling down the rabbit hole.

In an age of increasing misinformation and the continued temptation of conspiracism, when it is becoming more and more difficult to tell truth from fiction, Christians should be noticeably different from the rest of the world. This means diversifying where we're getting our information, taking in multiple and varied sources from different points of view. It means talking with one another, and genuinely listening to those with whom we disagree. It means breaking out of our homogenous silos and echo chambers and casting aside convenient yet far-fetched explanations. This is not supposed to be comfortable; seeking truth often isn't. If it is possible to rebuild the trust necessary for sustaining our political system—and not to be too negative, but it is a big *if*—this is a useful place for us to start.

Conspiracy theories tend to be rooted in fear, secrecy, and anger. Christians must cast aside these things, choosing instead the confidence, strength, and hope found in Jesus. In rebuffing the allure of conspiracy theories, we can point to something even more unbelievable by earthly

---

19. 1 Pet. 3:15.

20. Daniel Bennett, "We Need to Be Better Losers," *Christianity Today*, January 6, 2021, https://www.christianitytoday.com/ct/2021/january-web-only/christian-victory-election-loss.html.

21. Prov. 17:24.

standards: a victorious, resurrected Savior. There is no credibility in conspiracism. For the sake of our witness, Christians should be among the first to reject it.

References

Bennett, Daniel. "We Need to Be Better Losers." *Christianity Today*, January 6, 2021. https://www.christianitytoday.com/ct/2021/january-web-only /christian-victory-election-loss.html.

Boorstein, Michelle. "A Horn-Wearing 'Shaman.' A Cowboy Evangelist. For Some, the Capitol Attack Was a Kind of Christian Revolt." *Washington Post*, July 6, 2021. https://www.washingtonpost.com/religion/2021/07/06 /capitol-insurrection-trump-christian-nationalism-shaman/.

Cox, Daniel. "Rise of Conspiracies Reveals an Evangelical Divide in the GOP." American Enterprise Institute, February 12, 2021. https://www.aei.org /articles/rise-of-conspiracies-reveals-an-evangelical-divide-in-the-gop/.

Earls, Aaron. "Christians, Conspiracy Theories, and Credibility: Why Our Words Today Matter for Eternity." Lifeway Research, February 1, 2021. https://lifewayresearch.com/2021/02/01/christians-conspiracy -theories-and-credibility-why-our-words-today-matter-for-eternity/.

Edwards, Jonathan. "A QAnon-Obsessed Father Thought His Kids Would Destroy the World, So He Killed Them with a Spear Gun, FBI Says." *Washington Post*, August 12, 2021. https://www.washingtonpost.com/nation /2021/08/12/california-father-killed-children-qanon-illuminati/.

Flynn, Meagan. "Conspiracy Theorists Harass Sutherland Springs Churchgoers, Pastor Whose Daughter Was Killed." *Washington Post*, March 8, 2018. https://www.washingtonpost.com/news/morning-mix/wp/2018 /03/08/conspiracy-theorists-harass-sutherland-springs-churchgoers -pastor-whose-daughter-was-killed/.

Goldman, Adam. "The Comet Ping Pong Gunman Answers Our Reporter's Questions." *New York Times*, December 7, 2016. https://www.nytimes .com/2016/12/07/us/edgar-welch-comet-pizza-fake-news.html.

Heller, Zoe. "What Makes a Cult a Cult?" *New Yorker*, July 1, 2021. https:// www.newyorker.com/magazine/2021/07/12/what-makes-a-cult-a-cult.

Mason, Lilliana. *Uncivil Agreement: How Politics Became Our Identity*. Chicago: University of Chicago Press, 2018.

Pink, Sophia L., James Chu, James N. Druckman, David G. Rand, and Robb Willer. "Elite Party Cues Increase Vaccination Intentions among Republicans." *Proceedings of the National Academy of Sciences* 118, no. 32 (2021).

"The Relationship between Libertarians, the Tea Party and the Christian Right." Public Religion Research Institute, October 29, 2013. http:// publicreligion.org/2013/10/the-relationship-between-libertarians-the -tea-party-and-the-christian-right/.

Roose, Kevin. "What Is QAnon, the Viral Pro-Trump Conspiracy Theory?" *New York Times*, September 3, 2021. https://www.nytimes.com/article/what -is-qanon.html.

Srikanth, Anagha. "'The Birds Aren't Real' Movement Says Federal Government Replaced All Birds with Surveillance Drones." *Hill*, June 28, 2021. https:// thehill.com/changing-america/sustainability/environment/560583-the -birds-arent-real-movement-says-federal.

"Toward a More Responsible Two-Party System: A Report of the Committee on Political Parties, American Political Science Association." *American Political Science Review* 44, no. 3 (1950).

Turner, Joel. "The Messenger Overwhelming the Message: Ideological Cues and Perceptions of Bias in Television News." *Political Behavior* 29, no. 2 (2007): 441–64.

Walker, Andrew T. "A Pastor to Me through Text Message Just Now: 'I Pastor a Church of 1,500 in the Bible Belt and I Know One Guy Who Even Remotely Entertains the Idea of Q.' But Please, Continue with The Narrative.TM I Know Articles Need Written and Reputations Maintained." Twitter, June 25, 2021. https://twitter.com/andrewtwalk/status /1408422181835530244.

21

A CITY DIVIDED

Kaitlyn Schiess

A single letter took political conversations by storm in the spring of 2020: Q.

QAnon—the family of conspiracy theories centered around the claim that a secret cabal of pedophilic elites is running governments, media, and businesses around the world—has captured either the adherence or bewildered interest of many Americans. While the theory—named for the anonymous informant behind the unfounded claims, "Q"—grew on the Internet, it has had serious real-world effects, from the "Pizzagate" shooting in a Washington, DC, pizzeria to the January 6 attack on the United States Capitol.

This theory is not alone in combining elements of political participation or partisan loyalty with conspiratorial thinking. Even theories that do not seem explicitly political are often rooted in institutional suspicion, contain themes of government takeover by malicious elites, or feature narratives that fall along predictable partisan lines. Both Republicans and Democrats can believe conspiracy theories, but they aren't likely to believe the same ones. Conspiracy theorizing is often driven by partisanship—the greater a person's attachment to a political party, the greater that person's chances are of being socialized to accept theories that more easily fit with his or her political commitments. Political scientists Adam M. Enders and Steven M. Smallpage have described how conspiracy theories attract adherents by presenting theories that will discredit the political opponents of the group: conspiracy theories that harm Democrats (such as questioning Obama's citizenship or the results of the 2020 election) obviously find higher levels of support among Republicans, while conspiracy theories that harm Republicans (theories tying Donald Trump's 2016 campaign to the Russian government or the attack on 9/11 to the Bush administration) find higher levels of support among Democrats.[1] Especially as American Christians have increasingly found their identities and loyalties in politics or party affiliation, understanding the political nature and motivations of conspiracy theories is crucial to understanding how Christians can become captivated by them.

Christians face a unique challenge when it comes to addressing political conspiracy theories: we already believe in a cosmic conspiracy to ultimately defeat the evil that has infected all human hearts, communities, and institutions. American evangelicals face another challenge, as we have historically found ultimate value and meaning in politics and struggle to differentiate those electoral battles with the spiritual battle raging across time and cultures. How can we affirm the reality of systemic evil in the world, especially in human governments, without falling prey to the simplistic narratives and partisan fearmongering of conspiracy theories? How can we understand the way that the powers and principalities impact earthly concerns without placing that level of spiritual and theological meaning on legitimate political disagreements? We need more than correct facts to combat conspiracy theories; we need better political theology.

A Political Problem

American Christians have a problem with conspiracy theories, and we ignore the political element of their attraction at our own peril. The "Pizzagate" shooter was a Christian; many of the January 6 rioters used Christian language and symbols in the attack; many of the Q theories have described the coming persecution of Christians; and the strong identification of white evangelicals with the Republican Party has also included a subset strongly identifying with far-right political conspiracy theories like QAnon. But the connection is not merely political, it is also theological. An *Atlantic* article that introduced QAnon to many nonadherents noted that the "language of evangelical Christianity has come to define the Q movement. QAnon mar-

---

1. Adam M. Enders and Steven M. Smallpage, "Polls, Plots, and Party Politics," in *Conspiracy Theories and the People Who Believe Them*, ed. Joseph Uscinski (Oxford: Oxford University Press, 2018), 301.

ries an appetite for the conspiratorial with positive beliefs about a radically different and better future, one that is preordained."[2]

Plenty of theological errors prime Christians to be sucked into conspiracy theories: an unhealthy obsession with end-times predictions; inappropriate levels of political loyalty; a culture war mentality that fosters extreme suspicion of mainstream media, science, or institutions; and a misreading of verses like John 15:19–20 that promote a persecution complex. But one important theological error that often goes unnoticed when combating conspiracy theories among Christians is an undernourished political theology. We may enthusiastically affirm that our theological commitments shape our political participation, but we rarely articulate a robust political theology that broadly describes the relationship between earthly and spiritual authority, the simultaneous creative good and seductive evil present in governments, and what the death and resurrection of Christ mean for earthly nations.

Political conspiracy theories flourish where Christians have not adequately distinguished the temporal and the eternal, our earthly political work with our ultimate allegiances, and the powers and principalities from the human institutions that may be influenced by them but can also be instruments of creative good in the world. We need language and images to describe political work in this good-but-fallen creation that grapple with systemic evil in government without resorting to political conspiracy theories.

Easy Answers to Difficult Questions

Christian theology has always articulated a distinction between earthly and eschatological peace: between the cosmic battle of good and evil in which God promises ultimate victory, and earthly conflicts that are influenced by that larger conflict but not wholly representative of it. It has also struggled to describe this distinction and its relationship to earthly and spiritual authority. How should we think about our obligations to earthly authorities when our ultimate allegiance is to the coming kingdom of God? How can we understand the great depths of evil possible in human communities and governments and the great creative possibilities for believers seeking the material flourishing of their neighbors?

2. Adrienne LaFrance, "The Prophecies of Q," *Atlantic*, June 2020, https://www .theatlantic.com/magazine/archive/2020/06/qanon-nothing-can-stop-what-is -coming/610567/.

Conspiracy theories offer one set of answers to these questions. They present simplistic narratives in which the difference between spiritual warfare and earthly conflict is erased, the line dividing good and evil is easy to find and runs neatly between different human communities, and people or institutions take on the full weight of the "powers and principalities." Conspiracy theories avoid the difficult work of responding to our own political contexts—the particular time and place we inhabit—with nuance and humility by hardening and universalizing the difference between good and evil communities. Instead of recognizing moments of evil and flashes of goodness in the same communities and acknowledging that different moments might require different solutions, we create absolute categories of good and evil that persist in perpetuity. In other words, conspiracy theories answer complicated questions with easy answers: these are the "good guys," these are the "bad guys," and here is the clear way to respond. Rather than navigating the complicated landscape of applying Christian convictions to our political participation, conspiracy theories offer easy answers that ignore the ambiguity and complexity inherent in our fallen world.

The Model of the Two Cities

Throughout church history, theologians have answered those same questions quite differently. Many of them have used some version of "the doctrine of the two": Pope Gelasius I's "two swords" theory, Martin Luther's "two kingdoms," and contemporary theologian Oliver O'Donovan's "two ages" all attempted to describe the relationship between human rulers and God's rule, the different obligations Christians have to spiritual and earthly authorities in their lives, and the tension between God's current rule and his coming rule.[3] One of the earliest and more influential formulations of this idea, however, was Augustine's "two cities" as described in *The City of God*.

The City of God describes two cities—the earthly city and the city of God—in great detail: their origins, trajectories, and ultimate ends. Most importantly, it describes their different loves that bind them into two opposing communities. Augustine says,

3. "Proclaiming the unity of God's rule in Christ is the task of Christian witness; understanding the duality is the chief assistance rendered by Christian reflection." Oliver O'Donovan, *Desire of the Nations: Rediscovering the Roots of Political Theology* (Cambridge: Cambridge University Press, 1999), 82.

Although there are many great peoples throughout the world, living under different customs in religion and morality and distinguished by a
complex variety of languages, arms, and dress, it is still true that there
have come into being only two main divisions, as we may call them, in
human society: and we are justified in following the lead of our Scriptures and calling them two cities. There is, in fact, one city of men who
choose to live by the standard of the flesh, another of those who choose
to live by the standard of the spirit. The citizens of each of these desire
their own kind of peace, and when they achieve their aim, that is the
kind of peace in which they live.[4]

Augustine's concept of the "two cities," then, is not another way of talking
about the church and the world, or human governments and the kingdom
of God, or "Christian societies" and "non-Christian societies." Instead, the
two cities describe the difference in the orientation of all creatures: there
are those joined into a community by their mutual love of God (including
believers currently alive and throughout all history, and angels) and those
joined into an alternate community by their misdirected love of self or
temporal goods (including humans and demons).

At first glance, this important historical Christian doctrine might look
like it *encourages* conspiratorial thinking. It is an "us versus them" mentality, in which Christians are on the side of good and everyone else is on the
side of evil. But Augustine is careful to explain that this division between
the two cities runs between every human community, including political
and ecclesial communities. The city of God and the earthly city find their
members in both the government and the church. The real division in creation is not always easily discernible, and the real conflict is not between
the church and the rulers as much as it is between these two communities
of competing loves. It is a helpful picture of what Paul describes in Ephesians 6:12: "For our struggle is not against flesh and blood, but against the
rulers, against the authorities, against the powers of this dark world and
against the spiritual forces of evil in the heavenly realms" (NIV).

Augustine's two cities are a helpful challenge to the simplistic narratives
of conspiracy theories: in his telling, all human communities are a mix of
both cities, because members of any familial, national, or local community
are more foundationally a member of one of the two cities. The real division is not a national, political, or biological division but a division of love:

4. Augustine, *The City of God* 14.1, trans. Henry Bettenson (New York: Penguin,
1984), 547.

the earthly city was created by self-love that caused denial of God, and the city of God was created by love of God that caused denial of self.[5]

Conspiracy theories often rely on strong, confident judgments about what role countries, parties, or leaders play in the grand story of good and evil they have constructed. It's one of the reasons Christians have been uniquely susceptible to such theories—many of us are familiar with reading Revelation and seeing the parts the Soviet Union, China, or the United States play in these cryptic prophecies. We tend to be more comfortable assigning spiritual significance to earthly events, which is a good thing! But it can easily transform into assuming we have a perspective on history and current events that only God can have, assigning ultimate value and meaning to contingent historical events.

In Augustine's time, the rise and fall of the Roman Empire was often involved in such schemes. To some, Rome was destined to be the instrument through which God Christianized the whole world, and so the empire would inevitably survive any threat or attack. To others, her fall seemed imminent, so it must be a harbinger of the end times. Augustine, on the other hand, was perfectly willing to call Rome's fall a form of judgment, but he refused to give it the theological significance some of his contemporaries did.

The speculations at the time were not too far afield the way conspiracy theorists today read hidden meaning and spiritual significance into ordinary events. Political conspiracy theories about the 9/11 attack on the Twin Towers; the real use of the Area 51 air force base; the power of the "Illuminati," the deep state, or an international cabal to control government affairs—these all find sinister and secret meanings in ordinary events. For Christians, these deeper meanings almost always take on a spiritual dimension.

Augustine's "two cities" theology does not deny that earthly political problems are often both material and spiritual. The powers and principalities at work in the world do affect earthly institutions, and regular political problems can be sites of great spiritual battle. Believing that the coming kingdom of God is entirely separate from the concerns of earthly kingdoms ignores their great places of overlap: feeding the hungry, healing the sick, seeking justice and showing mercy. While Augustine's two-cities theology has been used to either promote withdrawal from earthly systems of government or justify injustice in the earthly city,[6] a proper understanding of

5. Augustine, *The City of God* 14.28; in Bettenson, 593.
6. For more on ways that overly harsh distinctions between the spiritual and

the two cities denies both options. It recognizes that the ultimate battle is not won in earthly politics, while dignifying that work as a significant place for citizens of the city of God to seek the temporal good they share with the earthly city. Christians facing an onslaught of challenging conspiracy theories need to recapture this Augustinian tension in our political theology if we want language and concepts to affirm the great systemic evil possible in government systems while refuting simplistic and dualistic conspiracy theories that ease that tension by ignoring the truth. It is a tension described in Scripture itself, between the good creation as a site of meaningful human work (Gen. 1:27–31; Jer. 29:4–7; Rev. 21:1–5) and the corruption of human communities that makes such work difficult and even dangerous (Gen. 3:17–19; 1 Sam. 8; Prov. 29:2; Mark 10:42).

The Two Ages and the Defeat of the Powers

Another theologian quite captivated by a "doctrine of the two," Oliver O'Donovan, uses different language to describe a similarly helpful idea. O'Donovan prefers to think about "two ages"—the slow end of the current age in which human rulers have a part to play in preserving peace and seeking justice, and the dawning new age that is inaugurated in Christ's resurrection, rehearsed in the life of his church, and coming in its fullest in eternity. The new age might not have fully arrived, but it still greatly impacts the ending age: "The coming era of God's rule held the passing era in suspension."[7]

What do the "two ages" have to do with conspiracy theories? To correctly understand the forces of evil at work in the world, we need to understand what the work of Christ on the cross means for political rule and our political participation. O'Donovan says this is the "primary eschatological assertion about the authorities, political and demonic, which govern the world: they have been made subject to God's sovereignty in the Exaltation of Christ."[8] In Colossians 2:15, after Paul describes what Christ's work on the cross meant for our sin and condemnation, he says: "having disarmed the powers and authorities, he made a public spectacle of them, triumphing over them by the cross" (NIV).

---

material or the earthly and the heavenly can cause political problems, see James Skillen, *The Good of Politics: A Biblical, Historical, and Contemporary Introduction* (Grand Rapids: Baker Books, 2014), 121.

7. O'Donovan, *Desire of the Nations*, 93.
8. O'Donovan, *Desire of the Nations*, 147.

In this central moment of all salvation history, Christ not only triumphs over the powers and authorities (both the physical power of the Roman Empire in crucifying him and the spiritual power of Satan over all creation), but he reveals their ultimate powerlessness. Their reign will not entirely come to an end just yet, but their subjection to Christ's ultimate authority is real even if not yet apparent to all creation. O'Donovan is careful to distinguish spiritual and temporal authorities while also forcefully describing their similar fate: both the powers and principalities and human governments were shown to be powerless on the cross. For the sake of God's purposes, he allows governments to continue to operate for the good of creation and the church's mission on earth (Rom. 13:1–7), but they cannot lay any claim to ultimate loyalties, identities, or meaning.[9]

Political conspiracy theories tend to slip into a denial of this subjection. They give great power to earthly governments, institutions, or mysterious international cabals. They rightfully recognize the ability of groups of fallen humans to do great evil, but they ignore the subjection of earthly power by Christ on the cross and the restraining power of the Holy Spirit and the Spirit-indwelled church. The resurrection reveals the folly and impotence of earthly powers, and while in the fading of their power they will use violence and force to try and maintain it, even those evil attempts reveal their own limited ability.[10] The kingdom of God, in contrast, does not require the weapons of the world.

The Ambiguity of Political Work

O'Donovan's "two ages" and Augustine's "two cities" both illustrate another important political theological truth: the ambiguity of political life in a creation that was made good, was distorted by sin, and is being redeemed by the power of God. Human history, on each of these accounts, is "secular" but not neutral: it is the theater of God's redemptive work against all evil, but no political development can either secure or threaten the coming kingdom of God.[11] The world contains both faithful seeking of flourishing and evil rationalization of injustice, both rightly ordered love toward God and neighbor and twisted love toward selfishness and abuse, the possi-

9. O'Donovan, *Desire of the Nations*, 147.

10. Luke Bretherton, *Christ and the Common Life: Political Theology and the Case for Democracy* (Grand Rapids: Eerdmans, 2019), 20.

11. Bretherton, *Christ and the Common Life*, 237.

bility of using political means to structure human communities in more God-glorifying ways and the possibility of using political means to further distort and destroy those communities.

This ambiguity is an important part of a political theology that can combat conspiracy theories. It recognizes the reality of the powers and principalities, including the way evil infects and influences cultures, institutions, and political systems, while also holding to a sense of creative possibility in the world God created. Theologian Luke Bretherton says it like this: a Christian conceptualization of the world requires seeing it as "a moral order that simultaneously contains the possibility and moments of its own inversion and dissolution."[12] Human leaders, institutions, and political structures can be both mediation of God's good gifts and instruments of the powers and principalities. In the face of a triumphant progressivism that denies the power of sin and separatist conspiratorial thinking that sees no room for working within imperfect systems, a sense of ambiguity can guide our careful but faithful action.

Faithful Political Participation

Oliver O'Donovan has a beautiful definition of political theology: it is theology that recognizes an analogy between the acts of God and human acts, as they both take place "within the one public history which is the theatre of God's saving purposes and mankind's social undertakings." Political theology looks at earthly acts of justice, liberation, and community building and sees "partial indications" of what God is doing, while also looking to the "horizon of God's redemptive purposes" in order to fully understand political events on earth. "Theology needs more than scattered political images; it needs a full political conceptuality. And politics, for its part, needs a theological conceptuality. The two are concerned with the one history that finds its goal in Christ, 'the desire of the nations.'"[13]

This is why faithful political theology is essential for responding to conspiracy theories in Christian communities. We need more than information about specific false claims; we need a correctly tuned sensibility that recognizes the depths of depravity and systemic nature of evil while rejecting simplistic narratives and false stories. We need to better understand the relationship between our worship of the true King and our obligations to provisional political orders—for the sake of better political participation,

---

12. Bretherton, *Christ and the Common Life*, 236.
13. O'Donovan, *Desire of the Nations*, 2.

but also for the sake of refuting dangerous conspiracy theories. Politics is an especially dangerous realm because of how it bends our hearts toward the wrong loves, how it instills ultimate values in us, and the way it inspires worship. We are constantly presented with the choice to trust in earthly leaders—whether that be the governments conspiracy theorists distrust or the "informants" or sources they do trust—or to trust God. Whom we choose to trust is never spiritually or political neutral.

Understanding and articulating a robust political theology is essential for combating conspiracy theories in our churches, families, and communities. Will it fix everything? No. But we must have a larger goal than merely slapping Band-Aids on the conspiracy theories of the moment. We need to know and teach and live into a larger and more robust political theology that can give us the sensibility we will need to deal with the next crop of conspiracy theories. We can refute the specifics of each one without dealing with the underlying theological problems. We can convince others that Q is a fraud but leave them with the same bad theology that sucked them into the theory in the first place. Rebuilding our public witness and healing the wounds in our communities will require the long-haul work of better, fuller, more vibrant teaching on what our political participation in the world looks like.

References

Augustine. *The City of God*. Translated by Henry Bettenson. New York: Penguin Press, 1984.

Bretherton, Luke. *Christ and the Common Life: Political Theology and the Case for Democracy*. Grand Rapids: Eerdmans, 2019.

Enders, Adam M., and Steven M. Smallpage. "Polls, Plots, and Party Politics." In *Conspiracy Theories and the People Who Believe Them*, edited by Joseph Uscinski. Oxford: Oxford University Press, 2018.

LaFrance, Adrienne. "The Prophecies of Q." *Atlantic*, June 2020. https://www.theatlantic.com/magazine/archive/2020/06/qanon-nothing-can-stop-what-is-coming/610567/.

O'Donovan, Oliver. *Desire of the Nations: Rediscovering the Roots of Political Theology*. Cambridge: Cambridge University Press, 1999.

Skillen, James. *The Good of Politics: A Biblical, Historical, and Contemporary Introduction*. Grand Rapids: Baker Books, 2014.

22

THEY ARE COMING FOR THE CHILDREN

Michelle Panchuk

I remember vividly the moment I discovered that there was someone you could call if your parents were hurting you. I was about eight years old. My heart began to race. A wave of heat crashed over me—then cold. I felt like I couldn't breathe. My mind raced with questions—would I be able to trust these unknown people on the other end of the line, whose number I still didn't know and had no way of finding? How bad was bad enough to count? The latter question was emphasized by the disapproving tone of the women I had overheard gossiping. It was clear that they were judging the child for "calling on his parents" and "claiming" that they had hurt him. The answer to this question would both trouble and elude me for many years, while an answer to the former question was more readily available.

I was soon old enough to take interest in the regular updates my family received from a group providing legal advice and representation for homeschooling families like mine. Few updates arrived without some story of plotting Department of Social Services (DSS) workers out to malign good, homeschooling, Christian families and unjustly separate them from their children. The organization encouraged families never to let Child Protective Services (CPS) into the house, never to allow their children to speak to a social worker alone, and to stonewall any investigation at every turn. My own family spoke often about how DSS and the government were trying to curtail our freedoms by making it illegal for children to be in public during school hours or by using our presences in public as a pretext to unjustly investigate us, which, despite considerable anxiety, never actually happened. These sentiments were reinforced by novels that I read as a preteen, such as Frank

Peretti's *Piercing the Darkness*, which tells the story of a single father and school principal whose school is sued after he paddles a child and tries to cast a demon out of her. In the process, his children are "unjustly" removed from his care by an overzealous and callous social worker. At one point the children are even injured by the social worker's reckless driving.

These warnings, instructions on self-protection, and fictional stories merely *insinuated* conspiracy against us, but more explicit conspiracy theories circulated within our community. For example, in 2004, Stephen Baskerville, who later became a professor at Patrick Henry College, founded by Home School Legal Defense Association leader Michael Farris, published an article arguing that DSS and the government were conspiring to steal children away from good Christian parents and then give or "sell" them to gay and lesbian couples, who, according to Baskerville, obviously could not have children by any means other than taking them from others.[1] I am not sure when I realized that the DSS workers described in these stories and the newsletters we received were the same people the church ladies had spoken of years before, but I had little doubt that they were the enemy of families like mine and that I could not and should not trust them.

While the epistemic (knowledge-related) contours of conspiracy theories are crucial for Christians to understand, in this chapter I will turn our attention to the practical and moral impact of these theories on Christian communities. In particular, I argue that conspiracy theories serve to shore up distrust of community outsiders, and in doing so contribute to moral and epistemic landscapes that render Christians vulnerable to religious trauma in three ways: (1) by making it easier for the trauma to be inflicted, (2) by occluding the victim's understanding of the abuse, and (3) by making it more likely that otherwise caring and loving Christians will fail to recognize and prevent, or even actively enable, the traumatization. I begin by explaining in more detail what I mean by religious trauma, and then explain how conspiracy theories function to shore up the in-group/out-group distinction that renders insiders vulnerable to abuse. I end by considering how neighbor love can serve as a defensive shield against the epistemic and moral harms of conspiracy theories.

Religious Trauma

"Religious trauma" refers to a broad range of traumatic experiences that a person can have in a religious context that negatively impacts their ability

1. Stephen Baskerville, "Could Your Children Be Given to 'Gay' Parents?" *WND*, July 1, 2004, https://www.wnd.com/2004/07/25349/.

to engage with religion or religious life in the future. While clergy sexual abuse most readily comes to many people's minds, and is indeed an all-too-common and devastating form of religious trauma, the term refers to many other things as well. It includes the extremes of religious-motivated physical abuse to medical neglect to religiously valenced emotional manipulation to persistent spiritual gaslighting that undermines the individual's sense of self and basic epistemic self-confidence. The central core of religious trauma that unites all of these experiences is that (1) the trauma is caused or inflicted by someone or something that the victim closely associates with their religion, as when inflicted by clergy, religious parents, or teachers; (2) the victim perceives the religion to have played a causal role in the trauma's coming about, because theology, tradition, or religious leaders endorse, or at least fail to condemn, the causes of the trauma, as when LBGTQ+ youth are shunned or made homeless by their religious parents; and (3) the posttraumatic effects of the experiences are religiously valenced, as when intrusive memories are triggered by religious practices.[2]

Trauma of any kind can leave deep scars on the survivor's nervous system, their sense of self, and their interpersonal relationships. Psychologist and trauma expert Judith Herman explains that psychological symptoms of trauma fall largely into three categories: hyperarousal, intrusion, and constriction. "Hyperarousal reflects the persistent expectation of danger; intrusion reflects the indelible imprint of the traumatic moment; constriction reflects the numbing response of surrender."[3] But the "purely psychological" effects are not the only, or even the primary, consequences of trauma. "Traumatic events have primary effects not only on the psychological structures of the self, but also on the systems of attachment and meaning that link individual and community."[4] And because religious trauma has uniquely spiritual and religious significance, it can harm the survivor's ability to relate to God, to relate to their religious community, and to trust their religious and spiritual judgments, beliefs, and desires. Prayer may become a source of anxiety rather than comfort. Religious practices may trigger body memories that send the survivor back into a reexperiencing of the trauma (what we often call "flashbacks"). Clergy may seem inher-

2. Michelle Panchuk, "The Shattered Spiritual Self: Philosophical Reflections on Religious Trauma," *Res Philosophica* 95, no. 3 (2018): 505–30.

3. Judith Herman, *Trauma and Recovery: The Aftermath of Violence—from Domestic Abuse to Political Terror* (New York: Basic Books, 1997), 34.

4. Herman, *Trauma and Recovery*, 51.

ently untrustworthy. In short, in addition to all of the "normal" impacts of trauma, religious trauma can undermine the survivor's ability and desire to engage in religious and spiritual life.

Epistemic Landscapes and Conspiracy Theories

Religious trauma can happen in any religious community, and anyone, regardless of their personal and social identities, can fall victim to it. However, certain epistemic landscapes are more conducive to religious traumatization than others. By "epistemic landscape," I refer to the features of our social worlds that shape our epistemic lives by constraining what we can come to know, the conceptual resources available to us, and what sorts of explanations seem plausible to us. Echo chambers are a powerful feature of epistemic landscapes that, when combined with conspiracy theories, make it incredibly difficult for people experiencing religious trauma to understand what is happening to them or to get help. For this reason, members of religious communities that have become echo chambers and embraced conspiracy theories are made especially vulnerable.

According to C. Thi Nguyen, epistemic bubbles arise when we are never exposed to the views of people who believe differently from us. Christians who have never been exposed to other religious belief systems are in an epistemic bubble. While they are bad for our epistemic lives, epistemic bubbles are incredibly easy to pop, especially living as we do in the information age. To pop an epistemic bubble, we simply have to expose ourselves to contrary points of view. Echo chambers are a more dangerous potential feature of epistemic landscapes. According to Nguyen, an echo chamber "is a social epistemic structure in which other relevant voices have been actively discredited."[5] While religious cults are perhaps the most extreme version of echo chambers (ones that often also involve epistemic bubbles), echo chambers can arise around any set of shared values and goals if those who don't share the values are actively discredited as malicious or duped by other malicious outsiders. The Paleo diet, the Curly Girl Method, a political pundit, a local church with a charismatic leader who doesn't tolerate dissent are all potential candidates for ideals or persons around which an echo chamber might develop. Less extreme echo chambers appear less dangerous than cults, as the members have access to outside information,

---

5. C. Thi Nguyen, "Echo Chambers and Epistemic Bubbles," *Episteme* 17, no. 2 (2018): 142.

they are not forbidden to engage with nonmembers, and the leaders don't control the members' every decision. But once in an echo chamber, it is extremely difficult to get out, because everyone who disagrees with the shared values of the echo chamber has been discredited. Furthermore, outsiders are often cast as actively out to get the members of the group. Under such conditions, exposure to outside information or evidence that runs contrary to the beliefs of the echo chamber can actually reinforce the individual's commitment to the shared values, since any attempt to discredit the views of the group is seen as an attack—an attack predicted by the narrative that paints outsiders as malicious.

Consider a Christian group that is skeptical of the need for and efficacy of the COVID-19 vaccine. They have observed many friends and family members struggle with overwhelming anxiety and depression as a global pandemic rages and church communities are largely isolated from one another due to lockdowns. Anxiety, fear, depression, loneliness, and isolation cannot be what God wants for God's people, they think. So, they encourage their fellow Christians not to live in fear. But if you want people to reject fear, it can be a short trip to trying to convince them that there is no cause for fear at all. And when an outsider presents the data that explains why their anxiety or caution ("isolation") is well founded, their explanations may start to sound like an attack. In other words, an echo chamber can start to develop.

I will follow Quassim Cassam in distinguishing between theories about conspiracies and Conspiracy Theories.[6] The former are explanations of actual conspiracies for which there exists some credible level of evidence. Conspiracy Theories, on the other hand, involve little to no evidence, and instead rely on coincidences, testimony of people who lack the relevant credentials (or a history of manipulating data), and the mere possibility of a conspiracy as support for its actuality. Conspiracy Theories are also often deployed to explain chaotic or random occurrences in the world via human agency, by putting a lot of apparently unrelated facts into tidy boxes that explain much and make the world seem less chaotic, but without providing actual evidence. Cassam further argues that Conspiracy Theories are a form of political propaganda. Whether this is an essential feature of Conspiracy Theories, it is certainly true that they often function as such, and also helps explain why Conspiracy Theories are a common companion to echo chambers.

According to Nguyen, Conspiracy Theories are common companions to echo chambers because they easily explain all of the facts about the evil

6. Quassim Cassam, *Conspiracy Theories* (Cambridge: Polity, 2019).

and misled outsiders, without the burden of evidence, since it is part of the conspiracy that evidence is hidden from the unenlightened. They also preemptively inoculate members of the echo chamber against contrary evidence that an outsider might offer (of course, doctors who want kickbacks from COVID diagnoses would say that COVID is a real threat!). In doing so, they help to shore up the in-group/out-group divide by breeding distrust and explaining (however superficially) why the outsiders are out to get the group members. Consider the above-mentioned group that is opposed to the COVID-19 vaccination. Conspiracy theories that claim that the vaccination actually includes a microchip for tracking the recipients reinforces an already existing skepticism. Claims that hospitals are intentionally misdiagnosing patients with COVID-19 for profit reinforces the belief that maybe COVID is not so bad after all. Claims that doctors and nurses are actively mistreating patients with COVID to hasten their death solidifies the idea that the medical establishment cannot be trusted. What started out as innocent and well-intentioned concern about spiritual and emotional well-being may become an echo chamber structured by conspiracy theories.

Conspiracy Theories and Religious Trauma

At this point, it is not difficult to see why people in echo chambers that use conspiracy theories to facilitate isolation from outsiders would render members especially vulnerable to religious trauma. In his book *Something's Not Right: Decoding the Hidden Tactics of Abuse and Freeing Yourself from Its Power*, Wade Mullen describes the way that abusive individuals and communities work to dismantle their victims' access to sources of understanding, such as information that might shed light on their experience of abuse, institutional support, and people and groups who have the authority or experience to name or stop the abuse.[7] If a victim is prevented from understanding that they are being harmed, they are less likely to resist, and if they don't know about or are led to distrust those that might offer protection, the victim is less likely to escape and to expose the abuser(s). While Mullen is interested in describing cases where there is an individual, or group of individuals, who actively abuse their victims, these two things— isolation from sources of knowledge and support—are also characteristic

---

7. Wade Mullen, *Something's Not Right: Decoding the Hidden Tactics of Abuse and Freeing Yourself from Its Power* (Carol Stream, IL: Tyndale Momentum, 2020), 70–75.

of communities where people are traumatized by structures, systems of belief, and practices rather than by individual abusers.

Conspiracy theories are both strategic and powerful tools for blocking access to relevant resources, because they apparently explain why trusting those whose beliefs do not align with the group's is dangerous. The isolation and blocked access look like they serve the best interests of potential victims. Rather than looking like a prison cell, the echo chamber looks like a bomb shelter. Believing that the medical establishment might not only misdiagnose you for profit but even actively facilitate their demise ensures that members of the antivaccination echo chamber will not trust the very people most equipped to give them good information about the risks and benefits of vaccination. It also discourages them from seeking treatment. One might wonder how an antivaccination echo chamber could cause religious trauma. But being told that "Jesus is your vaccine" and then told to trust God as you watch a vulnerable loved one die a painful, terrifying, and preventable death is precisely the sort of religiously motivated and enforced suffering that could constitute a religious trauma.

By convincing me that DSS, the US government, and most other outsiders to our community hated God, hated homeschoolers, and were out to find any excuse to take children away from families like mine, I was not only cut off from a potential source of help and protection; I was also preemptively immunized against any information that they might have given me that could have answered my pressing questions about whether I was being abused.[8] Of course *they* would tell me that I was being abused. They needed to convince me of that lie in order to justify their kidnapping. Furthermore, people of goodwill within my community who might otherwise have helped remained silent and failed to act because *they didn't know where to turn*. It wasn't that they didn't know that something was not right or that they didn't know that abuse-reporting lines existed. Rather, it was that they were cut off from sources of information and practical support through systematic distrust bred within the echo chamber established and maintained by such

8. I do not wish to suggest that Child Protective Services is a perfect institution or that they never remove children without sufficient cause. Like any human organization, Child Protective Services has deep flaws. Data shows that they are disproportionately likely to remove children from parents of color and disabled parents. What no data bears out is that Christian or homeschooling parents are being disproportionately targeted or that there is any conspiracy to "give" their children to adoptive parents in the LBGTQ+ community.

conspiracy theories. When neither you nor those who care about you have the resources to understand what is happening or to get help, this creates an environment where the trauma is likely to continue over a long period of time. Furthermore, studies repeatedly show that long-term or chronic traumatization is much harder to heal than single-event traumas.

It is important to note that it is not necessary for any members of the echo chamber to *know* that the conspiracy theory is likely false, or that anyone *intends* to cut victims off from sources of understanding and institutional support. Most members of echo chambers are not abusers or intentionally complicit in abuse. What matters is that echo chambers reinforced by conspiracy theories *do* have this effect, and as such they both make people more vulnerable to religious traumatization and increase the likelihood that they will experience the trauma for a longer period of time. Given that Christians have strong reasons to think that being harmed in one's relationship with God is a very serious harm, Christians should be especially concerned about participating in and fostering environments that make people more vulnerable to religious traumatization and themselves more vulnerable to enabling it.

Making the Escape

Echo chambers are often quite visible to outsiders, who may wonder how intelligent, rational people can choose to stay in them. But from within, it can be exceedingly difficult even to recognize that one is in a distorted epistemic landscape or to see escape as desirable, much less possible. Nguyen argues that it is as difficult to escape an echo chamber as to escape a cult. Indeed, he argues that nothing short of a social epistemic reboot—a complete reconsideration of all previously held beliefs about who is trustworthy and who is not—is necessary. Such an overhaul is often sparked by the formation of a bond of trust with an outsider, someone whom the echo chamber taught the member to distrust. Nguyen tells the story of Derek Black, a young man who grew up among neo-Nazis, who rejected the movement after becoming friends with a Jewish man on his college campus. Megan Phelps Roper, daughter of the late leader of Westboro Baptist Church, Fred Phelps, tells a similar story. The respectful, kind, and patient dialogue she encountered with some critics of her community on Twitter touched her in ways that the (justifiable) outrage toward them never did. These encounters eventually led to friendships that helped her realize that her church's practice of protesting funerals and carrying hateful signs that targeted LBGTQ+ folks, the Jewish community, and others was wrong.[9] The love shown toward her helped her to escape.

However, we have already seen that conspiracy theories can render it exceedingly difficult to establish such a relationship with an outsider. This might lead us to believe that there is little hope for religious trauma victims and other Christians of goodwill who have been unlucky enough to end up in an echo chamber. While I do not wish to diminish the difficulty or the personal, epistemic, moral, and physical risk that can come with escaping, the number of people who do escape, even without the help of an outsider, suggests that it is not always impossible. In fact, I wish to argue that it is often a value at the core of Christianity—love for one's neighbor as oneself—that sparks the escape. This solution may sound like an incredibly simplistic Christianese response: just love each other! But it is in fact exceedingly difficult, both epistemically and practically. We have already seen that echo chambers can contribute to misshaping the conceptual and moral landscape within a community, and whether any particular action constitutes a good expression of love depends not only on facts about the world—facts that can be obscured by Conspiracy Theories—but also on other related values that may be misshapen in the echo chamber. Refusing to give your underage child a lifesaving vaccine looks like an act of love if that vaccine carries greater risks than the disease it is supposed to protect against, or if it is actually part of a devious plot to control the world population. Beating a child can look like love if the community believes that children need to have their wills broken in order to be able to submit to the God who wants to save their souls. Sometimes abusers just use religious justifications to protect themselves when they know that they are harming their victims, but sometimes people of goodwill do harmful things sincerely believing that they are acting in love. Sincere love of neighbor, as the person understands it, does not guarantee that one will not end up being complicit in, or even causing, religious trauma. At the same time, many former members of echo chambers have found ourselves in distorted moral and epistemic environments and maintained enough of our moral intuitions to give us clues—if not outright knowledge—that something was not right. Even when someone is in the grip of conspiracy theories and has mostly accepted the distorted conceptual frame, there often remains

9. Megan Phelps Roper, "I Grew Up in the Westboro Baptist Church. Here's Why I Left," TED Talk, February 2017, https://www.ted.com/talks/megan_phelps _roper_i_grew_up_in_the_westboro_baptist_church_here_s_why_i_left?language=en.

something in that person that feels that beating a child just cannot be part of what love is, that standing by and watching loved ones die of a preventable disease during a global pandemic is not what God desires. Perhaps it is the true law of God written on our hearts.

Lilia Tarawa, who grew up in an abusive evangelical cult commune called Gloriavale in New Zealand, describes the way that the echo chamber she grew up in isolated her from sources of understanding, and in so doing encouraged her to systematically doubt her assessment of her own worthiness of love and respect. But not even this self-doubt could force her to accept the abuse of those she loved:

> When I was a child, they told me every day that I was a worthless sinner. It was my fault. I was evil. I was the one to blame. When people treated me badly I thought I deserved it. I struggled to think correct for myself because I was always second-guessing: What if it is my fault? What if I am to blame? Now, they may have beaten me down, but they messed up when they mistreated the people I loved. My fury against the injustices suffered by Grace [who was being forced into an arranged marriage], Jubilant, and Willing [who were physically abused] gave me the strength I hadn't been able to muster for myself. I couldn't stand by and watch someone I loved wrongly suffer. Love for others broke the chains that shackled me.[10]

The idea that love for others could help us break free of echo chambers where conspiracy theories have shackled us should be a source of great hope for Christians, but it is still not a simple answer. Human moral intuition is fallible, and Christians are reminded that we should not too easily trust ourselves. The heart is deceitful. God's ways are higher than ours. Everything in me screamed against my daughter's first set of vaccinations as an infant; letting the doctor hurt her felt exceedingly cruel. But, of course, I also knew that my gut reaction did not track what was actually loving. Many Christians believe that the Bible, Christian tradition, the work of the Holy Spirit, and human reason should all inform our understanding of what love is.

So, I am not suggesting that Christians of goodwill can always and everywhere recognize the signs of religious abuse and distorted epistemic landscapes by simply loving others and leaning into our moral intuitions

---

10. Lilia Tarawa, "I Grew Up in a Cult. It was Heaven—and Hell," TED Talk, July 9, 2020, https://www.ted.com/talks/lilia_tarawa_i_grew_up_in_a_cult_it_was _heaven_and_hell?language=en.

when they conflict with community beliefs and practices. What I am suggesting is that our love for others and ourselves can serve as both the grounds for and a compass through a moral epistemic reboot—a reevaluation of our moral values and how they should be practically worked out—when the values of community conflict with our intuitions about what love demands of us. It should give us reason to question, to scrutinize, to seek out additional evidence and views that we might not otherwise be open to considering or trusting. And that is often the first step in escaping the grip of a conspiracy theory. It is not easy, and it involves moral and epistemic risk, but love helps us to recognize that risk lies on both sides. Yes, there is moral risk in leaning into our moral intuitions and rejecting the values of our community. We could be wrong. But there is also great moral risk in standing by and becoming complicit in spiritual abuse that leaves people religiously traumatized. Perhaps love breaks the chains that shackle us.

References

Baskerville, Stephen. "Could Your Children Be Given to 'Gay' Parents?" *WND*, July 1, 2004. https://www.wnd.com/2004/07/25349/.

Cassam, Quassim. *Conspiracy Theories*. Cambridge: Polity, 2019.

Herman, Judith. *Trauma and Recovery: The Aftermath of Violence—from Domestic Abuse to Political Terror*. New York: Basic Books, 1997.

Mullen, Wade. *Something's Not Right: Decoding the Hidden Tactics of Abuse and Freeing Yourself from Its Power*. Carol Stream, IL: Tyndale Momentum, 2020.

Nguyen, C. Thi. "Echo Chambers and Epistemic Bubbles." *Episteme* 17, no. 2 (2018): 141–61.

———. "The Seductions of Clarity." *Royal Institute of Philosophy Supplements*. Forthcoming.

Panchuk, Michelle. "The Shattered Spiritual Self: Philosophical Reflections on Religious Trauma." *Res Philosophica* 95, no. 3 (2018): 505–30.

Roper, Megan Phelps. "I Grew Up in the Westboro Baptist Church. Here's Why I Left." TED Talk, February 2017. https://www.ted.com/talks/megan_phelps_roper_i_grew_up_in_the_westboro_baptist_church_here_s_why_i_left?language=en.

Tarawa, Lilia. "I Grew Up in a Cult. It was Heaven—and Hell." TED Talk, July 9, 2020. https://www.ted.com/talks/lilia_tarawa_i_grew_up_in_a_cult_it_was_heaven_and_hell?language=en.

23

PARENTING TEENAGERS
IN GULLIBLE TIMES

Bradley Baurain

In recent years, my wife and I have walked with our four children—particularly our three teenagers—through a contentious presidential election and a global pandemic. These events, which have become politically intertwined, have spawned a number of evidentially unsupported and often irrational beliefs, many of which have been accepted and even enthusiastically embraced by large swaths of the American church, particularly conservative white evangelicals (which we are). As one consequence, we have faced parenting challenges more difficult and intractable than any in our previous experience.

One of my responses is this chapter, written in part as an act of discovery. I needed to understand better what was happening and how to respond. I collaborated with my wife and our three teenagers during the writing process, discussing ideas and outlines with them as well as asking each to make comments on a full draft. They were my first editors. Genre lines have been intentionally blurred: narrative, argument, and reflection are all here. In general, I have embedded this chapter within a Christian approach to education, focusing especially on the idea of learning as a spiritual habit and as desirable change or transformation, but this foundation does not explicitly emerge until one-third of the way through.

For the sake of clarity, I should note that this chapter is written against a specific background of COVID-19 and vaccine resistance beliefs held by fellow Christians. For us, this group includes extended family members, church friends, and Christian academic colleagues and students, among others. In the past year and a half, we have been told that COVID-19 is not real or not serious. The numbers have been miscalculated or faked. Insurance companies have inflated the totals. The deaths would have happened from other causes. Our government and the liberal media are deceiving us. Hospitals are not overflowing. Intensive care units (ICUs) are not full. Ivermectin (a parasite medicine for animals) is the cure. Vitamin D is the cure. Household cleaners are the cure. This is a plot to take away our religious liberties. Masks will prevent enough oxygen from reaching the brain. Social distancing is against Scripture. We can ignore what medical experts say because they believe in evolution and global warming. We can ignore them because we do not live in a "spirit of fear" (2 Tim. 1:7). We should not take "the vaccine" because God intends for us to "share our germs." We should not take it because it will cause sterility. Thousands of people have died from taking it. We have been told, "My body, my choice," with no apparent irony. Personal rights are sacred. Defending them is our top spiritual priority.

These friends, family members, colleagues, and students do not see themselves as conspiracy theory followers, but rather as people who have penetrated the world's deceptions. Their pity for our family's naïveté has been palpable. Nonetheless, their opinions, positions, and beliefs regarding COVID-19 and the vaccines flatly contradict the available empirical data and research, reported evidence, and expert analyses. Their choices and actions based on these beliefs have demonstrably harmed themselves and others, yet they persist in their positions. This has not been happening "somewhere out there." We have encountered these beliefs at family gatherings, in church, at school, and at work.

Problems and Nonsolutions

The challenge has not been that our children are tempted toward conspiracy theory beliefs. They are not. Such opinions and actions are seen by our family as contradicting a biblical worldview, not to mention ordinary reason. Rather, the problem has been a feeling of isolation from the rest of the church, which in our region seems dominated by people pretending there is no pandemic. Frankly, it feels like we have slipped into another dimension filled with flat-earthers. Our challenge as parents has thus been to guide our teenagers in worshiping alongside and interacting with fellow believers who have accepted and advocated for absurd COVID-19 and vaccine claims such as those listed above. When what this group believes, says, and does can be evaluated as foolish, unloving, and idolatrous, how should we respond? When they resist biblical appeals, on what basis can conversations proceed? When they are closed to rational or evidence-based discussion, how can relationships be other than shallow? When they cannot separate their core identity from these kinds of beliefs, how can we best respect these brothers and sisters in Christ?

With regard to the pandemic, our teenagers have observed and drawn their own conclusions. Here is a composite of their thinking:

> *The church is responding to the COVID-19 virus based on partisan politics, while denying doing so. Many of the believers we know are not taking the death toll seriously, despite calling themselves "pro-life." Their main priorities seem to be personal liberties, convenience, and "getting back to normal," and these priorities outweigh if not erase the gospel and loving our neighbor. The only biblical issue being referenced is to what extent the church should submit to the government in this area. Believers look foolish and selfish; unbelievers look both smarter and more caring. If we try to live out our faith at school, others will lump us in with the former. We do not even want to reveal our Christian identities because of the stereotypes that now come along with it. Is this really how Christians think, speak, and act? Why would I want any part of this?*

These thoughts have been accompanied by strong feelings of confusion, sadness, and anger. Long gone are the days when my wife and I could successfully parent our way through a crisis with ice cream or by snuggling with our kids on the couch while reading *Thomas the Tank Engine* or *The Very Hungry Caterpillar*. Sigh. They are still our children, but now they are also emerging adults. How can we help them walk the path of godly pilgrimage and keep growing as followers of Christ when gullibility, to put it mildly, appears to be the status quo among many Christians we know?

For our family, then, the problem of conspiracy theories has emerged as a fellowship-focused issue: How do we respond to gullible, deceived, or sinning (pride, selfishness, foolishness, hypocrisy) fellow believers in this area? While we as parents have shared in these dilemmas, much of the guidance we and others have attempted to provide our teenagers has been inadequate:

> "Respect the person, not the opinion." This is obviously a recycled version of "Love the sinner, hate the sin." Fellow believers, even those who are

in bondage to conspiracy theory beliefs, continue to deserve our respect. They are made in God's image and are children alongside us in the family of God. This is true, but it does not help much. We might be able to separate the person from the opinion, but the persons themselves are often not able to do so. In our experience, those who accept and advocate for conspiracy theory beliefs identify strongly with those beliefs. Not only are they unwilling to consider the possibility that they might be wrong, they tend to view opposition as persecution. So the best this advice can do is prevent further damage.

"There are a lot of opinions out there. We can agree to disagree." Despite what many Americans like to think, truth does not always lie in the middle. Not all opinions have equal value or deserve equal respect. In practice, this guidance, then, is usually code for "Avoid conflict" or "Let's try to get along with as many people as possible."[1] In addition, "agreeing to disagree" limits or cancels the possibility of meaningful discussion. An absence of conflict is not the same as biblical unity.

"God is in control. Just keep your eyes on him." This advice is theologically sound, but again, it doesn't contribute much to building meaningful relationships. What our teenagers want to understand is why fellow believers believe as they do and make the choices they do. Here, again, is a composite of our teenagers' voices:

Why are many people at church acting as if there is no pandemic? Why would a homeschool family boast of ignoring current events? Why would an adult Christian uncritically accept a ridiculous "fact" about Ivermectin? Why do apparently mature believers avoid sources that challenge or contradict their opinions and accept less credible sources that tell them what they want to hear? Why is hostility or mistrust toward authority and expertise treated as a Christian virtue? Why do the "simple" seem willing to believe anything (Prov. 14:15)?

We have also texted our teenagers links to articles about the psychology of belief and discussed them as opportunities arose.[2] But understanding

---

1. This priority likely reflects an American cultural emphasis on "niceness." For an insightful treatment of this topic, see Sharon Hodde Miller, *Nice: Why We Love to Be Liked and How God Calls Us to More* (Grand Rapids: Baker Books, 2019).

2. I do not mean research articles in academic journals, as those were beyond our teenagers, but rather more popular articles from both mainstream and Christian publications. One of my favorite such pieces was a blog entry: Joe Forrest,

when and why people might go wrong in this area, while helpful, also does not contribute much to building fruitful relationships.

Learning as Transformation

Over time, as I have been processing and responding to these issues, learning theory has come to play an increasingly prominent role. Yes, that is completely nerdy, but we use what we have, and my doctorate is in education. The ways in which Christians accept and even cling to misinformation, as well as the accompanying failures in discernment and action, seem to me to be failures in education—not in education as a social institution but in education or learning as a priority and practice of the church. I see learning as a neglected spiritual discipline, one that we will be practicing into eternity. Experientially completed redemption will not make us all-knowing. Only God is or ever will be omniscient. In heaven, there will still be much to learn, mainly about God, which means infinitely more to learn. We will learn as we have never learned before, without the barriers of sin and death, and for the purposes God intended—primarily worship. In eternity, learning and worship will go hand in hand, perfectly so.[3]

If you are now imagining heaven as a "classroom in the clouds" with an eternity of pop quizzes awaiting, forgive me. "School" is what we have made of what God intended learning to be. Most children are curious and love learning but do not necessarily embrace formal education. School has other purposes, with socialization as perhaps chief among them. When I volunteered in my two oldest daughters' kindergarten classes years ago, I was struck by how much time was spent on "learning" to line up straight, walk quietly through the halls, sit "criss-cross applesauce" on the "story rug," and use the restroom at precisely scheduled times. Learning how to get along with others and how to be part of a group are legitimate lessons,

---

"Why Your Christian Friends and Family Members Are So Easily Fooled by Conspiracy Theories," *Instrument of Mercy* (blog), May 7, 2020, https://instrumentof mercy.com/2020/05/07/why-your-christian-friends-and-family-members-are-so -easily-fooled-by-conspiracy-theories/.

3. I have written a devotional Bible study for Moody Bible Institute's *Today in the Word* monthly devotional guide; see Bradley Baurain, "Learning from God: Growing in Wisdom and Godliness," *Today in the Word*, Moody Bible Institute, January 2022. Also available as a downloadable PDF at https://www.todayintheword.org /archives/.

but the emphasis on social conformity means that often the feeling most associated with classroom education is boredom. Similarly, as curricular content matures along with children, learning discipline for their curiosity is a good thing, but the key virtue needed to succeed in school turns out to be mere endurance.

How, then, does genuine learning take place? In their book *The Learning Cycle: Insights for Faithful Teaching from Neuroscience and the Social Sciences*, Muriel and Duane Elmer synthesize learning theory by describing five stages or levels:[4]

1. Recall, or "I remember the information." This includes memory, practice, and retention, as anyone who has ever crammed for an exam can tell you.

2. Recall with Appreciation, or "I value the information" (for more than its ability to earn me an A grade). As a teacher, I am sometimes depressed at how much of organized education never makes it even to this second stage.

3. Recall with Speculation, or "I ponder how to use the information." This is the start of applying new knowledge and includes creative attempts to envision a future different from the present.

4. Recall with Practice, or "I begin changing my behavior." Change is difficult and can feel awkward or embarrassing, but this is actually a good sign that progress is being made. Endeavoring to start new habits takes time, but repetition works because the process creates new or stronger neural networks in the brain.[5] The Elmers summarize: "The critical challenge in Recall with Practice is making a clear connection between the truth and practice of the truth. Only when the learner grasps the connection between truth and living and begins to practice the truth can we confidently assume that learning has actually occurred."[6]

5. Recall with Habit, or "I do consistently." The Elmers explain: "A transformed life presupposes new thinking, new attitudes, and new behaviors so automatic and so instinctual that they now characterize the person we have become."[7] For Christians, real transformation and sustained

---

4. Muriel I. Elmer and Duane H. Elmer, *The Learning Cycle: Insights for Faithful Teaching from Neuroscience and the Social Sciences* (Downers Grove, IL: IVP Academic, 2020).

5. Elmer and Elmer, *The Learning Cycle*, 134.

6. Elmer and Elmer, *The Learning Cycle*, 145.

7. Elmer and Elmer, *The Learning Cycle*, 161.

learning take place within the community of faith and are possible only with God's help. The ultimate goal is Christlike character, which is more than a "stage" and which lies at the heart of all true learning.[8]

Learning, then, is not merely the acquisition of knowledge. It is more even than the application of knowledge. The application must be such that behavior, habit, and character are all positively affected and transformed. If this is not the case, no real learning has taken place! Think of the kid in Sunday school who knows all the answers but disobeys his parents, or the adult who has been to Bible study after Bible study but whose spiritual walk remains stagnant.

Through eyes of faith, we must see authentic learning as a deeply moral and spiritual activity. And because this is so, learning, like all other human endeavors, can be derailed and damaged by sin. I see at least two ways in which this can happen—and it is here that the topic of conspiracy theory beliefs returns to center stage.

One way in which learning can be spoiled by sin is failure, that is, we fail to learn or to complete the learning cycle. Due to sin, we remain as we are and do not change as we should. Cain is a biblical example and warning in this area.[9] He knew about God. He had no doubt heard the creation and Fall stories from his parents, Adam and Eve. He understood that God deserves to be worshiped. When Cain's offering was rejected, God himself alerted Cain to the consequences of his next decision. He needed to learn from his failure and accept God's gracious offer of a second chance. Unfortunately, he didn't heed God's admonition to resist the sin crouching at his door. Instead, he "doubled down" on anger and rebellion by murdering his brother and denying the deed. This completed his failure to value life as God does and to love as God loves. He emphatically chose self over God.

A second way in which learning can be injured by sin is corruption, that is, we "learn" things that are not true. The learning cycle is completed or fulfilled, in a sense, but the results are negative rather than positive trans-

---

8. Two books that for me complement the Elmers' learning-cycle model are Howard Hendricks, *Teaching to Change Lives* (Colorado Springs: Multnomah, 1987), and James K. A. Smith, *You Are What You Love: The Spiritual Power of Habit* (Grand Rapids: Brazos, 2016).

9. Gen. 4:1–16. This example is drawn from the aforementioned *Today in the Word* devotional study (January 15, 2022).

formation. This is a significant failure in moral and spiritual discernment, but as in the case of Cain, it is also disobedience and rebellion. A jaw-dropping biblical example of this resistance to truth is found in the book of Jeremiah (Jer. 42-44). The people remaining in Judah after the exile in 586 BC came to Jeremiah and asked him to pray to the Lord for guidance as to what they should do next. They promised to do whatever he said: "Whether it is favorable or unfavorable, we will obey the LORD our God" (Jer. 42:6).[10] Jeremiah returned with God's answer, which was that they should stay in the land and not flee to Egypt. Despite their vow, the people accused the prophet of lying and forcibly took him along with them to Egypt. While they were there, Jeremiah delivered an oracle condemning them for their idolatry. Had they learned anything from God's judgment on Judah? Apparently not, for the people brazenly responded:

> "We will not listen to the message you have spoken to us in the name of the LORD! We will certainly do everything we said we would: We will burn incense to the Queen of Heaven and will pour out drink offerings to her just as we and our ancestors, our kings and our officials did in the towns of Judah and in the streets of Jerusalem. At that time we had plenty of food and were well off and suffered no harm. But ever since we stopped burning incense to the Queen of Heaven and pouring out drink offerings to her, we have had nothing and have been perishing by sword and famine." (Jer. 44:16-18)

In other words, not only will they not stop worshiping idols; they also give idols credit for their past blessings! Their beliefs had certainly transformed them, but in the wrong direction. They had "learned" a lie, embraced self-deception, and persuaded themselves to believe the opposite of what was true—just like today's conspiracy theory followers. In so doing, they broke the law and the covenant. Their idolatrous habits of thinking and practice withstood clear prophetic warnings as well as the evidence of their own experience (the Babylonian conquest and the deportation of most of their fellow citizens). Like Cain, they emphatically chose self over God and answered Jeremiah on the basis of their rebelliousness, foolishness, and pride.

As my family and I have interacted with fellow believers who are conspiracy theory followers, I have come to see them in these terms. They are

10. Scripture quotations in this chapter are from the New International Version.

fellow believers who are learning-impaired, that is, they have "learned" what is untrue. As a result, they are changing or transforming, but in the wrong direction. More plainly, they are backsliding into sins including foolishness and pride. They choose to call "light" what is dark and "good" what is evil (Isa. 5:20). In conspiracy theory terms, they call whatever they do not wish to believe "fake news." They accept absurd counterfactuals—Ivermectin is a cure for COVID-19, vaccines cause sterility—as true, "alternative facts."

In my weakness, it has been tempting to focus on what such people need to learn in order to return to true and active faith, and even to hope that God will appoint me to be their teacher (ha!). Instead, I have been graciously guided to better questions: How does God interact with prodigal believers who have become invested in various conspiracy theories or false beliefs and thus become captive to pride, foolishness, and idolatry? What do I need to learn in order to love them as he does? And how might my wife and I in turn promote this kind of godly learning in our children?

Learning God's Love

How does God interact with prodigal, backsliding, and conspiracy-theory-swallowing believers? He continues to love them, not because they deserve it but because faithful love is part of his character. We see this clearly in the book of Hosea. The Lord ordered the prophet to marry a prostitute, in part as an object lesson of his love for Israel (Hos. 1:2). Hosea obeyed and married a woman named Gomer. They had children together. At some point, though, she abandoned her family and committed adultery. At God's command, Hosea bought her from the slave market, reconciled with her, and took her home again as his wife (Hos. 3:1–3). God was not blind or duped. He knew exactly what kind of woman Gomer was. As Hosea loved her, so God loves his people.

In addition, God does not love prodigals in a pat-on-the-head, I-will-respect-your-foolish-and-sinful-choices sort of way. As our Good Shepherd, he loves us too much for that (see John 10:1–18). This means at least two things. First, there are no "acceptable losses." When sheep go astray, finding them becomes the Shepherd's top mission. He will "leave the ninety-nine to find the one." His love will go to any extent to find lost sheep and bring them home (Luke 15:1–7). Second, part of the Shepherd's care involves his rod and staff of discipline or correction. These tools are what an ancient Near Eastern shepherd used to bring a wandering sheep back to the right path. The psalmist found this a "comfort"—staying on the right path does not depend on us alone.[11]

Furthermore, God's love for prodigals is by any human measure extravagant to the point of incomprehensibility. The father in the parable did not welcome home his rebellious son grudgingly, but with a feast of celebration (Luke 15:11–32)! Moses learned this better than perhaps any other person in Scripture (excluding Christ). At the very moment when the people of Israel were most unfaithful and most disobedient—jumping both-feet-forward into the "golden calf conspiracy"—he interceded for them before the Lord (Exod. 32). His love did not come from trying to see the best in them. He knew well how fickle and rebellious they were. It did not come from his own finite and flawed heart. The only way in which Moses could have interceded as he did is by loving as God loved, that is, by drawing on God's love.

God's love, then, is individual. He does not give up on even one straying sheep. His love is faithful. He loves us no matter how stubborn or foolish we are and pursues us no matter how fast we run the other way. His love is extravagant. It in no way depends upon our deserving it. His love is truthful. It always sees us as we are, calls us to where we should be, and leads us to the grace of repentance.[12] I would like to love learning-impaired, prodigal believers as God does—but at present I do not. Instead, I feel angry or depressed. They are damaging my children's faith with their unbiblical, untruthful beliefs and politically determined, prideful choices.

How, then, can I learn to love as God loves? How can my wife and I teach such love to our children? How can we together love such believers? Biblically, I believe that the best way to learn more of the love of God—and in so doing to have my feelings (and more) transformed—is to draw near to him. So, during parts (only parts) of this pandemic, I have attempted to focus my prayer life on this one thing:

> One thing I ask from the LORD,
>   this only do I seek:
> that I may dwell in the house of the LORD

---

11. Ps. 23:4. This reading of the second half of the verse infers that the rod and staff are necessary because the sheep has wandered or gotten lost. I owe my understanding of this point to Kenneth E. Bailey, *The Good Shepherd: A Thousand-Year Journey from Psalm 23 to the New Testament* (Downers Grove, IL: IVP Academic, 2014).

12. As we know from the prophets at least, "speaking the truth in love" (Eph. 4:15) is not always "nice." See n. 1 above.

> all the days of my life,
>   to gaze on the beauty of the LORD
>   and to seek him in his temple. (Ps. 27:4)[13]

In doing so, I am coming to understand more of how God feels when sinners reject his love. He sent his Son to die for our sins, yet people insist on their own way, an "alternative set of facts" that will earn them an eternity in hell. Yet he loves them.

I am also coming to understand more of how God feels when his own children reject his love, that is, when we who have chosen to follow Christ slip back into sin by doing things in our own strength, believing according to our own "wisdom," and thus inevitably being ruled by our own selfishness and pride. For too many believers these days, the good news of the gospel and the authority of Scripture have been wretchedly replaced by the "insider knowledge" of conspiracy theories, the political idol of personal rights, and the prevailing authority of personal conviction.[14] Yet he loves us.

Sin hinders relationships, and so our desire to have meaningful, fruitful interactions with learning-impaired believers has largely been frustrated. We worship alongside them, but since the world in which they live accords with neither Scripture nor reason, deeper relationships will have to wait. This spiritual fact must be accepted, despite the emotional struggles it brings. Thank goodness he loves us!

This status quo does not leave us unable to love fellow believers. God's love cannot be blocked. If we are truly his children, even our own wrongdoing cannot permanently separate us from the love of Christ (Rom. 8:35–39). As we learn God's love, we can therefore move toward the learning cycle's goal of Christlike transformation by pursuing a life of biblical virtue, that is, by practicing obedience to biblical commands to love our brothers and sisters. Humility, gentleness, and patience will help us bear with learning-

---

13. During the pandemic, we have read as part of family devotions: Paul David Tripp, *A Shelter in the Time of Storm: Meditations on God and Trouble* (Wheaton, IL: Crossway, 2009). This book consists of fifty-two meditations on Ps. 27.

14. When a biblical rationale is offered for the latter, it is almost always Rom. 14. This chapter, however, does not make personal choice or conviction the bottom line, much less equal to Scripture, but simply instructs that when believers hold debatable convictions because they are weak in faith, believers stronger in faith should give up their freedom according to the "law of love." This is quite different from using one's personal or political convictions as a trump card.

impaired, prodigal believers in love (Eph. 4:2). Compassion, kindness, humility, gentleness, and patience will help us forgive them. Can I really forgive them for damaging my children's faith? Yes, because God has already forgiven them. How? Through his love, which binds these virtues together (Col. 3:12–14). In our pursuit of virtue, we must seek to imitate the example of Christ, the perfect, living model of godly love.[15] How can we help our children learn these virtues and this love? By learning and loving alongside them. Pilgrimage can be—and must be in these days when so much of the visible church in our context has strayed—a family journey.

We are now prayerfully seeking to move forward with this orientation: The best way in parenting to respond to the gullible times in which we live is learning, together with our children, God's gracious, truthful, never-lets-us-go heart of infinite love for his wandering, rebellious children. Surely his goodness and love will pursue us relentlessly all the days of our life, and we will dwell rejoicing in his presence forever (Ps. 23:6; see also Ps. 84).

Reader, we are in process. The learning cycle is ongoing. We are being transformed. We have much to learn. This chapter is not a pat solution, much less a song of victory. Our teenagers' faith struggles caused by pandemic-disbelieving and vaccine-resisting prodigal fellow believers remain real. Our parenting challenges caused by such brothers and sisters in the faith continue to trouble us deeply. Nonetheless, we persevere in faith, confident in what we hope for and assured of what we do not yet see—because God loves us and because he loves them, too (Heb. 11:1; James 1:2–4).

References

Bailey, Kenneth E. *The Good Shepherd: A Thousand-Year Journey from Psalm 23 to the New Testament*. Downers Grove, IL: IVP Academic, 2014.

Elmer, Muriel I., and Duane H. Elmer. *The Learning Cycle: Insights for Faithful Teaching from Neuroscience and the Social Sciences*. Downers Grove, IL: IVP Academic, 2020.

Forrest, Joe. "Why Your Christian Friends and Family Members Are So Easily Fooled by Conspiracy Theories." *Instrument of Mercy* (blog), May 7, 2020. https://instrumentofmercy.com/2020/05/07/why-your-christian-friends-and-family-members-are-so-easily-fooled-by-conspiracy-theories/.

15. That is to say, Christ perfectly fulfilled 1 Cor. 13. See Phil Ryken, *Loving the Way Jesus Loves* (Wheaton, IL: Crossway, 2012).

Hendricks, Howard. *Teaching to Change Lives*. Colorado Springs: Multnomah, 1987.

Miller, Sharon Hodde. *Nice: Why We Love to Be Liked and How God Calls Us to More*. Grand Rapids: Baker Books, 2019.

Ryken, Phil. *Loving the Way Jesus Loves*. Wheaton, IL: Crossway, 2012.

Smith, James K. A. *You Are What You Love: The Spiritual Power of Habit*. Grand Rapids: Brazos, 2016.

Tripp, Paul David. *A Shelter in the Time of Storm: Meditations on God and Trouble*. Wheaton, IL: Crossway, 2009.

24

JESUS WAS ALSO CONSPIRED AGAINST, YET HE WAS WITHOUT SIN

Steven L. Porter

Matthew's Gospel records, "Then the chief priests and the elders of the people . . . conspired to arrest Jesus by stealth and kill him" (Matt. 26:3 NRSV). When it comes to threats from powerful persons and groups, Jesus has some skin in the game. He was conspired against by members of his own religious group. He was thought insane by his family and largely misunderstood by those he came to help. One of his ministry companions betrayed him for financial gain, and the rest abandoned him hours before his death. He was handed over to a corrupt, foreign government, where he was beaten, mocked, and executed on false charges. He suffered all these and other indignities as the only person in the entirety of human history who was actually innocent. And yet, he never responded to any of this in a manner that was mean-spirited, unkind, or less than fully loving. Jesus was conspired against as we are, yet without sin.

For Jesus, to be "tempted in all things as we are, yet without sin" (Heb 4:15 NASB) means that even though Jesus desired to set his opponents straight, he refused to lash out against them in a malicious manner (Matt. 26:53). He didn't ridicule or misrepresent their position. He didn't demean or wish harm on those who successfully plotted against him. Instead, from the cross he prayed, "Father, forgive them, for they do not know what they are doing" (Luke 23:34 NIV). In his own pain and loss, Jesus was able to empathize with his conspirators, asking God to let them off the hook due to their lack of comprehension. While Jesus had his share of stern rebukes, carefully reasoned retorts, and even angry protests, in all of it he pursued the genuine good of those who opposed him.

At the center of what Jesus taught—at the core of his very being—is enemy love. In the Sermon on the Mount, Jesus says, "You have heard that it was said, 'Love your neighbor' and 'hate your enemy.' But I say to you, love your enemy and pray for those who persecute you, so that you may be like your Father in heaven, since he causes the sun to rise on the evil and the good, and sends rain on the righteous and the unrighteous" (Matt. 5:43-45 NET). For Jesus, loving our enemy means that we want and willingly pursue good things for those intent on doing us harm. In so doing, we are acting like God the Father, who sought our good while we remained in sinful opposition to him (Rom. 5:8, 10; cf. Col. 1:21). This doesn't mean that we never defend ourselves or others from harm, but it does mean that when we take a stand, we do so lovingly in the name or character of Jesus.

When it comes to the idea that we are being conspired against by government, media, political parties, or some other organized group, Christians face two main challenges. The first challenge is common to everyone, whether Christian or not, which is to avoid being duped by dubious conspiratorial claims. This involves the hard work of thinking clearly, carefully, and humbly. The second challenge, uniquely applicable to Christians, is to respond in a Christlike way when we believe we are being conspired against. This involves the hard work of learning from Jesus how to live and love like he did, no matter our circumstances. The point here is that even if our way of life is threatened by a person or group, this does not justify demeaning, manipulative, or hate-filled treatment of them. Again, Jesus's teaching and example are clear, "Love your enemies, do good to those who hate you, bless those who curse you, pray for those who mistreat you" (Luke 6:27-28 NIV).

In this chapter I begin by showing that Jesus's core attitude toward those who opposed him was compassionate love. Key to this is demonstrating that Jesus's attitude of love is consistent with, for instance, calling the Pharisees "a brood of vipers" or turning over tables in the temple courts. That is to say, Jesus was compassionate, gracious, and patient even when he spoke and acted in ways that were direct, immediate, and forceful. After presenting Jesus as our example of loving response to conspiratorial threats, I suggest a prayer practice that will help us become more like him in the face of our own persecution.

Jesus's Example of Enemy Love

We need to make clear that Jesus's central message and example was one of compassionate love toward those with whom he disagreed, which was just about everyone. Jesus, being fully God and fully human, was the most countercultural person to have ever lived. We tend to think of his main opponents as the religious leaders and Roman officials, which is true. But, in addition, Jesus often differed from those who knew him best. His family was embarrassed by him (Mark 3:21), John the Baptist questioned his identity (Matt. 11:3), his hometown rejected him (Matt. 13:53–58), many of his followers turned away from him (John 6:66), and his specially chosen disciples continually misunderstood him (Matt. 16:22). And yet, a careful reading of the gospel accounts makes clear that Jesus consistently responded to those around him with patience, kindness, compassion, and love. Jesus said of himself that he "did not come to be served, but to serve, and to give his life a ransom for many" (Matt. 20:28 NIV). Jesus regularly thought about what he could do to help meet the needs of those around him and not so much about his own needs.

But what about his more obvious opponents—the scribes, Pharisees, and religious leaders? Certainly Jesus saved his harshest words and actions for those who conspired against him and plotted his demise. Perhaps the two clearest examples are when Jesus uses strong language toward the scribes and Pharisees and when he turns over the tables in the temple courts. Don't we see in these cases a Jesus who is in beast mode, no holds barred, giving his enemies a taste of their own medicine? And does this not justify our own ridicule, harsh critique, and angry protest of those who stand against us?

Let us first consider that there is no reason to think that love—desiring and pursuing the well-being of others—is inconsistent with firm speech and immediate intervention. Indeed, there are times when seeking the well-being of those around us requires quick correction in order to prevent harm. For example, no one questions the love of the parent that urgently commands the child to stop at the edge of the busy street. When someone's safety is at stake, love is firm, clear, and loud if need be. If strong words and actions are needed to get the attention of those in imminent danger, then that is the loving thing to do. But notice that while we do not question the parent that cries out when the child's safety is at issue, we do question the parent that goes on to berate or demean the child who is no longer in immediate danger. Using firm language out of loving concern for others looks much different than an angry, bitter, demeaning rant.

What about the situations when Jesus used charged language and forceful action? The clearest example of strong language is Matthew 23, when Jesus refers to the scribes and Pharisees as "hypocrites" (v. 13), "blind guides" (v. 16), "blind fools" (v. 17), "whitewashed tombs" (v. 27), "snakes" (v. 33), and a "brood of vipers" (v. 33). Does this not show that following Jesus is consistent with name-calling and otherwise demeaning one's opponents?

First, it bears noting that Jesus starts his rebuke by recommending that his followers respect and observe the scribes and Pharisees due to their office (Matt. 23:1-3). Jesus respects their authority even though he critiques how they use it.

Second, the heart of Jesus's criticism in Matthew 23 is that the religious leaders' legalistic and hypocritical behavior epitomized Israel's historical rejection of God's redemptive plan, which was to establish an inner righteousness that would naturally lead to an outward righteousness (Matt. 23:3, 25-26; 9:13; Rom. 10). Jesus makes clear that Israel's long-standing resistance to God's grace had repeatedly led to violence against God's prophets and would soon lead to his own unjust execution (Matt. 23:34-35; cf. 12:7). This was a situation in which Jesus was addressing the tragic end result of thousands of years of Israel's rebellion against God and violence against those whom God sent. Similar to the parable of tenants (Matt. 21:33-46), Jesus is pointing out that the religious leaders are on the verge of committing the greatest injustice in human history. In terms of time line, Jesus is having this debate a few days before his arrest.[1] The scribes and the Pharisees are not just running toward the edge of the busy street, they are about to run off the edge of a great abyss. We would have reason to question Jesus's goodness if he did not call out clearly, directly, and forcefully for the scribes and the Pharisees to come to their senses. Indeed, Jesus's challenge for them to admit their own outward pretense and inner emptiness—that they were indeed "hypocrites," "blind guides," "whitewashed tombs"—was exactly what was needed for them to recognize that Jesus was the long-awaited Messiah who was able to clean the "inside of the cup" (Matt. 23:26).

Third, the context of Matthew 23 makes clear that Jesus was motivated by loving concern over Israel's long-standing resistance to God's grace. Jesus concludes his rebuke by saying, "O Jerusalem, Jerusalem, the city that kills the prophets and stones those who are sent to it! How often would I have gathered your children together as a hen gathers her own brood under her wings, and you would not!" (Matt. 23:37 ESV). We see in this lament that Jesus's strong language is not motivated by anger, contempt, and hos-

---

1. For an excellent exposition of Matt. 21-23 and a timeline of these events, see Michael J. Wilkins, *Matthew: The NIV Application Commentary* (Grand Rapids: Zondervan, 2004).

tility. Rather, it is motivated by grief, compassion, and love likened to a mother hen gathering her chicks under her wings. Jesus is calling his wayward children to return. He's not so much angry; he's lovingly pained.

Fourth, when considering strong speech and protest, Christians should remember that Jesus turned to these methods very rarely. For instance, Matthew's Gospel recounts about fifteen distinct times Jesus interacted with the Jewish authorities, and in only one of these interactions (Matt. 23) does Jesus use such strong language. Although many occasions are not recounted in Matthew's Gospel, what is revealed is a ratio of 1:15. This should at least lead us to consider that if we are using harsh rhetoric more often than not, or even half the time, we are more caustic than Jesus ever was. This should be particularly troubling for us, seeing that Jesus was perfectly wise and his judgment was always just, while we often lack wisdom and misjudge the situations we are in.

Fifth, Jesus's language within his historical context was not cruel or demeaning. Jesus's use of the term "hypocrite" was akin to calling someone an actor, someone who was putting on a front. It was a metaphor to get at Jesus's central critique that the religious leaders' righteousness was only external. There is nothing mean about calling one's conspirators "actors" if we have good reason to think they are putting on an act. Similarly, "blind guides" and "whitewashed tombs," as Jesus called the scribes and Pharisees, were metaphors that provided poignant images of Jesus's central critique. The Pharisees were not good guides because they were blind to the way of God. By comparing the scribes and Pharisees to "whitewashed tombs," Jesus was appealing to a common enough object (an ossuary) that looked beautiful on the outside but held impure death on the inside.[2] Jesus's reference to them being like "snakes" and the "offspring of vipers" was meant to call up images of a malicious, deceptive creature in Israel's history who misled God's children just as the scribes and Pharisees were doing now. Jesus, we might say, was speaking truth to power, but he was not using demeaning language.

Perhaps the term that sounds most unloving is "fools" (v. 17), which Jesus uses to refer to the scribes and Pharisees. Interestingly, the Greek word used here for "fools" (*mōroi*) is the plural form of the same word that Jesus warns his disciples not to use to refer to others in Matthew 5:22. There Jesus says, "But I say to you that everyone who is angry with his brother will be liable to judgment; whoever insults his brother will be liable to the council;

---

2. Wilkins, *Matthew*, 755.

and whoever says, 'You fool!' will be liable to the hell of fire" (ESV). This seeming contradiction is extremely helpful in understanding why Jesus's use of "fools" in reference to the scribes and Pharisees is not derogatory.

For one, the Greek word *mōroi/mōros* could be translated "godless," which does not have much in the way of harsh connotations. More importantly, the context in Matthew 5 involves Jesus's teaching about how outward righteousness (do not murder someone) is not equivalent to inward righteousness (do not angrily think or say insulting things to someone). Jesus is describing a situation where someone is so angry that he or she completely devalues someone else. The tone is a disdainful one. Something like "you are a good-for-nothing dumbass." The point of Jesus's teaching is not to exchange one external law (do not murder) for another (do not call someone a fool). Jesus is after the attitude and intent of the human heart. What Jesus is saying in Matthew 5 is that if you call someone a "fool" in an angry, insulting, demeaning manner, then you are murdering your brother or sister. You are ripping his or her value to shreds. But we have already seen that this is not Jesus's attitude toward the scribes and Pharisees in Matthew 23. Jesus is utilizing the language of "fools" to awaken them to the injustices they have already committed and are about to commit. They are truly acting foolish.

This turns us to perhaps the most important point in looking to Jesus as a model of enemy love. Jesus was not a fallible representative of God on earth like we are. Rather, he was the perfect image of God on earth (Heb. 1:3). He had a perspective on things that we will never have. And Jesus is not confronting a particular political, moral opponent, or even global conspiracy. Jesus is critiquing the entirety of humanity's sinfulness as epitomized in the scribes and Pharisees. In Matthew 23, Jesus was God incarnate addressing the sins of humanity from Adam and Eve to his impending crucifixion. To think that we are anywhere near having his point of view or that the issue we are opposed to is the entirety of human sin is itself a case of being foolish. In other words, if anyone can utilize strong language lovingly, it's Jesus and not us. If he did so sparingly, perhaps our best bet is to refrain altogether.

Interestingly, something similar is at stake when Jesus overturns the money changers' tables and drives out those buying and selling in the Jerusalem temple (Matt. 21:12–13). Jesus wasn't against open air markets or even first-century consumerism. The Jerusalem temple symbolized the real presence and action of God on earth, and it was meant to have been "a house of prayer" (21:13). Utilizing it as a place of commerce was not a break in purity laws but was once again a sign of the failure of God's chosen people to administer his grace to the world. Once again, these money changers and buyers/sellers in the temple epitomized the failure of God's people to recognize God's overtures across human history. That Jesus's cleansing of the temple was an act of kindness is seen in the response. Matthew notes that "the blind and the lame came to him in the temple, and he healed them" and that children were "crying out in the temple, 'Hosanna to the Son of David!'" (21:14, 15 ESV). Jesus was not intent on destruction or even protest; he was intent on making his Father's house a place of blessing.

Practicing Enemy Love

Now someone might say, "Well, good for Jesus that he was so thoughtful when he was conspired against, but that's not me." Precisely. The first step is to admit that *it is not us* because the character of Jesus—his inner life—*is not fully formed in us*. But although admission is the first step, it cannot be the last step. When it comes to making efforts to develop more and more of the character of Jesus, we cannot opt out. Jesus didn't just save us from the consequences of our sins, he saved us from having to sin constantly. "Are we to continue in sin so that grace may increase? May it never be!" (Rom. 6:1–2 NASB). The Lord Jesus invites us into an overall way of life with him in his Father's kingdom by his Spirit. Over time, that way of life— walking in the Spirit—will produce traits in us such that even when we are being threatened by our enemies, our pervasive experience will be one of love, joy, peace, patience, kindness, goodness, faithfulness, gentleness, and self-control (Gal. 5:22–23). Jesus made available a life with him and his Father such that we gradually become the kind of person whose knee-jerk reaction to persecution is "Father, forgive them; they do not know what they are doing."

So, here's a twofold Christian response to conspiracies or, really, threats of any kind. First, try to assess the situation clearly and carefully in order to determine the reality and level of the threat. Second, however you perceive the degree of threat, plan a loving response to your opponents that is motivated by the desire to bring about their good as much as or perhaps more so than your own.

Of course, this is easier said than done. How do we become increasingly like Jesus such that we consistently love our enemies? Others have described the way of Christian formation far better and more completely than I can here.[3] But in the wee bit of space I have remaining, I want to suggest Jesus's Gethsemane prayer as a way to respond when we are under threat of harm. This practice is tried and true because it was the practice Jesus engaged when the footsteps of his conspirators drew near.

Shortly after Judas is outed as the inside man, Jesus goes to the garden of Gethsemane and takes with him his inner circle—Peter, James, and John (Mark 14:33). We are told that Jesus is "greatly distressed and troubled," and Jesus himself says that he is "very sorrowful" (14:33, 34). In Gethsemane, Jesus takes up that emotion, lays on the ground, and prays the following: "Abba, Father, all things are possible for you. Remove this cup from me. Yet not what I will, but what you will" (14:36 ESV). After the first instance of praying these words, Jesus returns to find the three disciples asleep. Jesus tells them to stay awake and "pray that you may not enter into temptation. The spirit indeed is willing, but the flesh is weak" (14:38 ESV). He then retreats again and prays something similar a second and third time. Many commentators on this passage suggest that Jesus is clearly recommending to Peter, James, and John the same sort of prayer that he himself is praying so that when the conspirators arrive, Peter, James, and John won't succumb to the temptation to hurt somebody. When he finds them sleeping, Jesus diagnoses their predicament as the "spirit indeed is willing, but the flesh is weak" (Matt. 26:41 ESV). Jesus sees that Peter, James, and John are wanting to stay spiritually awake with God, but they have a stronger, embodied tendency to fall asleep. Because they fail to practice Jesus's Gethsemane prayer the way Jesus did, they very soon succumb to violence, fear, and deception in the face of opposition.

How about you and me? How might Jesus's exhortation to "stay awake and pray that you might not fall into temptation" echo down through the centuries to us when it comes to those threatening our well-being, the well-being of those we love, or the well-being of our faith? What would it look like for you and me to stay spiritually awake and practice Jesus's Gethsemane prayer in response to these threats?

It seems we can do no better than to follow after Jesus to a garden or park where we can be alone with God. Perhaps we can ask a few friends to pray with us from their own places. We can express our distress and sorrow about the situations that threaten. Then, if we can, we can lie prostrate on

---

3. To learn more about the Jesus way of transformation, I highly recommend Dallas Willard, *Renovation of the Heart: Putting on the Character of Christ* (Colorado Springs: NavPress, 2002).

the ground like Jesus and pray, "Abba, Father, all things are possible for you. Remove this cup from me. Yet not what I will, but what you will" (Mark 14:36 ESV). We might want to elaborate on each phrase, for no doubt there was much going on in Jesus's mind as he prayed these words. We don't simply want to repeat his prayer; we want to enter into what he meant and felt when he prayed. It is important to remember that this is not a prayer of passivity. "This is what I want, God, but go ahead and do what you want." Rather, this is a prayer of resignation. We let God know how we want things to go as we struggle to resign ourselves to God and entrust ourselves to him, come what may. In this prayer, we gradually come to lay down in the loving arms of God, whether the threat is taken from us or not. A prayer practice such as this, taken on with serious intent, will dramatically transform how we respond to the conspiracies and threats that we perceive around us. Jesus was conspired against as we are, yet he was without sin.

Conclusion

Do we really want to become like Jesus? Do we really want to love our enemies, those intent on doing us harm? If so, we need to practice the way of life Jesus practiced. When he was conspired against, when his well-being was threatened, he laid himself on the ground and prayed, "Abba, Father, all things are possible for you. Remove this cup from me. Yet not what I will, but what you will" (Mark 14:36). As you turn from reading this chapter, I want to challenge you to choose something in your life about which you feel distressed. Perhaps it is some person, group, or situation that feels threatening to you and your way of life. Take a moment right now and find a place to talk with God. Go to him in your concern and slowly talk through Jesus's Gethsemane prayer. The one who first prayed it promised that he would be with us always, even to the end of the age (Matt. 28:20).

References

Wilkins, Michael J. *Matthew: The NIV Application Commentary*. Grand Rapids: Zondervan, 2004.

Willard, Dallas. *Renovation of the Heart: Putting on the Character of Christ*. Colorado Springs: NavPress, 2002.

APPENDIX:
CAREFUL REASONING GUIDE

This is a short selection of logical fallacies and critical thinking tools that are relevant to the evaluation of conspiracy theories. We hope you find them helpful in your quest for the truth.

Ad Hoc Explanation

As Stephen T. Davis and Eric T. Yang say in chapter 1, explanations are *ad hoc* if they "lack independent support for accepting them other than the fact that they save the theory from the objections" (p. 3). An example of an *ad hoc* explanation employed to defend a conspiracy theory can be seen when Mark Sargent, a famous flat-earther, explains why we discover molten rock under the earth's surface. He proposes that the creator of the earth placed molten rock furnaces at a depth of fifty miles at intervals across the surface of the earth to discourage us from digging too far and discovering the truth.[1] In contrast, the scientific explanation says that the heat has to do with the earth's formation, pressure, and friction, which is supported by evidence from experiments conducted on the surface of the earth.[2] The flat-earth explanation is *ad hoc* because it's accompanied by no independent evidence.

1. Mark Sargent, "Under the Dome," YouTube, July 12, 2015, https://youtu.be/fk4YqPtvJao.
2. Quentin Williams, "Why Is the Earth's Core So Hot? And How Do Scientists

Ad Hominem Fallacy

When someone points to an irrelevant factor about the arguer, such as the arguer's employment, and claims that this disproves his or her argument, it is an *ad hominem* fallacy. An example of this is saying we can't believe what Dr. Fauci says about COVID-19 because he works for the government. The fact that someone works for the government, by itself, isn't relevant to whether the argument is right. To evaluate an argument, we need to focus on the evidence. It's possible, however, that one's employment could create a situation of bias, but even this alone doesn't discredit the argument. As George Wrisley points out, we need to further ask whether "the bias also interfered with [the arguer's] ability to argue fairly."[3] It's possible for a biased person to be right.

Appeal to Ridicule

To ridicule a point of view is to make fun of it. To commit the appeal-to-ridicule fallacy is to argue against a point of view solely on the basis that it sounds crazy. The problem with this kind of reasoning is that something sounding crazy isn't evidence that it's false. Many things believed by Christians sound crazy to non-Christians, but this doesn't mean that the beliefs are false. For example, the resurrection of Jesus sounds crazy to many people, but the truth of this doctrine is central to the faith. Non-conspiracy theorists are often guilty of this fallacy because it's easier to mock a strange-sounding conspiracy theory than to take it seriously, consider the evidence, and take the time to build a case against it.[4]

Confirmation Bias

Confirmation bias means being closed to evidence that doesn't confirm what we already believe. Being biased is natural, and so is seeking confir-

---

Measure Its Temperature?" *Scientific American*, October 6, 1997, https://www.sci entificamerican.com/article/why-is-the-earths-core-so/.

3. George Wrisley, "Ad Hominem: Bias," in *Bad Arguments: 100 of the Most Important Fallacies in Western Philosophy*, ed. Robert Arp, Steven Barbone, and Michael Bruce (Oxford: Wiley, 2019), 71–76.

4. For more on this fallacy, see Gregory L. Bock, "Appeal to Ridicule," in Arp, Barbone, and Bruce, *Bad Arguments*, 118–20.

mation of our biases. We love to read and listen to points of view we agree with, and we feel most comfortable in our "echo chambers." As natural as this is, however, it can cause us to miss the truth because contrary points of view get left out, and if our echo chamber is wrong about something, we may never notice. This doesn't mean that we have to unsubscribe from our favorite Facebook groups, but it does mean that we should implement some strategies that make us more aware of other viewpoints. For instance, consider subscribing to the *other* news site, the one your favorite site criticizes. Also, consider following authors that you disagree with.

Conspiracy Fallacy

In this fallacy, nefarious intentions are inferred without evidence—only on the basis that the outcome of events benefits the alleged conspirators. For example, the 9/11 conspiracy theory claims that the 9/11 terrorist attacks made it possible for the United States to invade Iraq; therefore, the United States was behind the 9/11 attacks. David Paxton, who possibly coined the fallacy, says it's based on paranoia. He describes the fallacy in the following way: "Since event x caused event y, event x must have been instigated to bring about event y."[5] This is a fallacy because the claim is made without evidence and overlooks other, more plausible explanations, such as coincidence.

Curiosity

The Intellectual Virtues Academy lists curiosity as a virtue. It says, "Curiosity is a disposition to wonder, ponder, and ask why. A thirst for understanding and a desire to explore."[6] It's an intellectual virtue because those who cultivate it tend to have more true beliefs than those who don't. Non-conspiracy theorists who simply accept the received view because it's the received view may lack this virtue. It isn't necessary to research every challenge to the standard account. Who has time for that? But those who have the virtue of curiosity would, it seems, spend at least some time thinking about why conspiracists hold the beliefs that they do. For exam-

5. David Paxton, "The Conspiracy Fallacy," The Gerasites, September 13, 2014, https://thegerasites.wordpress.com/2014/09/13/the-conspiracy-theorists-fallacy/.

6. "Master Virtues," Intellectual Virtues Academy, accessed June 23, 2022, https://www.ivalongbeach.org/academics/master-virtues.

ple, when challenged to reconsider whether the moon landings actually happened because, as some claim, the astronauts would have died when they passed through the Van Allen (radiation) belts, a curious person would want to learn more about these belts and find out how the astronauts could have survived.[7]

False Dilemma

Also known as the either-or fallacy or the black-and-white fallacy, a false dilemma occurs when the arguer incorrectly limits (intentionally or not) the number of available choices. For example, a conspiracy theorist might say that you must either think for yourself (and embrace the conspiracy theory) or have blind faith in the government. The assumption is that trusting a source outside oneself is an act of blind faith. But there's a third possibility—trusting a source after carefully thinking through the reasons for doing so.[8]

Falsifiability

A testable theory is a falsifiable one, meaning that it can be shown to be false. If there is no way to determine whether it's false, then there is no way to determine whether it's true, and thus there is little reason to accept it, let alone get worked up about it. Many conspiracy theories seem unfalsifiable. For example, in the documentary *Behind the Curve*, flat-earthers attempt to test their theory with a ring laser gyroscope test and a laser experiment. The results of their tests contradict their flat-earth hypothesis, but they refuse to accept the conclusion.[9] This seems to indicate that these flat-earthers hold an unfalsifiable theory and aren't open to the truth.

7. Amy Shira Teitel, "Apollo Rocketed through the Van Allen Belts," *Popular Science*, September 19, 2014, https://www.popsci.com/blog-network/vintage-space/apollo-rocketed-through-van-allen-belts/.

8. For more on this fallacy, please see Jennifer Culver, "False Dilemma," in Arp, Barbone, and Bruce, *Bad Arguments*, 346–47.

9. Courtland Lewis and Gregory L. Bock, "Falling Off the Edge of the Earth," in *Conspiracy Theories: Philosophers Connect the Dots*, ed. Richard Greene and Rachel Robison-Greene (Chicago: Open Court, 2020), 59–69.

Intellectual Humility

Intellectual humility is a virtue of the mind that often seems in short supply. As human beings, we have limits related to what we can know. All too often we deny those limits, cover up our mistakes, and seek some sort of intellectual status or prestige. Intellectual humility instructs us to accept those limits, to own up to them, and to reject any concern for and pursuit of intellectual prestige.[10] This isn't just a virtue for academics or others whose career has to do with certain kinds of knowledge. This is a virtue for everyone. Wherever we are, and whoever we are, we should admit what we don't know, both to ourselves and to others. This can be difficult, but it can help us in many ways. First, it might cool down a heated exchange. Not only can this sort of humility undermine an emotionally charged discussion; it can also put the truth, rather than the ego, at center stage. When we admit our limits, our mistakes, and our own fallibility, we are more likely to learn from others, as well as learn more about what the truth of any matter is. Once the ego, the self, is more out of the way, we can more clearly see the truth.

Intellectual Autonomy

Intellectual autonomy is a virtue. It is commonly expressed in the saying "Think for yourself!" However, the lengths to which it is employed by conspiracy theorists makes you wonder whether it is, in fact, a virtue. In the name of autonomy, they reject evidence from scientists, health officials, NASA, etc. Aristotle, however, defines a virtue as a mean between two extremes. It is the middle way. If he's right, then you can take autonomy too far, having too little or too much of it. So, be on the lookout for the abuse of this virtue.[11] It's possible to be intellectually autonomous and trust what experts have to say. In fact, it may be an act of autonomy to trust an expert when you've determined that the expert is, indeed, an expert.

---

10. "Master Virtues"; see also Nathan L. King, *The Excellent Mind: Intellectual Virtues for Everyday Life* (New York: Oxford University Press, 2020), 106-30.

11. For more on this virtue in the context of conspiracy theories, see Lewis and Bock, "Falling Off the Edge," especially 66-69.

Occam's Razor

Named after William of Occam (1287–1347), Occam's razor is a principle that says that the simplest explanation is often the best explanation. The principle works by "shaving off" unnecessary assumptions or entities. In other words, given two explanations that are equal in every respect except that one makes only one assumption and the other makes more than one, the first should be preferred. For example, there are two explanations of the moon landing: (1) we actually landed on the moon, and (2) it was a big hoax. The hoax theory is problematic because it makes so many assumptions. As Jeff Cervantez writes, "If the hoax is going to work, the thousands of people working at NASA and many others working for the US government at the time of the Apollo missions would have to be involved in a deep cover-up. These same people would have to continue to deceive other people for years, without ever telling another person of their deception."[12] These assumptions, and many more, make the hoax theory more complex than the standard account, so we should reject the hoax theory.

Open-mindedness

Open-mindedness is the inclination to learn new things or change one's mind. It's a virtue because open-minded people are more likely to believe the truth when they encounter it. Of course, once you find the truth, your mind should, in a sense, close around it; however, having strong beliefs is compatible with remaining open-minded because we can always come to a better understanding of what we think we know, and sometimes we are flatly mistaken about what we are sure of. There's a lot of closed-mindedness these days, and it's important for conspiracy theorists and non–conspiracy theorists alike to remain open because sometimes conspiracy theorists are right (Watergate, Edward Snowden, etc.). And sometimes they're not (flat-earth theory, lizard people, etc.). Another reason you should be open-minded is that you're less likely to persuade the other side if you won't sincerely listen to them first. Who knows? You may even change your mind.

12. Jeff Cervantez, "That's . . . One Giant Joke on Mankind?" in Greene and Robison-Greene, *Conspiracy Theories*, 71–77.

CONTRIBUTORS

Chase Andre is instructor in Communication Core and Digital Learning for the Department of Communication Studies at Biola University, where he has taught since 2014. He focuses his research on how communicative acts shape and reshape society, the ethics of intercultural interaction, Martin Luther King Jr., and ways in which the church can pursue justice and shalom in the public sphere. Chase presents at national conferences, including the American Academy of Religion, the National Communication Association, and the Student Congress on Racial Reconciliation.

Michael W. Austin is professor of philosophy at Eastern Kentucky University and Senior Fellow at the Dietrich Bonhoeffer Institute. He has published twelve books, including *Being Good: Christian Virtues for Everyday Life* (Eerdmans, 2012), *Humility and Human Flourishing* (Oxford University Press, 2018), and his latest, *God and Guns in America* (Eerdmans, 2020).

Bradley Baurain is associate professor of TESOL (Teaching English to Speakers of Other Languages) at Moody Theological Seminary and Graduate School in Chicago. He has been teaching for more than thirty years in China, Vietnam, Canada, and the United States. Many of his academic publications can be accessed via Academia.edu. He also writes for the *Today in the Word* devotional guide and recently authored *On Waiting Well: Moving from Endurance to Enjoyment When You're Waiting on God* (Moody Publishers, 2020).

Daniel Bennett is associate professor of political science and assistant director of the Center for Faith and Flourishing at John Brown University. He researches the intersection of law, religion, and politics in the United States. He is the author of *Defending Faith: The Politics of the Christian Conservative Legal Movement* (University Press of Kansas, 2017) and has published articles on public opinion and constitutional rights, the politicization of religious freedom, and federal judicial selection. He has also written for *Christianity Today*, *Religion and Politics*, and the *Gospel Coalition*.

Gregory L. Bock is assistant professor of philosophy and religion and program director of the Philosophy, Religion, and Asian Studies Programs at the University of Texas at Tyler. He is also director of UT Tyler's Center for Ethics. His areas of research include bioethics, the ethics of forgiveness, and the philosophy of religion. He is editor of volumes 3 and 4 of *The Philosophy of Forgiveness* (Vernon, 2018, 2019) and coeditor of *Righteous Indignation: Christian Philosophical and Theological Perspectives on Anger* (Fortress, 2021).

Chad Bogosian is a philosophy instructor at Clovis Community College in Fresno, California. As a proponent of public philosophy, he founded CCC's Ethics Bowl Team and their Philosophy and the Good Life events, and has appeared on multiple philosophy podcasts. He writes on ethics and moral development, epistemology, and philosophy of religion, and he enjoys speaking on these topics to groups ranging from teens to seniors.

Kevin Carnahan is professor of religion and philosophy at Central Methodist University. He specializes in Christian ethics and questions of political theory. In addition to numerous articles, his books include *Reinhold Niebuhr and Paul Ramsey* (Lexington Books, 2010) and *From Presumption to Prudence* (Routledge, 2019).

Jason Cook is pastor of men and theology at Grace Community Church in Tyler, Texas. He is also the ninth-grade Bible teacher at Grace Community School. His research interests include Biblical Hebrew, Old Testament narrative, and biblical theology.

Scott Culpepper serves as professor of history at Dordt University. He specializes in the fields of early modern Europe and the Americas, with a particular emphasis on the interaction of politics, religion, and popular cultures in the Atlantic world from 1400 to the present. He is the author of *Francis Johnson and the English Separatist Influence: The Bishop of Brownism's Life, Ministry, and Controversies* (Mercer University Press, 2011) and is currently working on a historical study of "satanic panics" in American history and popular cultures.

Stephen T. Davis is the Russell K. Pitzer Professor of Philosophy, Emeritus, at Claremont McKenna College. He specializes in the philosophy of religion and analytic theology. He is the author of over eighty academic articles and author or editor of some seventeen books, including *Encountering Evil* (Westminster John Knox, 2001), *Christian Philosophical Theology* (Oxford University Press, 2006), *Rational Faith: A Philosopher's Defense of Christianity* (InterVarsity Press, 2016), and (with Eric T. Yang), *An Introduction to Christian Philosophical Theology: Faith Seeking Understanding* (Zondervan, 2020).

Garrett J. DeWeese is professor at large, Department of Philosophy, Talbot School of Theology. His philosophical interests are philosophy of science and philosophical theology. He is the author of several books and articles, including *God and the Nature of Time* (Ashgate, 2001) and *Doing Philosophy as a Christian* (IVP Academic, 2001).

Marlena Graves is a PhD student in American cultural studies at Bowling Green State University. Her focus is on white evangelical Christianity and inequality—specifically in the areas of race, immigration, and gender. She has also taught spiritual formation courses as an adjunct seminary professor and is the author of five books and over two hundred articles.

Shawn Graves is associate professor of philosophy and chair of the Department of Religious Studies and Philosophy at the University of Findlay. He has published articles in epistemology, philosophy of religion, the ethics of love, sports ethics, and animal ethics. Along with Marlena Graves, he is the coeditor of *The Gospel of Peace in a Violent World: Christian Nonviolence for Communal Flourishing* (IVP Academic, 2022). He has published papers in places such as *Oxford Studies in Philosophy of Religion, Faith and Philosophy,* and *Sport, Ethics, and Philosophy,* in addition to contributing chapters in volumes published by Oxford University Press and Mercer University Press.

David A. Horner is professor of theology and philosophy at Talbot School of Theology, Biola University, where he has taught since 2001. He is the author of *Mind Your Faith: A Student's Guide to Thinking and Living Well* (IVP, 2011) and numerous articles and book chapters in ethics, apologetics, and ancient and medieval philosophy.

Dru Johnson is associate professor of biblical and theological studies at The King's College in New York City. He also directs the Center for Hebraic Thought and hosts *The Biblical Mind* and the *OnScript* podcasts. He has written several monographs, academic books, and trade books on the intellectual world of the Bible, including *Biblical Philosophy* (Cambridge University Press, 2021).

Nathan L. King is professor of philosophy at Whitworth University. His research interests include intellectual character, the epistemology of disagreement, and the philosophy of religion. He is author of *The Excellent Mind: Intellectual Virtues for Everyday Life* (Oxford University Press, 2021).

Rick Langer is a professor of biblical studies and theology at Biola University and the director of the Office of Faith and Learning. He specializes in the integration of faith and learning and has also published in the areas of bioethics, theology, and philosophy. His recent books *Winsome Persuasion: Christian Influence in a Post-Christian World* (IVP, 2017) and *Winsome Conviction: Disagreeing without Dividing the Church* (IVP, 2020) deal with the challenges of communicating Christian convictions—whether in the public square or within the church. He served for over twenty years as a pastor before joining the faculty of Biola in 2005.

Christian B. Miller is the A. C. Reid Professor of Philosophy at Wake Forest University. He is the author of over one hundred academic papers, as well as *Moral Psychology* with Cambridge University Press (2021) and four books with Oxford University Press, *Moral Character: An Empirical Theory* (2013), *Character and Moral Psychology* (2014), *The Character Gap: How Good Are We?* (2017), and *Honesty: The Philosophy and Psychology of a Neglected Virtue* (2021). He is a science contributor for *Forbes*, and his writings have also appeared in the *New York Times*, *Wall Street Journal*, *Dallas Morning News*, *Slate*, the *Conversation*, *Newsweek*, *Aeon*, and *Christianity Today*.

Tim Muehlhoff is a professor of communication at Biola University in La Mirada, California, and is the codirector of the Winsome Conviction Project, which seeks to reintroduce humility, civility, and compassion back into our public disagreements. He is the cohost of the *Winsome Conviction*

Podcast, and his latest books are *Winsome Conviction: Disagreeing without Dividing the Church* (IVP, 2020) and *Eyes to See: Recognizing God's Common Grace in Unsettled Times* (IVP, 2021).

Michelle Panchuk is an assistant professor of philosophy at Murray State University. Her research interests include philosophy of religion, philosophy of trauma, feminist philosophy, and philosophy of disability. Michelle is coeditor of *Voices from the Edge: Centering Marginalized Perspectives in Analytic Theology* (Oxford University Press, 2020) and has published in such venues as *Hypatia*, the *Journal of Analytic Theology*, *Res Philosophica*, and *Religious Studies*.

Susan Peppers-Bates is an associate professor of philosophy at Stetson University. Her research interests include early modern philosophy, the philosophy of religion, the philosophy of race, and feminist philosophy. As such, she has published *Nicholas Malebranche: Freedom in an Occasionalist World* (Continuum, 2009), as well as articles, including "Doubly Other: Black Women's Social Death and Re-enslavement in America's Genocidal Prison Nation," in *Feminism and Philosophy* (Spring 2018), and "The Satanic Nature of Racist 'Christianity,'" *Journal of the Black Catholic Theological Society* 4 (2012).

Steven L. Porter is senior research fellow and executive director of the Martin Institute for Christianity and Culture at Westmont College. He remains an affiliate professor of spiritual formation and theology at Biola University. Steve teaches and writes on Christian formation, psychology and theology, and philosophical theology. He is coeditor of *Neuroscience and the Soul* (Eerdmans, 2016), *Psychology and Spiritual Formation in Dialogue* (IVP, 2019), and *Until Christ Is Formed in You* (ACU Press, 2018). He also serves as the editor of the *Journal of Spiritual Formation and Soul Care*.

Kaitlyn Schiess is the author of *The Liturgy of Politics: Spiritual Formation for the Sake of Our Neighbor* (IVP, 2020), and her writing has appeared at *Christianity Today*, the *New York Times*, *Christ and Pop Culture*, *RELEVANT*, and *Sojourners*. She has a ThM in systematic theology from Dallas Theological Seminary and is currently a doctoral student in political theology at Duke Divinity School.

J. Aaron Simmons is professor of philosophy at Furman University and president of the Søren Kierkegaard Society (USA). In addition to numerous articles and essays, Simmons is the author or editor of many books, including *God and the Other* (Indiana University Press, 2011), *The New Phenomenology* (Bloomsbury Press, 2013), *Christian Philosophy* (Oxford University Press, 2019), and *Kierkegaard's God and the Good Life* (Indiana University Press, 2017).

Domonique Turnipseed is a PhD student at Marquette University focusing on medieval philosophy, metaphysics, philosophy of language, philosophy of religion, and histories of racism. Domonique defines his work as an effort to bring together Thomas Aquinas and W. E. B. Du Bois, Saint Augustine, and Frederick Douglass, and the insights of medieval metaphysics as aids to furthering racial considerations. In practice, he questions how to understand Aristotelian and Avicennean essence realism in light of language and social categories of race.

Rachel I. Wightman is currently the associate director for instruction and outreach at Concordia University (MN), St. Paul Library. She has been a librarian for over ten years, working in academic libraries in the United States and abroad, and has written and presented on a variety of library-related topics. She is the author of *Faith and Fake News* (Eerdmans, 2023) and partners with churches to offer classes on the intersection of faith and misinformation. For more information, see www.racheliwightman.com.

Keith D. Wyma is professor of philosophy at Whitworth University in Spokane, Washington. He also coaches Whitworth's three-time national-champion Intercollegiate Ethics Bowl team. He has written on weakness of will, moral responsibility and its limits, and financial ethics, and he is currently working on the divine law ethics of the Ten Commandments.

Eric T. Yang is an associate professor of philosophy at Santa Clara University. He specializes in metaphysics and philosophy of religion. Along with several journal articles and book chapters, he has published (with Stephen T. Davis) *An Introduction to Christian Philosophical Theology: Faith Seeking Understanding* (Zondervan, 2020).

INDEX